Turnaround Challenge

Turnaround Challenge

Business and the City of the Future

Michael Blowfield and Leo Johnson

OXFORD
UNIVERSITY PRESS

Great Clarendon Street, Oxford, OX2 6DP,
United Kingdom

Oxford University Press is a department of the University of Oxford.
It furthers the University's objective of excellence in research, scholarship,
and education by publishing worldwide. Oxford is a registered trade mark of
Oxford University Press in the UK and in certain other countries

© Michael Blowfield and Leo Johnson 2013

The moral rights of the authors have been asserted

First Edition published in 2013

Impression: 1

Published in the United States of America by Oxford University Press
198 Madison Avenue, New York, NY 10016, United States of America

British Library Cataloguing in Publication Data

Data available

ISBN 978-0-19-967221-9

Printed in Great Britain by
Clays Ltd, St Ives plc

Contents

Acknowledgements   ix

Abbreviations and Glossary   xi

List of Figures   xv

List of Boxes   xvii

1. Introduction   1

2. Turnaround Challenge: Escaping the Petropolis   7
    The Rhetoric of Extinction   7
    A View from a Bridge: Does the Rhetoric have a Rationale?   8
    Under the Bonnet of Capitalism: the Model T Ford   10
    And after Ford . . . is there a Next Great Surge?   13
    Anatomizing the Crisis   14
    Transformational Crises   15
    The Crisis of Governance   22
    Can we still Afford a Ford?   23

3. Megatrends: Mapping Business's Key Challenges   25
    Wicked Problems . . .   25
    . . . and Their Illogical Solutions   26
    Climate Change   27
    Climate Change: the Background for Business   28
    The Challenge of Aviation   33
    Demographic Change   36
    The Economic Crisis and Geo-Political Shift   46
    Governance Crisis   52
    The Privatization of Regulation   53
    The Governance Gap   55

4. Ways Out? The Oracles   63
    Mass Production and the Technological Cycle   63
    Exit from Petropolis   67
    Market Moderation, Market Solutions, or Market Exit?   69
    The Oracles   70
    Market Solutions   79

Contents

Evaluating the Oracles 80

Reviewing the Oracles 92

5. The Dynamics of Transition: Techno-economic Paradigms 97

Waiting for the Wave to Break 97

Reclaiming the ICT Revolution 100

Internal and External Congruence 102

The Evolving Norms of Business 107

Incongruence and its Impacts on Transition 109

How Congruence Happens: the Schumpeterian Approach 110

Installation Period 112

Turning Point 113

Deployment Period 114

The Uses of Techno-economic Paradigms: Mapping an Economy
on the S Curve 116

The Strange Life of the ICT Era 118

From Producers to Consumers 124

Plausible Options 125

6. Cyburbia 129

Songdo: 'Everything one could possibly want' 129

The Benefits of Cyburbia 133

Questioning Cyburbia: How Smart is Smart? 135

7. The Return of the Optimist 143

Beyond Petropolis and Cyburbia 143

Techno-Optimism Revisited 144

Colliding Mega-trends: Rising Chinese Labour Costs . . . 150

. . . and Decreasing Costs of Local Manufacturing 152

Structural or Surface Change 155

Drogba and D.Light 161

Lessons for Business: Innovation Aligned with the Market 168

Innovators and Incumbents 170

Scanning for the Disruptors 171

Business Implications: Resolving the Crises of the Quadrilemma 175

8. The City of the Future: A Place for People 185

From Smart Cities to Smart Citizens 186

The Great Texas Blackout 186

Co-designing the New Energy Economy 189

Accelerating Transition 192

From Laboratory to City 193

From Consumer to Producer 197

Challenge 1: The Car-shaped City 198

Challenge 2: Political Engagement and Results from Government   199
Challenge 3: Good Jobs   202

9. Transition: The Turnaround   209
    Innovation and the Entrepreneurial State   209
    Three Cities of the Future   212
    Synergy and the Role of the Entrepreneurial State   215
    Moving to Producer Capitalism   223
    Reasons for Optimism   226
    Annex: The Grassroots FabLab Instructable   228

References   231
Index   241

Acknowledgements

The origins of this book are in a series of lectures the authors gave at Oxford University's Smith School of Enterprise & Environment and to the Sloan Fellows at London Business School. The authors would like to thank the participants in both lecture series, as well the faculty at Oxford, LBS, and Middlesex for their companionship, ideas, and constructive critique.

We believe that lectures, like cities, grow from the bottom up, through the contributions and reactions of participants, and it is in this spirit that we have written this book. Addressing the challenge of long-term economic and social transformation, by definition cuts across issues and timeframes. What we hope is not to thump the table with a tome that says 'This is how it is!', but to give a framework to stimulate more thought and discussion.

While the authors take all responsibility for errors, special thanks go to the following for contributions that helped to make the book happen: Sir Martin and Lady Smith, benefactors of the Smith School, Sir David King and Gordon Clark, the founding and current Directors of the Smith School, Megan Cole and the Business Fellows at the Smith School as long-running sparring partners. Special thanks go to our valued colleague Anne Augustine. A number of the cases and characters, from Mama Felix in the Mathare slum to Neill the genderless cyborg, came to light as part of research for BBC World News documentaries presented by Leo Johnson. Thanks go to Paul Gibbs, Mary Wilkinson, Emma de'Ath, and Jonathan Brunert as Commissioning Editors and Executive Producers of One Square Mile, Down to Business and World Challenge. Thanks also go to the late Robert Lamb, Gus Lamb, Rob Gould, Rob Finighan, and Alex Posada at One Planet Pictures. The Sustainability & Climate Change team at PwC has proven a vital resource for testing the business perspective. Thanks go to Malcolm Preston, Emma Cox, and the whole team, with special thanks to the authors of the Low Carbon Economy Index.

Many others have given us glimpses into what is possible in terms of transformation, not least Carlota Perez and Frank Geels. The authors would like to highlight the influence of the Skoll World Forum, the New Economics Foundation, the Green Alliance, and the teams at the IFC/FT Sustainable Finance Awards and FT Boldness in Business Awards. Our families have put up with a lot in terms of cluttered houses and late nights, and our special thanks and love go to them. Finally, we see this book as the start rather than the end of a journey, and so we thank in advance all of those who feel inspired or provoked enough by these ideas to want to be part of that future.

Mick Blowfield and Leo Johnson
Oxford 2013

Abbreviations and Glossary

ABBREVIATIONS

BAU	business as usual
BRICS	Brazil, Russia, India, China, South Africa
EROEI	energy return on energy invested
GBAU	green business as usual
GDP	gross domestic product
GHG	greenhouse gases
GPT	general purpose technology
ICT	information and communication technology
IFPRI	International Food Policy Research Institute
MOOC	massive open online courses
OECD	Organization for Economic Co-operation and Development
ppm	parts per million
PWG	prosperity without growth
ROA	return on assets
SLEPT	social, legal, economic, political, and technological (elements/ institutions of society)
TEEB	the economics of ecosystems and biodiversity
TEP	techno-economic paradigm

GLOSSARY

absolute decoupling	reducing the total greenhouse gas emissions without affecting economic growth.
behavioural economics	a strand of economic and psychological theory investigating why people make choices that are irrational from an economic viewpoint. Has been developed to propose ways of making consumer behaviour more economically rational.

bottom billion capitalism the market-led provision of goods and services targeted at the needs of the poorest people in the world.

business primarily used in this book to mean the activity of commerce undertaken in order to generate a profit. It can also mean the organizations that carry out those activities, such as companies.

capex capital expenditure

capitalism an economic system in which private wealth is used to produce goods and services for profit, and the free market is the main determinant of prices (narrow sense). More broadly, capitalism is a social system heavily influenced by profit and free market principles, but with the intention to deliver prosperity and well-being to society as a whole, not only to the owners of financial capital.

capitalist someone who invests their capital assets for profit.

carrying capacity the size of population (human and other life-forms) that an ecosystem can sustain in the long run.

CO₂ carbon dioxide

crisis a state of affairs in which a decisive change is required.

crisis of humanity a crisis that tests people's sense of humanity including issues of justice, well-being, and belief.

decoupling see *absolute decoupling* and *relative decoupling*.

demographic change shifts in size and patterns of population over time.

ecosystem a biological system composed of all the organisms found in a particular physical environment, interacting with it and with each other. (*Oxford English Dictionary*)

emerging economy a national economy once considered poor or under-developed that is enjoying rapid economic growth.

existential risk a risk threatening the entire future of humanity.

general purpose technology a category of technology responsible for creative destruction (Schumpeter) and techno-economic paradigm shifts (Perez).

global hectares a unit to measure the demands humans place on the Earth's *carrying capacity*.

institution An established law, custom, usage, practice, organization, or other element in the political or social life of a people; a regulative principle or convention subservient to the needs of an organized community or the general ends of civilization. (*Oxford English Dictionary*)

overshoot	the condition when a population demands more than its environment/ecosystem can provide.
quadrilemma of crises	the interplay of the four major crises of climate change, demographic change, geo-political shift, and governance change.
relative decoupling	resource intensity for every unit of production/output is reduced.
steady state growth	an economy structured to find an equilibrium between production growth and population growth.
stationary state	an economy with levels of consumption and population that remain below the *carrying capacity* of its natural environment. (cf. *steady state growth*).
techno-economic paradigm	a period of capitalism characterized by a particular type of technological and financial innovation during which the norms of capitalism and business are altered to create a new era. (cf. *general purpose technology*).
transformational crisis	a crisis with the power to fundamentally and irreversibly alter the way business is done, and what is meant by business success.

List of Figures

2.1 A view from a bridge 9

2.2 Carbon intensities required to meet 450ppm target 16

2.3 Return on assets and USA unemployment rate (1976–2010) 19

2.4 Relationship between GDP and finance industry and other industry profits, 1990–2007 21

3.1 World prices of major grains under different climate change scenarios 26

3.2 Navigating the numbers 27

3.3 The trillion tonne budget of carbon emissions 29

3.4 Towards low carbon intensity: are we making progress? 30

3.5 Costs and investment to achieve a low carbon economy 31

3.6 Primary energy mix by 2030 32

3.7 The aviation industry's path to carbon neutrality 34

3.8 Predicted commodity demand growth 2010–2030 39

3.9 International financial reserve accumulation prior to 2008 financial crisis 49

3.10 The evolution of governance and risk 54

3.11 Selected United Nations General Assembly resolutions 2011 56

3.12 Mega-trends Quiz: Answers to Figure 3.2 59

4.1 Overview of the Oracles 71

4.2 Bentley and Electric Car 76

4.3 Mapping the dreams of the Oracles 81

4.4 Oracle goals versus the long-term potential outcomes 93

5.1 The techno-economic paradigm: Internal congruence of GPT and institutions 103

5.2 Justifications of capitalism 104

5.3 External congruence of TEP and external environment 108

5.4 The five techno-economic paradigm shifts of the capitalist era 111

5.5 Phases in a techno-economic paradigm 112

5.6 Changing relationship between the real economy and asset values, 1971–1999 120

6.1   Push and pull factors affecting the shift to Cyburbia   132
6.2   Current account situation of major economies, 2011   133
7.1   The logic of mass production   149
7.2   Hidden costs of outsourced mass production   151
7.3   The logic of additive manufacturing across the value chain   153
7.4   Technology and the shrinking barriers to entry to manufacturing   156
7.5   Apple value chain: the logic of late stage mass production   158
7.6   The intensive and extensive economy   167
7.7   Creative destruction at the maturity phase   167
7.8   Potential invested capital to fund selected BoP businesses over the
      next 10 years in US$ bn.   169
7.9   The impact of intervention—with/without analysis for solar power   170
7.10 Rural productivity—countering urbanization   171
7.11 Managing the transition: strategic implications for business   178
7.12 Principles of mass versus distributed economy   181
7.13 Shifting economics of local production   182
8.1   Structural challenges with the power grid   188
8.2   Waves of production   191
8.3   The virtuous circle of productive cities   196
8.4   ICT and empowerment   204
9.1   Technological waves   210
9.2   Konza Technopolis   213
9.3   Accelerating transition: phases of government support   217
9.4   Institutional moves across technological cycle   220
9.5   Resolving the quadrilemma of crises   223

List of Boxes

2.1 The quadrilemma of crises   16

3.1 Climate Change: the background for business   28

3.2 Demographic change: the background for business   36

3.3 Limits to population growth   43

3.4 Economic crisis: the background for business   46

3.5 Business background: the governance crisis   52

4.1 Relative and absolute decoupling   78

4.2 Types of geo-engineering   79

8.1 Key success factors for Barcelona's Fabcity   194

1

Introduction

This book is about the rights to optimism. Can capitalism deliver for us all? Let's be more specific. Your neighbour, the person closest to where you live. What are the basics they are looking for? What are the some of the building blocks for them of a good life?

Let's say you come up with some of these:

- Jobs, good ones, for them and their families
- Health care
- Education
- Security, in their lives and from major changes like climate change
- Quality of life, with a community that is flourishing

That was the first part of a thought experiment. Perhaps you have come up with other ideas, but the chances are you would be wary of any social system that could not supply those building blocks.

The second part of our thought experiment is more challenging. Is capitalism—today's dominant social system—on track to provide these basic elements of a prosperous, civilized society for the foreseeable future? Does society—do you, your friends and neighbours—have the rights to optimism?

'The future,' as William Gibson (self-appointed prophet of cyberpunk) once commented, 'is already here—it's just not very evenly distributed.' This book is an exploration, an examination of the present to see what it can tell us about the futures that capitalism could create for business and all of society.

The contours of three different possible cities of the future have started to emerge. The first is *Petropolis*: the city of fossil fuel driven mass production and consumption that is decreasingly resilient, and has Hurricane Katrina as its norm. The second is *Cyburbia*. This is Petropolis rebuilt: smart and green but censored and sensored, embodied in the shimmering towers of the eco-city. The third city is a city for its people; a city without a blueprint, but where new approaches from small scale manufacturing, to participatory budgeting and micro grids, help communities make the city they want.

Each of these cities has to be built on foundations that have already been laid, formed by the megatrends of climate change, demographic change, and shifts in global wealth and power. So, where does the logic of capitalism point us? Which city looks set to emerge as the dominant model? Is it a city that delivers for its people? Is it a city that allows business to flourish? And what are the challenges and opportunities, the new rules of the road for commerce and government?

We start our examination with a health check in Chapter 2. Amid the twenty-first century's rhetoric of extinction and the laments of the apocalyptoholics, what stands out as business and the rest of society's most pressing challenges? What are the economic, social, and environmental megatrends confronting us? And do they constitute a turnaround challenge for business? Is fossil fuel driven mass production—the engine of twentieth-century globalization, the workhorse of poverty reduction—now threatening to become the prime driver of escalating social inequality, economic stagnation, and environmental instability?

Furthermore, what are the consequences of a deeply embedded way of life finding itself at odds with—i.e. incongruent with—major crises and its own promises of well-being? If the current configuration of the good life is the cause of some of the crises that confront us, what approaches will be fit for purpose? Before looking at the options that are on offer, Chapter 3 digs deeper into the nature of the challenges. Just how tough a situation do we find ourselves in? How intractable, how 'wicked' is the set of challenges we have to deal with? And what constitutes an approach that could work?

Chapter 3 tests the resolve of even the most strident optimist. It sets out a twin hurdle for any proposed solution. Any viable way ahead has to clear an adequacy test, addressing the external challenges of climate change and inequality against a backdrop of economic uncertainty and changes in global governance. It also has to clear an achievability test; it has to stand a chance of getting implemented by business and government at the speed and scale required.

Chapter 4 then looks at the 'Oracles': the fashioners of ideas intended to help surmount our multiple challenges. Do any of them pass the above test of fitness for purpose? We explore the range of approaches that get batted about as possible alternatives to the path we are on, whether by unleashing, mitigating or abandoning the market. The first is 'business as usual' (BAU). BAU has one core assumption: if there are any costs to social and environmental challenges, the next generation, richer than us, can pay. The second approach is 'green business as usual' (GBAU), addressing the carbon challenge either by the hard yards of decarbonizing 80 per cent by 2050, or by the technological silver bullet of large-scale geo-engineering. The third is prosperity without growth (PWG), moving to an economy that does not attempt to pursue limitless growth on a finite planet.

Despite the positives that each of these approaches offers, none of them, Chapter 4 concludes, meets the twin challenge of being both adequate and achievable. GBAU presents no solution to the social challenge of the instability of inequality; PWG appears to fail the market test of being achievable by business and government in the available timeframe. Our conclusion is that the current trajectory, given the lack of viable alternatives, steers society by default back towards the city of Petropolis.

So is this the future: the decreasingly resilient megacity, buffeted by the impacts of climate change and social instability? Do we have to relinquish any rights to optimism? Chapter 5 presents a counterview with the potential to upend this logic. Economic growth, as the Austrian economist Schumpeter observed, has rolled out in waves, with a sequence of general purpose technologies (GPTs), from water power to the steam engine to electricity and the combustion engine, that usher in successive great surges of development. These GPTs sweep forward new people with new powers to accomplish new things. They have the potential to transform productivity, but the existing techno-economic paradigm—the entrenched set of institutions and incentives that rolled out the previous GPT—resists them. Society's institutions only realign to support a new GPT when productivity gains from its predecessor have been exhausted.

What does this imply for optimism? Our excavations reveal a paradox in which the darkest hour may be the prelude for dawn. The long-standing declines in productivity observed over the past few decades may signal not the end of growth, but the potential emergence of a new paradigm. But what is this new GPT? Chapter 6 looks at the revolution in Information and Communications Technology (ICT). Does it present not just a new GPT but one with the potential to meet the congruence test of adequacy to the challenges we face and achievability given the institutions we have available? But if ICT is the new general purpose technology, then why, as Nobel Prize winning economist Robert Solow points out, have the productivity gains of ICT shown up *everywhere but in the statistics.*'

To answer this question, Chapter 6 examines some of the directions in which the set of ICT innovations have been deployed, from sushi-slicing robots and voice-activated popcorn dispensers to super-computers that accelerate image processing for deep-water drilling, to hyper-accelerated financial trading, and the complex derivatives of the subprime crisis. Its conclusion is that ICT, under its current path of deployment, far from displacing the GPT of fossil fuels and mass production, is being used to extend its life cycle.

The latest techno-economic paradigm, then, is one that has blended the fossil driven mass production era with that of ICT. In place of the Petropolis, we see its successor, Cyburbia: blueprint smart cities that insulate a minority of privileged groups from social instability, and introduce environmental efficiency both as a cost-saving and a source of legitimacy. If Petropolis represents the city that is disconnected, socially, economically, and environmentally, then Cyburbia is the city that is hyper-connected, but virtually more than physically. What happens when your neighbour's lights blow a fuse in Cyburbia? You are unable to help. The smart technology is for the expert to install and maintain. Cyburbia is a city, both sensored and censored, that reduces people to digital factors of production.

Chapter 7 looks for other options. Is there another road that ICT innovation could go down? Can it deliver on its promise as a GPT, bringing new powers to new people to do new things? Chapter 7 identifies two grounds for optimism. The first is a colliding set of trends around manufacturing. Rising Chinese labour costs, shipping price volatility and decreasing domestic wage bills are rebalancing the economics of production in favour of local manufacturing. Can new micro-manufacturing techniques, from nanotech and 3D printing to open source and agile manufacturing, put production back in the hands of small businesses? If the Model T Ford defined the era of fossil fuel driven mass production, a different car, Wikispeed's C3, illustrates the emergence of its diametric opposite in manufacturing. It employs crowd-sourced finance, seven day invention cycles, and open source software and hardware to create a car capable of 100 miles per gallon and switchable to electric power.

What Wikispeed represents, at the extreme end, is the advance of micro-manufacturing. New ICT tools, protocols, and processes such as CAD/CAM lathes, rapid prototyping, and 3D printing are putting the capabilities that used to require high capex automated plant into the hands of small businesses. The chance to capture value from production is being distributed. Control of the means of production is shifting hands, with the potential for an emergence of a new form of producer capitalism in which the producer shares in the surplus value they have created.

The impact of these new technologies, as with Stephenson's Rocket or Ford's Model T in the past, is to break open new markets. The evolution of ICT in Kenya gives an example of how new technology is creating new market opportunities. M-PESA uses mobile technology to allow the unbanked to transfer money. M-KOPA then couples this advance to the D.Light portable solar light, with SIM cards embedded in the lamps that allow people to lease them. Kilimo Salama uses solar powered mobile towers to monitor weather conditions, and is part of a system that allows farmers to buy weather insurance for crops, and to receive instant claims payments through their mobile phones. Micro-insurance in turn lets the poor make investments in land and tools for further productivity, including technologies such as Slingshot's solar micro-desalination units and Kickstart's hand-pumps to tap the underground water table for less than they would spend on paraffin and firewood.

What this represents is a model of growth and deployment of ICT that is the opposite of the subprime, towards a market that is **big** (1.6 billion people, for example, are without power); **growing** (it is in these emerging markets that the 3.2 billion people will be added between now and 2050); **willing to pay** (the world's poorest pay an estimated US$36 billion a year for paraffin alone, and **elastic on supply** (delivering goods and services into these markets raises productivity and incomes, enhancing the ability to pay back and invest in additional productive goods). The logic of capitalism today points towards this extensive economy, rather than to the subprime derivatives of the recent past.

But there is one key question remaining. The economic model this presents may help address what your neighbour asked for in our initial thought experiment. But will this model get implemented? Over the last 200 years, as Carlota Perez has identified, there have been five *'great surges of development'*: from water power, weaving looms and canals to coal, steam locomotives and railways; from steel, electricity and transmission lines to automobiles, oil and highways. Each great surge has coincided with a new type of power being harnessed and distributed, allowing large groups of people to improve their productive capacity. Chapter 8 looks at the third emerging city on the hill: a distributed city of producer capitalism and engaged, prosperous citizens. It looks at technological advances that may accelerate the evolution of this new city. The examples of power blackouts in India and Ohio show the structural problems of centralized power grids: ageing, increasingly expensive to maintain, routine outages, and high costs for consumers. However, this need not be the only model on offer. Although the prospects for replacing the energy demands of the Petropolis with cleaner renewable sources seem bleak, the success of the distributed city does not depend on sustaining the outmoded and dysfunctional. A smart micro-grid is emerging and energy-independent communities are producing and selling distributed clean power from Texas to South Korea.

Today, smart micro-grids, falling solar panel prices, and other advances are creating an energy internet that has the capacity to introduce and distribute new sources of energy that are globally and freely available (e.g. solar, wind, rivers, sea). In the same way that centralized electricity generation enabled manufacturers to rethink their entire modus operandi, so the energy internet enables business to rethink production, productivity, and prosperity.

Kentaro Toyama tells us that technology is not the answer but the amplifier of intent. As the example of a local power grid in Austin, Texas shows, one effect of the neighbourhood co-production of power is to catalyse civic intent. To test this hypothesis, Chapter 8 examines three stubborn problems for a city: the social impact of the car, political engagement, and good jobs. Can ICT act as an amplifier of intent to help create a city in which the people flourish? What emerges is ICT's potential to help the city thrive through forms such as liquid democracy, participatory budgeting, and crowd sourced corruption monitoring, and then to drive local political engagement and direct funds to the projects the community wants. The impact of these advances, singly and collectively, is to increase civic engagement, the commitment and capacity of the community to shape the space they will thrive in.

The final question is, what is next? In Chapter 9, we look at the prospects of the three cities against the quadrilemma of environmental, social, economic, and governance crises that we set out at the start of this book. While the new direction of growth does not immunize society against the full challenges of climate change, and its evolution is inherently unpredictable, it appears to perform better than its alternatives on the twin test of delivering increases in productivity, and providing a dematerialized and distributed growth model that responds to the social and environmental challenges. But will this be the city that thrives? And what are its accelerators? Chapter 9 looks at the roles of business and government. What are the challenges and opportunities? Who is doing what? And what, specifically, is being done in programmes such as Barcelona's network of FabLabs in order to gain advantage by accelerating the transition of the new GPT, and restoring the economy to productive growth?

What our exploration unearths is a portrait of the possible. The alternatives we describe are not inevitable, and crises are by definition moments of decision and action. But it is a portrait that maps a range of the real challenges and opportunities for business in a world that is already certain to be fundamentally different to the one we are used to. The thesaurus found in Microsoft Word (one of the current ICT giants) says that the opposite of an optimist is a realist. By contrast, we believe that realists have the rights to optimism, but in an age of multiple tipping points and crucial moments of decision, realism has to be snatched from tired thinkers and put in the hands of imaginative actors. In other words, into the hands of optimists everywhere.

2

Turnaround Challenge: Escaping the Petropolis

IN THIS CHAPTER

The turnaround challenge for business. Why the current business model has run its course. Is this a cause for optimism or pessimism? The changing meaning of business success.

> *'When you think of the good old days, think one word: dentistry.'*[1]
>
> P.J. O'Rourke

The Rhetoric of Extinction

When the Mayan prophesy of the apocalypse failed to come true on 21 December 2012 it joined a long list of eco-apocalyptic announcements, covering the gamut from the air we breathe to the food we eat:

- Hundreds of millions of people will soon perish in smog disasters in New York and Los Angeles...
- The oceans will die of DDT poisoning by 1979...
- USA life expectancy will drop to 42 years by 1980 due to cancer epidemics.[2]
- Humanity's greatest challenge may soon be just making it to the next harvest.

For the Mayan apocalypse, the French Government had troops on standby, '(T)here can be a danger of psychological collapse,' a spokesperson said, 'If fragile, vulnerable people expect an event like the end of the world and it doesn't happen, they can feel let down and in anguish.'

While some would argue that on occasion these announcements have themselves helped ward off dire outcomes, the reality is that the worst has not yet happened. Between 1958 and 1962, thirty-six million Chinese died of famine; since the economic and industrial reforms in 1981, 600 million of their descendants have been lifted out of poverty. As Stephen Pinker, Matt Ridley, and others have commented, capitalism may not be perfect, but around the world child mortality has fallen; war between free market economies is almost non-existent; and people live longer, are better educated, and enjoy more material wealth than ever before. Since capitalism began to take hold as the dominant social system in the late eighteenth century, it has stimulated an unprecedented amount of technological innovation, enabling 97 per cent of all human wealth to be created in just 0.01 per cent of human history.[3]

But when executives look out at the world around them, they see numerous crises that seem to require business to think and behave differently than it has in the past. The turnaround challenge they face is to understand whether optimists like Pinker and Ridley have got it right, or if there is a genuine need for an alternative approach to business. In 1830, Thomas Macaulay posed what seems a rhetorical question: *'On what principle is it that, when we see nothing but improvement behind us, we are to expect nothing but deterioration before us?'* In the following sections, we will explore if the answer is as obvious as it once seemed, or if there is something different about the crises already in our midst.

A View from a Bridge: Does the Rhetoric have a Rationale?

Let's stress test Macaulay by taking a concrete example. Take a look at the photo (Figure 2.1).

Imagine you are an archaeologist from another galaxy and this snapshot is the only remnant you have of life on Earth at the start of the twenty-first century. First off, the big picture: would you want to live in that place? Next, do you know where it is? The answer is in the richest economy in the world, the United States of America. More specifically, it is New Orleans in the aftermath of Hurricane Katrina.

Let's dig deeper. What, if this one photo was your data set, could you guess about the economic system? Are there, for example, any glitches you see?

First of all, look at the people. There seems to be a large group of people stretched along the left side, some of them shielding themselves from the sun with umbrellas. They are crowded behind some kind of barrier. Some have white skin but the majority is black. What conclusions can be drawn about their economy? There are some issues around equality, with differences in resilience against natural disasters across ethnic groups. Perhaps some people

Figure 2.1: A view from a bridge

had safe havens to go to and fled there in private cars. Others, maybe, did not and are stuck immobile behind concrete barriers.

Next let's look at the natural environment. What you notice about it chiefly is that it is not there. The mangrove swamps of New Orleans have been concreted over. Then look for the evidence of government's role. The police look fairly settled in. Although this picture was taken days after the storm, the police are still there observing what is going on. There are lorries lined up behind a barrier, with palettes delivering emergency supplies to the stranded. On the lorries is the blue badge of Wal-Mart. The central role in emergency response appears to be being delivered by the supermarket chain. Armed police guards, and the repositioned concrete lane divider protect the Wal-Mart distribution team.

What are we to make of this roadside scene?[4] Is it an anomaly we should not read much into? Or does this roadway huddle depict the first of our cities of the future? Does it outline the contours of Petropolis, the unequal and decreasingly resilient city for which Katrina and subsequent storm events in the USA and elsewhere are no longer the exception but the norm?

To answer this we need to go back to a turning point in the development of twentieth-century capitalism and the arrival of something that is only at the periphery of our picture, the car.

Under the Bonnet of Capitalism: the Model T Ford

When Henry Ford introduced the Model T Ford in 1908, he came up with a contraption we would not even call a lemon. The petrol tank was a firebomb in waiting right under the seat. The vehicle had no heater or windows. You had to start it with a crank handle. Hold this the wrong way and you risked breaking your thumb or arm. (To remedy this, the Non-Kick Device Company of Kansas City, Missouri, developed an improved starting handle marketed under the caption 'Broken Arms Prevented.') The car crept forward as soon as you cranked it, often before you had the chance to climb on board. The cast iron steering column pointed directly at your heart. Moreover, once you were under way, there were no real roads to travel on: With a 10-gallon tank and 20 miles per gallon fuel economy, the first Model T had a range that was 45 miles more than the combined total of 155 miles of surfaced roads in the whole of the USA at the time.

The car, as we know from history, sold like hot cakes. When the ten millionth Model T rolled off the production line, 50 per cent of all cars in the world were Fords. The Model T was so successful that Ford did not purchase any advertising between 1917 and 1923; more than 15 million Model Ts were manufactured, reaching a rate of over 9,000 cars a day in 1925, or two million annually.

Transforming manufacturing . . .

Ford took the combustion engine, a technology that had been underperforming for 30 odd years as a plaything for the rich, and he democratized it for the masses. The Model T was a tool that increased people's productivity, whether it was used as a car, tractor, flatbed truck, or fishing boat. And it was a tool people could afford. Ford's approach—counter-intuitive as the USA's economy recovered haltingly from the Panic of 1907—was simple: to expand the market. He would take the painstakingly hand-crafted status symbol that was the automobile, and commoditize its production until the purchase price dropped to a level his workers could afford. 'I will build a motorcar for the great multitude,' he proclaimed. And he did.

Ford's methods of standardized parts and mass production, inspired by the overhead conveyor 'disassembly lines' of the Chicago slaughterhouses, transformed efficiency. According to Womack, Jones, and Roos, '[T]he assembler . . . had only one task—to put two nuts on two bolts or perhaps to attach one wheel to each car. He didn't order parts, procure his tools, repair his equipment, inspect for quality, or even understand what workers on either side of him were doing' (Womack, 1990: 31).

By 1914, this evolving assembly-line process had reduced the time for building an individual car from 12 hours to 93 minutes. In 1909, the standard four-seat open tourer cost $850. In 1913 the price dropped to $550 and in 1915 to $440. In 1914, an assembly line worker could buy a Model T with just four months' pay. By the 1920s, the price had fallen to $260 driven by volume and increasing efficiencies of assembly line technique. By 1927, the Model T's last year, Ford was producing them at a rate of one every 24 seconds.

Ford transformed the automobile itself from a luxury to a necessity. He also reshaped the industrial landscape beyond his sector. He showed the potential to apply electricity to mass production. In the steam era, a giant engine had powered a central rotating shaft, and machine tools ran off pulleys in long linear factories with decreasing functionality. In the new electric model of production, small motors could be arranged on the factory floor. It was an early industrial version of the move from centralized to efficient, distributed processing.

... and transforming markets

In terms of industrial evolution, this was the best of all possible worlds. Technological innovation brought economies of scale that drove step-function improvements in productivity and continual reductions in unit costs.[5] Each reduction in the unit price of electricity opened up the possibility of new uses that brought further reductions because the high fixed costs of plant investment could be spread over greater sales volumes. What were once luxuries (e.g. the light bulb) became commodities as a train of advances lowered costs and increased sales.

One can argue that personal computers, mobile phones, and the internet are the latest manifestation of the luxury to commodity process, and to an extent they are because they rely on the vast centralized manufacturing processes that Ford pioneered at the Rouge complex near Detroit. He also reshaped labour relations, introducing the five dollar day in a bid to reward workers with purchasing power and reduce high turnover rates. 'I have heard it said, in fact, I believe it's quite a current thought, that we have taken skill out of work,' he said. 'We have not. We have put a higher skill into planning, management, and tool building, and the results of that skill are enjoyed by the man who is not skilled.'

But Ford's influence didn't stop there. As much as he transformed manufacturing, he transformed markets. Cars for the masses also reconfigured the relationship between rural and urban communities. The revolution in production and consumption inaugurated by the railway age had been essentially an urban revolution, bypassing any rural communities more than a horse and trap's ride from a railway station. Motor transport, aided by seven successive USA administrations that built a total of 435,000 miles of road, integrated rural regions into the marketplace, at the same time laying the rails for a revolution in mass communications driven by the rollout of radio and then TV.

On 27 September 1908 the first Model T emerged from the Piquette Plant in Detroit, Michigan. Eighteen years later, on 26 May 1927, the 15 millionth rolled off the assembly line at the Highland Park, Michigan. In the intervening years, Ford's high capex investments had netted him a sum estimated to be US $190 billion in today's terms. It had also laid out the contours for a new form of capitalism, replacing craft and artisanal techniques with an economy based around fossil fuel-driven mass production and consumption. This transition transformed the living standards of communities in the USA and around the world, putting within reach of most a quality of life that had been the preserve exclusively of the rich.

The rubber hits the road: the legacy of Fordism

The economic model of fossil fuel-driven mass production and consumption resulted in a great surge of development to rival and exceed that of earlier phases of the first Industrial Revolution. It is a defining feature of twentieth-century capitalism, globalized by Robert McNamara, briefly President of Ford, during his Presidency of the World Bank. It is to Ford that we owe the lorries and helicopters that brought aid to Katrina's victims as well as the leisure time, bright lights, and electronic music that made New Orleans the entertainment mecca it was. It also underpins however some of the environmental, social, and economic challenges revealed in the roadside scene captured in our snapshot of New Orleans. On the environmental side, mangrove swamps made way for the suburban real estate and highways that accompanied the car. This paving over of natural capital had more than an aesthetic cost: the mangrove swamps also performed an economic function: they were buffers against tidal surges, serving as sponges that soaked up water and stopped it swamping a city that has 49 per cent of its territory below sea level. The post-Katrina cost of paving over this natural capital came to more than 1,400 deaths, 70,000 lost jobs, and an estimated US$125 billion in damages.[6] Costanza's assessment of New Orleans' mangroves estimates their annual economic contribution at US$6 billion.

Man-made climate change, created by increasing concentrations of fossil fuel-driven carbon dioxide in the atmosphere has been frequently cited as a factor behind Katrina and subsequent storms along the US East Coast. It was, some allege, partly due to fossil-fuel dependency that 3,000 of the National Guard were unable to assist in New Orleans. While Wal-Mart delivered emergency services, the Guard was engaged in a war in Iraq to secure the oil supply essential to the US global production and logistics chain.

Katrina reveals more, however, than the environmental dimension of the mass era. Early adopters of mass production now have to deal with a range of social challenges, from automation, job insecurity, and stagnant wages for many workers, to the dominant role of retail giants such as Wal-Mart as the provider of emergency goods and, post Katrina, a de facto social safety net. When Katrina hit, the average income of the lowest earning 90 per cent of the population in the USA had fallen 0.1 per cent in 20 years, just when the 1 per cent was reaching roughly 20 per cent of the total (including capital gains) compared to under 10 per cent in 1985.[7] Against that backdrop, one of Wal-Mart's central achievements at a time when real wages were barely rising for large segments of the population was to keep down the cost of living.

The same logic of mass—driving down price to push up volume—underpinned Wal-Mart's business strategy of outsourcing production of those goods to low-cost producers, and the economic consequences that followed. The model of low-cost mass consumption pushed manufacturing and jobs overseas, to countries where the national narrative was not about mortgage-fuelled debt and stagnant wages, but about industrialization, economic growth, an emerging middle class, and national savings looking for international investment opportunities. The standards of living of the people in our photograph had been maintained by an industrializing China and other emerging economies and the reinvestment of their trade surplus in the USA's debt. Soon, rather than relying on spiralling house prices, those same people would be reliant on China's continuing economic growth so that China and other emerging economies would keep buying sovereign debt even when it reached 120 per cent of GDP in 2010.[8] By then, the economic impact of a struggling mass era was being felt far beyond the USA, and a model of growth that had defined business success was looking in need of turnaround.

And after Ford . . . is there a Next Great Surge?

In Aldous Huxley's 1932 book *Brave New World*, Henry Ford, 'Our Ford' has a messianic status. Graveyard crosses are truncated to Ts, in honour of both Ford's best-selling model and his cost cutting. The era is named not AD (Anno Domini) but AF (After Ford). Huxley's analysis is one-sided. Ford's model of consumer capitalism transformed the living standards of the people on the roadside a legacy ignored by Huxley. But it also laid some of the foundations for a city that, after a long period of prosperity, would end up with depleted natural resources, vulnerability to flooding, income inequality, persistent low pay, underemployment, subprime houses doubling as ATMs to fuel a consumption boom and a manufacturing capacity that had been outsourced for cost reasons to China.

Katrina is not just a picture of the USA or even of the economic giants of the Organisation for Economic Co-operation and Development (OECD). It is a snapshot of a possible future for today's mass-based economies. There are many good reasons for wanting that era to continue, for wanting its benefits to be enjoyed by the Earth's growing population. That is why many people in politics, academia, business, and the media insist that the norms and values of that era be rolled out around the world. The Katrina photo shows they are wrong, because it shows that the conditions which allowed mass to deliver a surge in welfare no longer apply. The risk now is if society persists in treating the mass era as the zenith of capitalism and its model of growth as immutable. That vision is a dangerous one for society, but it is also a bleak one for business that cannot flourish in a floundering society. In the words of Fabio Barbosa, then President of Banco Real, Brazil, 'a bank is only as healthy as the society around it is healthy.'

Capitalism, as Kondratiev first observed, evolves in waves. Its genius is its capacity to hunt out new technologies that deliver prosperity to its citizens. This book asks two central questions. First, do the emerging social, environmental, and economic challenges suggest that the current model of capitalism is no longer fit for purpose? Second, if there are challenges, is there a new model of capitalism that addresses them? Is there another wave of growth ahead? For naive optimists, the answer to the first question is a resounding no. There are no structural challenges that the market cannot resolve and we should get on with enjoying things. For pessimists, there are challenges and the logic of capitalism is to amplify them. We are headed, at best, for what Tyler Cowen refers to as 'the great stagnation.' Between these two extremes sit reluctant optimists: those who recognize that there are structural challenges, but believe the logic of capitalism is not to aggravate them but to address them.

Gramsci talks of pessimism of the intellect but optimism of the will. As authors, our job, as best we can, is to have agnosticism of the intellect. We want to celebrate capitalism's historic triumphs, but also examine its current challenges and prospects for delivering once again the surges of development that it has driven in the past.

Anatomizing the Crisis

The origins of the word crisis are in the Greek word for 'choice' or 'decision' (κρίσις). A crisis wasn't just about a state of affairs, it was about decisive action to respond to that state. The difference is one of agency. States of affairs aren't handed down to us (unless you are an extreme determinist). We aren't their consumers: we also help to produce and adapt them.

Crisis is an overused word that can be found underscoring a range of moments of intense difficulty escalating from wardrobe crisis to mid-life crisis to crises of humanity.[9] If one looks from the window of the executive suite today, there are crises from here to the horizon. Financial crisis, sovereign debt, conflict, unemployment, global warming, water shortages, commodity prices, inequality, religious zealotry, decline of the old powers, poverty . . . The list is long, and each crisis has ramifications for business, not just because it affects investment, production, and consumption, but because as the representative social institution (to use Peter Drucker's term) business, if it is to retain its social licence to operate, is expected to respond to and address them. Consequently, an executive can gaze from the C-suite and wonder how food insecurity in developing economies will affect his business, but he can also think how to respond as a representative social institution; not necessarily because it is morally creditworthy but because institutions that do not perform the functions society assigns to them are at risk.

Transformational Crises

Not all crises or decision points are equal. Crises can be differentiated on different axes, for example, by their theme, their magnitude, and the agents involved. Our focus is on business as an agent, and on the key decision points it faces if it is to continue to deliver prosperity. Amid the welter of crises the modern CEO or board member has to grapple with, we propose to focus on what we would term the transformational crises: the decision points that affect the nature of capitalism—what the capitalism of the future, one that delivers for its citizens, can look like.

These *transformational* crises have a number of characteristics. They have the power to fundamentally change the way business is done. They are *crises* because they not only present decision points, they are acute. They mark the moment at which decisions have to be made; decisions that can't be put off, or left to the march of history to sort out. They are, finally, global not just local in nature. They affect business internationally, and in doing so they have ramifications for society as a whole.

We have singled out four crises (Box 2.1). Many readers interested in modern business will be familiar with the themes, and we offer a more detailed overview of each one in Chapter 3. What we want to emphasize for now, though, is how the crises relate to one another. Each one is a moment of decisive change in its own right, but their full significance stems from the way they interact. Take any one by itself and it presents business with numerous dilemmas. Take them together, though, and business confronts a 'quadrilemma' of crises. Under this quadrilemma, what might be a rational response to one crisis can

15

Box 2.1 THE QUADRILEMMA OF CRISES			
TYPE	**CRISIS**	**THREAT**	**DECISION POINT**
Economic	Declining productivity	Ongoing economic stagnation	Credit-driven consumption vs. productive economy
Environmental	Climate change	Feedback loops leading to existential risk	High carbon vs. low carbon growth
Social	Demographic change and rising unmet needs	Crisis of humanity	Intensive economy vs. extensive economy, addressing unmet needs
Governance	Path-dependency	Lock-in	Centralised vs. distributed forms of governance

become irrational or unfeasible given the other crises that are unfolding. A perfectly logical response to climate change, for instance, may make no sense at all in the context of population growth, and moreover could be implausible given shifts in global wealth and power.

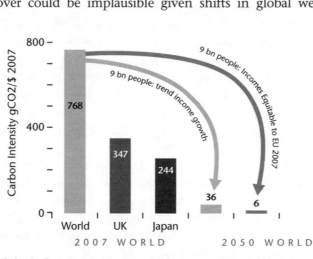

Figure 2.2: Carbon intensities required to meet 450ppm target
Source: Adapted from Jackson 2009

Nowhere is this clearer than in Figure 2.2 (based on Jackson's analysis[10]). In a world of nine billion people enjoying a roughly stable climate and the same trend income growth as in recent years, the amount of carbon used for each US $ of GDP (carbon intensity) would need to fall from 768 grams of carbon dioxide (gCO_2) in 2007 to 36 in 2050. In that same world but with everyone enjoying incomes similar to those in the European Union in 2007, carbon intensity would need to drop from 768 to 6 gCO_2 per US$ GDP. In other words, maintaining the status quo would require a sharp improvement in carbon intensity, but a more equal world of the kind emerging nations demand requires even more drastic changes.

Climate change and existential risk

The first crisis we will examine is around climate change. If Katrina gave early indications of this crisis, the years since have turned up the volume. In November 2012, at the end of a year which saw record states of climate-driven emergency declared in counties across the USA, Hurricane Sandy battered the East Coast of New York. Mayor Bloomberg of New York, on the eve of the US election commented, *'It's the climate change.'*

Climate change, the most transformational of the numerous environmental crises, represents a long-term existential risk to human society and some of the Earth's ecosystems. Put simply (and we will elaborate on this in the next chapter), there is overwhelming evidence that greenhouse gas emissions are increasing at a rate that, if unchecked, will lead to catastrophic climate change. This increase was accelerated by the mass era throughout much of the twentieth century, and continues today. It will take an unprecedented social, technological, and economic effort to stabilize the climate at a point at which the rise in global average temperature poses a minimal risk to human existence. The clear implication is that society cannot address this existential risk without adapting the model of fossil fuel-driven mass production and consumption. Society, if the evidence is right, faces a decision point if it is to confront this existential threat, either to scale back growth or to find a low emissions alternative that decouples growth from carbon.

Demographic change and a crisis of humanity

The second crisis, a social one, is anchored in the complexity of demographic change: from population growth, low infant mortality, ageing, urbanization and migration, to malnutrition, obesity, and rising inequality. Demographic change is not an existential risk but a crisis of humanity that raises issues not just of well-being and prosperity, but of fairness: just what does business produce and for whom? Failure to address these demographic changes (leaving 1.6 billion people without a reliable supply of electricity, or 1.4 billion without access to potable water, for example) harms people if not humanity. The events of the 'Arab Spring' in 2010 illustrated the instability of this inequality and its potential to destabilize regional government and business.

The crisis of demographic change is, however, not simply about poverty and marginalization. In October 2005, a Citigroup analyst issued a memo to investors dividing the world's major economies into two blocs: one egalitarian

17

(e.g. continental Europe, Japan), the other comprising 'plutonomies' in which the economy is driven by a small group of the wealthiest citizens (e.g. USA, UK, and Canada). The initial memo and two subsequent ones in 2006 found their way into the public domain and became highly controversial.[11] Amongst investors, coming at a time when bonds connected to subprime mortgages were at their peak, the plutonomy memos might have been seen as unremarkable, another way of breathing some life into equities—and the researchers behind them highlighted how stocks of companies such as Richemont and Bulgari, that primarily served the rich, outperformed others. But the impact of the memos has been far greater than normal research analysts' reports, spurring a debate around 'plutonomy' as a form of market-led growth.

The plutonomy debate was taken up by various anti-capitalist movements, including in recent years the Occupy Movement and the campaign for the 99 per cent, i.e. the vast majority who it is claimed have received limited benefits from recent financial boom times. The Occupy Movement built their protest campaign around the richest 1 per cent, which in the UK means anyone with an income of £143,000 or more and in the USA US$344,000.[12] Disparities in wealth, the closing gap between rich and middle income countries and the growing gap between the rich and poor in OECD countries are all part of the backdrop against which the transformational crises are unfolding.

However, the exact definition of plutonomy is a secondary issue. The take-away from the 'Plutonomy' memos is the dispassionate analysis that a relatively small number of people own a vast amount of wealth (far larger than the target market of the bottom billion capitalism of C.K. Prahalad and others[13]) and that this market is a logical investment opportunity. The core issue, the one that Citigroup's analysts were correct to identify, is that business in the mass era is set up around a growth model that focuses on stimulating and serving demand for products and services for those who can afford to be served. The expectation is that this group will expand, thanks to the employment opportunities created by market growth, and one of the claims made about the mass era is that, as it has spread globally, it has lifted unprecedented numbers of people out of poverty. However, as the mass era has evolved, job creation has become a by-product of business, and, in OECD countries in particular, an uncertain one characterized by job insecurity and stagnant wages exacerbating the consequences of demographic change. This is in marked contrast with Ford's theory that he could grow his company by increasing his customers' and workers' prosperity. Hence, a decision point today is whether to focus on those who can afford to be served, or consciously expand the market through goods and jobs that enhance prosperity. We characterize this as the choice between the intensive and the extensive economy.

Economic crisis of declining productivity

The third crisis relates to the global economy. There is an ongoing economic shift of historic proportions around productivity. Ford's production lines increased workers' productivity and allowed labour and investors to benefit. Over time, labour came to be seen as a substitutable factor of production that found itself in competition with automation as much as a globally distributed labour pool. As a result, all manner of management decisions with a negative impact on workers were justified by appeal to productivity benefits that increased returns on investment. Now, however, orthodox thinking about productivity is itself being questioned. Return on assets (ROA) is a measure to assess a company's profitability as a ratio of its assets, and therefore the productivity of those assets. In its 2012 *Shift Index*, used to create Figure 2.3, the consultancy firm Deloitte showed a 45 year decline in ROA, from an average of just under 3 per cent in the late 1970s to 0.5–1.7 per cent in the period since 2007.[14] Any upticks in ROA, Deloitte argued, were due to the short-term measure of laying off workers. Yet even this has not prevented the long-term fall in ROA.

Scraping the barrel: technological maturity and declining returns . . .

This decline is symptomatic of the decreasing incremental productivity that accompanies the approach of any technological era towards maturity. Each such era has its general purpose technology (GPT), a concept we explore more in Chapter 6. A GPT brings huge benefits in terms of productivity and cost, as was the case with the fossil fuel-based combustion engine. Over time, however, as the GPT is fully deployed, these benefits diminish making productivity gains

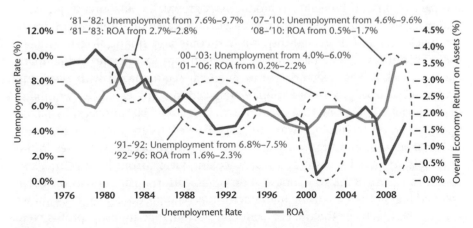

Figure 2.3: Return on assets and USA unemployment rate (1976–2010)
Source: Hagel 2011

harder and more expensive to achieve. One can see this by looking at estimated energy return on energy invested (EROEI). While many theorists have commented on peak oil and the long-term availability of oil and natural gas, a factor that affects industrial productivity is the return on oil—the excess energy you get out of oil, net of the energy it takes to extract it. The oil that powered Ford's Model Ts was easy oil, with an EROEI of approximately 100. Dig a hole and gush it, you 100 times more energy than you put in. This abundant and cheap energy is one of the main reasons the mass era business model served society so well. Excitement about the positive impact shale gas will have on energy prices needs to be tempered by the fact that this is an energy intensive extraction system with an EROEI of 5:1. Even in the few prospects where one can still drill a well that will produce over 100,000 barrels of oil per day, like the deepwater Gulf of Mexico, the EROEI varies from 4 to 14.[15]

The more society relies on sources with a low EROEI such as biofuels, nuclear power, deep water drilling, and tar sands, the more costly energy becomes, and therefore less and less affordable to increasing numbers of people. Furthermore, a low EROEI means more energy and more financial capital is being eaten up to cause a net energy decline. Mearns calls this a 'net energy cliff' and argues there is an exponential drop in the energy available to society once EROEI falls below 10:1.[16] The ratios are controversial and are only just starting to be rigorously tested,[17] but they add to the evidence too much faith is being put on maintaining a high energy—even if lower carbon—society, when there is little reason for such confidence.

. . . and the business response of offshoring

Part of industry's response to these two factors, as mapped in the *Shift Index*, has been to offset this decline in productivity growth by outsourcing, job cuts, and wage freezes, leaving communities with increased unemployment, lower pay packages, and decreased disposable income and financial resilience. In OECD countries, this helped provide the conditions for changes in the financial sector. Like manufacturing, the financial sector, faced with declining profitability from its conventional transactions, increased its emphasis on financial engineering to secure returns. One financial innovation enabled by information technology was mortgage-backed securities, involving portfolios of subprime mortgages. Tranches of mortgage-backed securities (MBS) were sold to global investors similarly seeking yields, from local councils to Iceland's Glitnir Bank to Chinese state organizations. The returns on these were far higher than anything manufacturing could produce: Figure 2.4 shows that at the height of the dot.com bubble, non-finance industry profits were already lagging behind those of the finance industry, but by 2007 there was no correlation at all.

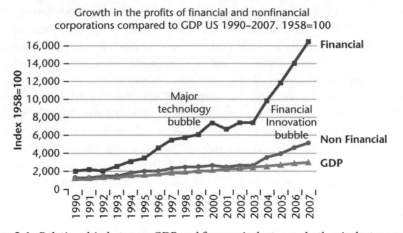

Growth in the profits of financial and nonfinancial corporations compared to GDP US 1990–2007. 1958=100

Figure 2.4: Relationship between GDP and finance industry and other industry profits, 1990–2007

Source: Perez 2009

The rise of MBS, credit default swaps and collateralized debt obligations, and its consequences for global finance has been told numerous times. What is important in terms of the transformational crises that define business's turn-around challenge is that for perhaps the first time in history lenders no longer prioritized their borrowers' ability to service debt and manage the risk that entailed. Instead, their primary interest was maximizing the volume of mortgage transactions. As Ritholtz comments, 'the history of commercial credit has, for millions of years, been based on the borrower's ability to service the debt. What took place from 2002 to 2007 is that the borrower's ability to service the debt was replaced with a new standard for making loans... the ability of the lender to sell that debt to a Wall Street securitizer.'[18] In the words of Warren Buffett to the Financial Crisis Inquiry Commission: 'There was the greatest bubble I've ever seen in my life... The entire American public eventually was caught up in a belief that housing prices could not fall dramatically.' The escalation of the subprime crisis into a financial crisis, and then via bank bailouts into an ongoing economic and ultimately political crisis is not the focus of this book. What is central is the decision point revealed by the roots of the subprime crisis, whether to maintain an economic model that fuels growth through unsustainable consumption or move to a model that drives growth through advances in productivity.

Governance and path dependence

The first three transformational crises centre on specific external challenges that confront society and business in particular. The fourth and final crisis is

21

an internal challenge to do with governance concerns our ability to respond to crises. Does society have an economic, political, social, and legal system whose direction just cannot be shifted? This governance crisis reveals itself in relation to specific crises. 'New Orleans,' the *New Scientist* had warned in 2001, 'is a disaster waiting to happen.'[19] In September 2003, at a hearing of the House Financial Services Committee, Congressman Ron Paul predicted the impacts of the housing bubble, 'Like all artificially-created bubbles, the boom in housing prices cannot last forever. When housing prices fall, homeowners will experience difficulty as their equity is wiped out. Furthermore, the holders of the mortgage debt will also have a loss.' The *Economist* magazine in June 2005 stated, 'The worldwide rise in house prices is the biggest bubble in history, prepare for the economic pain when it pops.'[20]

The Crisis of Governance

It is not just voices in the USA that get ignored. Adair Turner, then chair of the UK Financial Services Authority, announced that 'Growth...needs to be dethroned.' *Financial Times* columnist, Martin Wolf, announced that 'Another god, capitalism, has fallen.' One time Russian oligarch, Mikhail Khordokovsky, stated, 'Oil is a thing of the past.' The then president of France, Nicolas Sarkozy, declared, 'We must change the insane system of capitalism.'

Yet, over five years later, the same model of capitalism was in place, delegitimized and yet not weakened. The reason for this is path dependency. Values and beliefs change over time, but at any given moment they have a huge effect on what happens next. Path dependency is another way of saying that history matters: society's responses are governed by its experiences. Thus, a society that sees the car as an essential part of leisure, family, work, and status is not going to abandon it overnight no matter how compelling the evidence for climate change may be. Likewise, the new middle class in emerging economies has been brought up on the promise of material prosperity and will pursue the path that fulfils that dream.

Geopolitical shifts

The first aspect of this path dependency is the geo-political shift which is changing the balance of international power in ways not seen since the Cold War. This is discussed in more detail in the next chapter, but it refers not only to the growth of emerging economies and their importance to business, but also to the influence many of those countries have over the decisions of advanced economies, not least because they own those countries' debt. This shift in turn affects what are plausible responses to our other crises so that, for instance, calls in the name of combating climate change to deny poor people the material benefits associated with economic growth will go unheeded in ways they might not have previously. Equally, the sight of Western politicians pleading to emerging economies for energy intensive industries such as steel to come to their shores (as happened in 2012 for instance when British politicians appeared to ask India's Tata Steel to move its steel plants from France to London[21]) is likely to become more common as countries try to grow their way out of debt.

Government vs. governance

The other aspect of path dependency is the changing nature of governance itself. In addition to a geo-political shift, how society is governed is altering. Governance is no longer synonymous with government, and companies and civil society have considerable influence on the way society is organized. As the Wal-Mart lorries in the Katrina photo showed, government does not have a monopoly on logistics and infrastructure. Some people feel that business has too much influence over government, be that through political financing, participation in drafting legislation, delivering government services, or self-regulation. However, even the largest companies struggle to manage their reputation and credibility at a time when global communications enable innumerable civil society groups around the world to act as regulators. The challenges around governance mean that forms of state intervention used in the past to direct and accelerate transitions have less currency today. Civil governance, liquid democracy, post-financial crisis capital constraints, and the legitimacy crisis of conventional government in Western democracies, all constrain responses to the underlying environmental, social, and economic challenges. The risk is one of lock-in; that business and the rest of society continues to march in step towards a destination it doesn't collectively want to reach. The decision point is one around intervention. Does society maintain the status quo, where governance has become diffused, or recognize the acuteness of the challenges and empower institutions to accelerate responses?

Can we still Afford a Ford?

Business as the representative institution of modern society confronts four major crises. Taken individually, these have the power to transform the world that business is a part of: taken together they represent a far more complex challenge compounded by their intricate and often contradictory interrelationship. They are a quadrilemma of crises, and their resolution has significant implications for business. They lay the grounds for the argument that we will develop in the coming chapters that the conventions of the mass era are now harmful not only to society but also to business. There is nothing particularly novel in our claim that society is on an unsustainable trajectory. Where we differ, though, is in saying that a transition is possible and that business is key to changing this situation. But for business to address the quadrilemma of crises successfully, it needs a more detailed understanding of the challenges. It is this we turn to now.

Notes

1. http://libertarianquotes.net/O/PJ-O-Rourke.html, accessed November 4, 2012
2. (Ehrlich 1969)
3. (Beinhocker 2007)
4. (Giles, Bates 2005). The figures on losses are from Munich Re, see below
5. (Thurow 1999)
6. Vigdor, Jacob, 'The Economic Aftermath of Hurricane Katrina,' *The Journal of Economic Perspectives* 22 (2008): 141
7. (Palma 2009)
8. Figures are from the IMF, presented in a series of lectures by Valpy Fitzgerald on the Global Financial Crisis and Developing Countries, University of Oxford, 2010.
9. One theory, explored in discussion with Emma Howard-Boyd, on the Board of the UK Green Investment Bank, is that the compulsion of many middle aged men to talk at length about the insolubility of climate change is in fact a projection of their own mid-life crisis
10. (Jackson 2009)
11. (Kapur, Macleod, Singh 2005, 2006; Kapur, Macleod, Levkovich 2006)
12. http://www.bbc.co.uk/news/magazine-15822595, accessed 25 September 2012
13. (Prahalad 2002)
14. (Hagel 2011)
15. (Moerschbaecher 2011)
16. (Mearns 2008)
17. For example Moerschbaecher 2011
18. (Barry 2009)
19. *Scientific American* (October 2001), p.70
20. http://www.economist.com/opinion/displaystory.cfm?story_id=4079027
21. (Elliott, Pagnamenta 2012)

3

Megatrends: Mapping Business's Key Challenges

IN THIS CHAPTER

The external crises in detail: climate change, demographic change, and declining productivity. Examining the internal crisis: Geo-political shift and the changing nature of governance. How these crises relate to social prosperity and business success. Defining the criteria for a response.

> *'The best scientists aren't the ones who know the most data: they're the ones who know what they're looking for.'*
>
> Noam Chomsky

Wicked Problems . . .

Chapter 2 identified a quadrilemma of transformational crises that will shape what is meant by business success, going forwards (Box 2.1). The era of mass and the consumer capitalism that underpinned it delivered a great surge of global development, but it appears there are good reasons to doubt if it is still capable of bringing long-term prosperity. These crises or decision points represent an opportunity for business not just to respond to the economic, environmental, and social side-effects of the maturity of the model of fossil fuel-driven mass production and consumption, but to unleash a new wave of growth.

As noted already, the crises are quite different in nature, but each one affects and is affected by the other three. They have been called 'wicked problems' because they may require contradictory solutions. Like the moles in whack-a-mole, you hit one and another seems to pop up. What looks like the solution to challenge A only worsens challenge B.

Food prices, for example, are expected to increase considerably as climate change takes its toll on rainfall and temperatures. Analyses such as those by International Food Policy Research Institute (IFPRI) show the changes

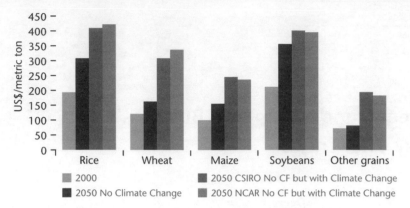

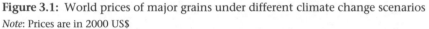

Figure 3.1: World prices of major grains under different climate change scenarios

Note: Prices are in 2000 US$

Source: International Food Policy Research Institute (2009) 'Climate Change—Impact on Agriculture and Costs of Adaptation', http://www.ifpri.org/sites/default/files/publications/pr21.pdf

in average maximum temperatures possible by 2050.[1] Based on these predictions, the price of major grains will double or triple compared to 2000, increasing the food security risk of the world's growing and changing population. Figure 3.1 shows first the increase in prices even if climate change did not occur. The third column, factoring in climate change, is an estimate from the National Center for Atmospheric Research (USA) assuming no CO_2 fertilization; the fourth is an estimate from the Commonwealth Scientific and Industrial Research Organization (Australia) for the same set of conditions. The New England Complex Systems Institute has demonstrated a correlation between rising food prices and the incidence of riots, reminding us of Francis Bacon's comment in the sixteenth century that rebellions of the belly are the worst.[2]

... and Their Illogical Solutions

Yet according to the mass era model, the logical solution to food insecurity is to raise yields by increasing energy use and oil-based fertilizer and pesticide inputs. Thus, in order to increase agricultural productivity so as to meet demand and keep down prices, the risk of higher temperatures and changes in precipitation is worsened, which in turn will have a negative effect on yields and prices. Figuring out the response to this wicked set of problems, then, takes a deep understanding of not just these challenges, but their interdependencies. This chapter aims to synthesize a fairly wide and complex body of literature into something clear and concise for the business reader. Many readers may already have a detailed grasp of these issues, and may want to jump to the end of this chapter. Figure 3.2 with answers at Figure 3.12 is our

MEGATRENDS BY THE NUMBERS

What do any of these refer to?

- 450 and 2
- 0.1%
- 5.1%
- 20% 2030
- 9 tonnes : 10 tonnes
- 1.6 billion
- 7.91 – 2 – 1.44

- 1 in 16; 1 in 3,500
- 3.1 billion
- 3 – 7 – 9 billion
- 68.3% – 51.8%; 2.6% – 16.5%
- 120%
- 220%
- 55 in 1900; 196 in 2012

NB Answers are in Figure 3.13

Figure 3.2: Navigating the numbers

litmus test—if these numbers aren't familiar, parts of this chapter might provide some context to the challenges and ways forward. Otherwise the narrative, gradually building in optimism, continues with Chapter 4.

Climate Change

There is an overwhelming scientific consensus that (a) greenhouse gases (GHG) have reached unprecedented levels, (b) this rise is essential for explaining the global warming seen in the past few decades, and (c) the GHG increase can only be explained with reference to human beings. 'Human activity is to blame for the rise in temperature over recent decades... There are plenty of areas for debate in the global warming story but this is not one of them.' (Walker, King 2008: 37). This is more fully discussed in Box 3.1.

If global average temperatures continue to rise, the Earth's climate will change significantly. If the rise is limited to less than 2°C compared to the start of the Industrial Revolution, the changes will be considerable but not unpredictable. If we go beyond that 2°C line, scientists believe we will have entered a period of unpredictable and perhaps catastrophic change.

Two broad strategies have dominated climate change discussions: mitigation (i.e. preventing temperatures rising by 2°C) and adaptation (i.e. responding to the consequences of global warming including the increasingly unpredictable changes should temperatures rise by more than 2°C). There are examples of both strategies in the response of business to climate change, but mitigation accounts for the majority of actions so far. Mitigation can be subdivided between different efforts to reduce GHG emissions; technical innovations to prevent emissions, financial innovations to change damaging behaviours, and experiments in creating a new type of low-carbon economy. As a result there have been private sector investments in energy efficiency,

Climate Change: The Background for Business

Box 3.1 CLIMATE CHANGE: THE BACKGROUND FOR BUSINESS

Climate change has become part of the vocabulary of everyday life. Some fear it, some doubt it; it is talked about both as a threat to humanity and as a hoax; it informs government policy and management practices; it inspires local community action and drives people into the streets in protest. Yet, in spite of its high profile, its significance is still often misrepresented, so we will begin with the facts.

The greenhouse effect, long targeted as the culprit behind global warming, is in itself a good thing. Without the greenhouse effect, the warmth of the planet would pour into space, the UK would be in the grip of frost, and the Earth would have the climate of Mars or Venus. In a greenhouse, sun shines through the glass and heats the inside. Whatever is inside the glass glows with warmth, and pours out infrared light. Some of that light remains inside, however, and overall the light and heat inside is more than that which pours out.

Greenhouse gases such as carbon dioxide, water, and methane act as the Earth's glass, and they trap just enough infrared light to stop the world freezing or boiling. Water is the largest GHG but it is not important in the climate change context because it is already so plentiful that any changes would be like a bucket tossed into the ocean. CO_2 and methane comprise less than 0.1 per cent of the atmosphere, and any changes in that amount are akin to pouring buckets into a bath. In other words, human activity can affect these particular GHGs in significant ways.

The greenhouse effect was discovered by Joseph Fourier in 1827, but we can understand previous climate changes by looking at ice cores, tree rings, coral, the pollen in lake mud, and, at least since 1659, through temperature records. These different sources of evidence reveal that the Earth's climate changes, but for the past 10,000 years (i.e. since the start of the Neolithic era) there has been a period of relative stability. That appears to be changing, quickly. Higher levels of carbon dioxide are found in the atmosphere than at any time in the last 650000 years, and certainly in the 50000 years of Homo sapiens' occupation. For the last 400000 years according to ice core data the amount of CO_2 in the atmosphere varied in cycles between about 175 parts per million (ppm) and about 300 ppm. Now it is 400 ppm, well above the 350 ppm figure initially presented as the safe upper limit for CO_2. Even achieving stabilization below 450 ppm requires major reductions in fossil-fuel emissions, and the decoupling of economic growth from carbon.

Although burning wood and crops also emits CO_2, the real danger lies in unlocking ancient stores of CO_2 as this leads to a drastic change in the balance of the atmosphere. Volcanoes may erupt and naturally occurring wildfires are part of sustainable ecosystems, but only the release of CO_2 through the use of hydrocarbons can realistically explain what has happened with the Earth's atmosphere since the Industrial Revolution. This is the overwhelming conclusion of global climate models, and while there is disagreement about what will happen (e.g. articles published by the Royal Society in 2010 predict a 4°C rise in temperature by 2060), there is no scientifically robust evidence that the causes are anything other than man-made.

low-carbon and renewable energy sources, geo-engineering, and carbon trading, all designed to reduce the amount of GHG used per unit of economic output. Large companies such as Unilever, General Electric, and Vattenfall have put climate change at the heart of their strategic thinking, and growth in sectors such as solar panels in China, battery electric vehicles in Japan, and eco-efficient buildings in Scandinavia is climate change driven.

Climate Change: Deeper Dive

THE SIZE OF THE CHALLENGE
The size of the challenge is immense as Figure 3.3 shows. The world effectively has had a trillion tonne carbon emissions budget that it can spend without increasing temperatures by 2°C. Since the onset of the Industrial Revolution it has used up half of that, and at current rates the budget will be spent by the early 2040s. According to PwC's Low Carbon Economy Index, the world now needs to improve the carbon intensity of growth by 5.1 per cent a year until 2050, a rate society has not yet achieved for a single year, never mind every year for the next 38 years (Figure 3.4).[3]

Nothing that has happened so far to combat climate change gives grounds for confidence that we will stay below the 2°C threshold. According to PWC's

Figure 3.3: The trillion tonne budget of carbon emissions
Source: trillionthtonne.org, accessed 3 December 2012

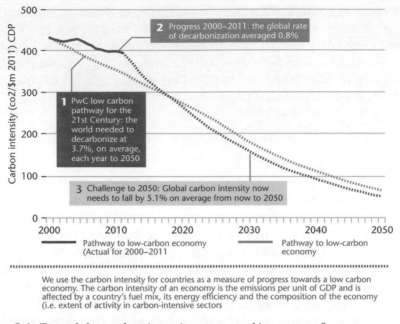

We use the carbon intensity for countries as a measure of progress towards a low carbon economy. The carbon intensity of an economy is the emissions per unit of GDP and is affected by a country's fuel mix, its energy efficiency and the composition of the economy (i.e. extent of activity in carbon-intensive sectors

Figure 3.4: Towards low carbon intensity: are we making progress?
Source: PwC 2011

Index, even if we quadruple the current rate of decarbonization from 0.8% to 3.2%, we are still on track for 1200 ppm by 2050. An important part of the climate change crisis may be dealing with the consequences of severe climate disruption. It needs to be stressed, however, that whether mitigation or adaptation defines the course for the future, the impact on business will be profound. This fact is usually lost when climate change is talked about as a political or economic issue. Most politicians, it is fair to say, hope that the transition from a high carbon to a low carbon economy will be fairly smooth: renewable and nuclear will become the backbone of an energy supply that continues to grow, investments will flow into the opportunities a green economy provides (hopefully stimulating national economies in the process), technological innovation will make the world more resource efficient, taxes and offtake contracts of different kinds will stimulate behavioural change, and above all economic growth will continue unabated. In place of business-as-usual, in other words, there will be green business-as-usual.

An energy problem?

Climate change is often treated as an energy problem. Each era of industrialization has been linked to energy breakthroughs, and except for water power

In order to stabilize CO2 emissions at 2000 levels by 2050	In order to reduce CO2 emissions to 50% below 2000 levels by 2050
Cost: $50 per tonne of CO2 saved	Cost: $38–117 per tonne of CO2 saved depending on technological progress
Investment: $17 trillion total energy sector investment	Investment: $45 trillion total energy sector investment
Investment: $400 billion per year, equivalent to GDP of Holland	Investment: $1.1 trillion per year, equivalent to GDP of Italy

Figure 3.5: Costs and investment to achieve a low carbon economy
Sources: Data from IEA 2008; IEA 2010; OECD 2011

in the early Industrial Revolution, these advances have involved carbon fuels. For instance, the railway era depended upon, and created a huge demand for, coal; the era of automobiles and mass production (the mass era) was inextricably linked to oil and electricity, and, as noted in Chapter 2, was made possible by low cost energy generated in large power plants distributed through national grids. The challenge today is how society replaces conventional, high-carbon energy sources with alternative, low-carbon ones. Furthermore, how does it achieve this while increasing the overall energy supply in response to population and economic growth?

The challenge of supply

If climate change is treated as a standalone energy problem, the cost and investment to convert to a low carbon economy is immense (Figure 3.5). According to BP, a doubling of global GDP and a 20 per cent rise in population will push energy consumption up by 39 per cent to about 16 billion tonnes oil equivalent by 2030.[4] That is in a sense an encouraging figure because it reflects the considerable advances made in energy efficiency since 1980, making every dollar of GDP much less carbon intensive. However, it is difficult to argue, based on current practices and trends, that the economy in 2030 will be genuinely a low carbon one. Increased demand, the nature of the installed base, the relative cost of different parts of the energy mix, and the market-readiness of different energy types all lead analysts to conclude, as Figure 3.6 indicates, that oil, coal, and gas—non-renewable, high carbon sources—will make up the largest shares of primary energy. Renewables will grow rapidly, and nuclear and hydro will be important, but they are set to account for 20 per cent of global primary energy at a time when we could be less than 15 years away from using up our trillion tonne carbon budget.

If the projections of industry analysts and climate scientists are right, then by 2030 business will have to operate successfully in one of the following scenarios:

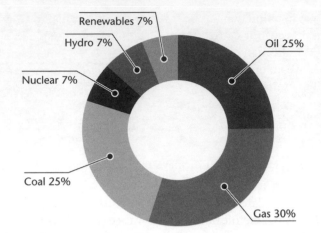

Figure 3.6: Primary energy mix by 2030
Sources: Conn 2012; HSBC 2011

A. *Ongoing adaptation*. The global economy grows, exceeding the carbon budget, and increasing amounts of GDP have to be invested in climate change adaptation as we breach the 2°C limit.

B. *Last gasp mitigation*. Late attempts to tackle the demonstrable consequences of climate change result in heavy-handed regulation, public unrest, and financial uncertainty, leaving companies with stranded assets and no basis for making long-term investment decisions.

C. *Preventative slow-down*. Global economic growth is deliberately stalled in an attempt to reduce GHG emissions.

One can debate which of these is more likely, or whether there are other scenarios on offer, but the message to business is clear: society is not currently on a smooth transition to a low-carbon, green business-as-usual economy of the kind most politicians and many economists envision. Society cannot grow its way out of the crisis in the way it has before if economic growth exacerbates climate risk. Economist Nick Stern's original macro-analysis estimated that mitigation would cost about 1 per cent of GDP, but he later adjusted that figure to 2 per cent, and others put it at 3 per cent.[5] This is the difference between a growing and a non-growing OECD economy.[6] Analysis such as McKinsey's GHG abatement cost curves shows that tackling climate change is not necessarily a cost, but, such calculations take no account of barriers at the individual, firm, and national levels to transferring away from fossil fuels.

More than an energy problem

From a business perspective it would be ideal if climate change proved to be a standalone energy problem, with climate-harming energy sources displaced by alternatives in a timely manner. The mass era described in Chapter 2 could continue, and even if it caused localized or temporary crises as it has in the past it would hold many attractions. However, as we have seen there is no reason to believe an energy switch will happen in time to prevent overspending our carbon emissions budget, even if one uses the slightly more generous 2050 timeline favoured by politicians.

The energy gap

So to frame climate change as just an energy crisis is mistaken. The transition to a cleaner energy mix can be accelerated if we invest in nuclear power, renewable energy generation and distribution, energy efficiency, and not least the number of engineers: this will help create a more energy efficient economy, but it will not be a low-carbon one. Treating climate change as a fossil energy problem, even if the most optimistic scenarios are used, could leave an annual shortfall between supply and demand of 400 exajoules by 2050—equivalent to the industry's entire output in 2000.[7] As we will show in the next chapter, quite different solutions have been proposed to deal with this. Some experts want to accelerate the supply of cleaner energy; some point to energy technology breakthroughs from fracking in the here and now to nuclear fusion in the distant future. There are other experts who want to control the demand for energy and other resources in ways the market does not seem capable of: they point to the failure to decouple emissions from economic growth, in spite of the efforts of some companies and industries to do more with less.

The Challenge of Aviation

Let us look at a real world conundrum, however, before evaluating theoretical options. The airline industry provides a clear example of the decoupling dilemma facing many sectors. Air travel accounts for up to 3 per cent of anthropogenic GHG emissions—much more if radiative forcing and other consequences are also factored in. Modern aircraft are 70 per cent more fuel efficient than those of 40 years ago, and the airline industry has various initiatives in place to improve this situation further including reducing fuel consumption per unit of thrust by 15 per cent, introducing biofuels, improving aerodynamic efficiency, and operational efficiencies such as better managed arrivals and flight paths. All told, these could result in future planes having 28 per cent less emissions than today's.

But reducing the carbon intensity of flights by a projected 1 per cent a year (the industry's goal) will not lead to a decrease in total aviation emissions if the industry continues to grow by 5 per cent per annum. The global air fleet has

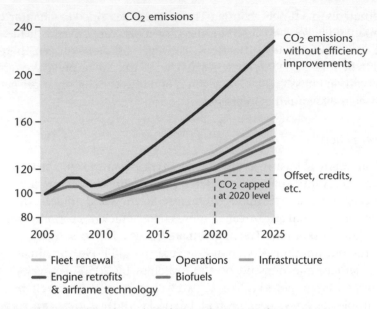

Figure 3.7: The aviation industry's path to carbon neutrality
Source: IATA 2009, Aviation and Climate Change: Pathway to Carbon Neutral Growth in 2020

more than tripled since 1978, meaning that even with efficiency savings, the industry would have needed to cut emissions by more than 50 per cent in thirty years to avoid an absolute emissions increase. 'It may be that the Airbus A380 is much more fuel-efficient than the Comet, but, with a sevenfold rise in passenger numbers over the last forty years, greater efficiency is still inconsistent with higher resource utilization.' (King 2010: 21).

In response, in 2009, the industry announced its four pillar climate protection strategy intended to deliver carbon neutral growth by 2020.[8] However, in Figure 3.7, the industry's figures show that if all its efforts are successful, absolute emissions will be nearly 20 per cent higher in 2020 than they are today. Consequently, the industry's pursuit of carbon neutrality will depend on other industries reducing their own emissions to the extent of generating enough carbon credits to allow airlines to offset emissions.

Implications for business

Climate change rears up as an energy challenge, and no sooner do we as a society bombard it with renewables than it changes its form into an economic, or a technological, or a moral challenge. What is more, our efforts seem to consistently fall short of what is required whether it be how quickly we adjust the energy mix, how much we drive down carbon intensity, how rapidly we develop and bring online new technologies, or how ready we are to create a low carbon economy.

Tackling climate change will be increasingly a key driver of government policy and public attitudes. Carbon taxes and carbon pricing, however volatile, are early examples of this, and company market research suggests companies believe policy levers remain in play.[9] In one way or another, companies will be under ever greater pressure to stop treating GHG emissions as externalities. Already, the voluntary Carbon Disclosure Project asks companies to measure and disclose their emissions, and the data are used by 500 investors with over US$71 trillion under management.

Such changes are only coming after a long struggle, but from a business perspective they are less threatening if they create an impartial level playing field applying to all companies. However, there are two areas in which the implications are more profound. First, at the macro-level, to the extent that improved carbon intensity and alternative technology do not lead to an absolute reduction in emissions, tackling climate change is likely to have a negative influence on economic growth. Humanity will not be able to continue the mass production philosophy of making anything in any amount provided it is profitable, unless it is willing or able to live with the consequences of profound climate uncertainty. Essentially this means throwing large chunks of current economic thinking into metaphorical landfill. Ecological economists have made this claim for a long time, and its potential ramifications have made it highly controversial. We will talk about the growth/no growth stand-off in depth later in this book, and it is a pivotal issue in understanding the turnaround challenge for business. For now, though, we will simply state that given the current situation, a major implication for business of the climate change crisis is that growth—the shibboleth of business and society—may be at risk.

Undermining valuations

The second malign implication of the climate change crisis, at the micro-level, is how it will affect certain industries: their prospects and their valuation. Cement manufacturing, which produces nine tonnes of carbon dioxide for every ten tonnes of cement, or steel production averaging over two tonnes of carbon per tonne, could be seriously penalized by, for instance, taxing their energy consumption to pay for investments in clean energy. The Carbon Trust did an early assessment of how climate change would affect different industries, posing a threat, for instance, to oil and gas, increasing demand for building insulation, and increasing the volatility of the price of beer.[10] More recently, granular analysis of the implications for particular industries has been conducted. Campanale & Leggett, for example, have calculated that the fossil fuel reserves held by the top 100 listed coal companies and top 100 listed oil and gas companies represent potential greenhouse gas emissions of 745 $GtCO_2$. If all of these reserves were used, the resultant emissions would take the world

180 GtCO$_2$ over its remaining emissions budget. 'This means that using just the listed proportion of reserves in the next 40 years is enough to take us beyond 2°C of global warming' (Campanale, Leggett 2011: 2). As a result, they estimate that listed companies may only be able to use 20 per cent of their current reserves, exposing investors to the risk that a major part of the value of these companies could never be realized without causing catastrophic climate change. This, and subsequent analysis by HSBC, highlights a threat to investors who will inaccurately price firms, but is also a reminder that companies could end up with stranded assets if they continue to pursue their current strategies.[11]

Demographic Change

Box 3.2 DEMOGRAPHIC CHANGE: THE BACKGROUND FOR BUSINESS

If climate change presents a potential existential risk, a range of demographic factors threaten to amplify its impacts.

- **Population increase:** The first is increasing population. World population has risen from 2.5 billion in 1950 to over 7 billion today and is expected to reach 9.4 billion by 2050.

- **Increasing per capita consumption:** The second is rising consumption per head, driven by a range of forces including the historic growth of China and India's middle classes. As a result of population increases, and shifts in consumption patterns, global demand for food estimated to increase 25 per cent by 2030 and water by 40%.

- **Shifts in diet:** The third is a rise in the carbon intensity of consumption, with people not just consuming more food per head, but shifting towards water and carbon intensive meat in their diets. As a result of these, shifts, the amount of land globally available per capita to supply food, water, materials, and other essentials has dropped from the equivalent of 7.91 global hectares in 1900 to about two global hectares per person today. By 2050 when the population exceeds nine billion, it could have fallen to 1.4 hectares per person.

- **Technological plateau:** The fourth is the apparent emergence of a technological plateau. Where technological advances have in the past proven Malthusian projections of scarcity to be false, the combination of societal resistance to innovations such as Genetically Modified Organisms and lagging investment in agricultural technology have reduced investment into breakthrough agricultural technologies.

- **The instability of inequality:** Other demographic shifts are translating this scarcity of basic resources into social instability. Urbanization, at times accelerated by the climate driven breakdown of local subsistence farming, creates concentrations of the unemployed in slums at the borders of megacities. Social media has shown its potential to act as an accelerator of social disruption. A direct correlation between food prices and food riots has now emerged, with 220 riots in the price peak years of 2008 and 2011 against 140 in each of the preceding years.

Demographic change: deeper dive

However, climate change's most serious implications for business come from interdependencies with other crises. Business does not confront a single crisis: rather, as explained in Chapter 2, it must deal with a quadrilemma of crises, any one of them significant for business success, but the combination of which defines the turnaround challenge. Demographic change—the social dimensions of shifts in size and patterns of population over time—offers many examples of the dichotomies these crises throw up. As we will show, the rise in populations puts absolute pressure on national resources and may increase overall poverty (demographic pessimism). Depending on how demographic change is managed, it can 'boost' national economies and social well-being (demographic optimism). Growing markets with affluent people are hugely attractive to business. However, serving booming markets while simultaneously managing natural resource constraint is a new territory for business. We are treating demographic change as a crisis of humanity because how it is addressed will often be an expression of human values such as fairness, morality, and belief. For instance, in an era of climate change, how will humanity ensure that the growing population of poor countries does not suffer from rising sea levels or land degradation? Equally, what right have the rich countries originally responsible for man-made warming to impose restrictions on emerging economies that want to enjoy the benefits of industrial growth?

According to some philosophers, a crisis of humanity is inherently different to one involving existential risk because no matter how severe the impact of events such as famine and conflict on specific groups of people, the outcomes can never be as grave as a crisis threatening the existence of humankind.[12] For our purposes, though, what is important about these different types of crisis is that they reveal why what is ethical and logical when addressing one set of events is unethical, illogical, and indeed unworkable in the context of another set. In this chapter, for instance, we have discussed the energy problem associated with climate change, but as we noted in Chapter 2, for 1.6 billion of the poorest people in the world the real energy problem is that they do not have reliable access to electricity. Conversely, one could argue that this kind of injustice is one business can address because it is a market opportunity. Opening the eyes of business to the opportunities that exist because of poverty is the essence of 'bottom billion capitalism' of the kind pioneered by C.K. Prahalad and Stuart Hart.[13] Yet, as soon as one applies a mass production solution to this problem, one reverts to actions such as centralized fossil fuel-driven manufacturing that are incongruent with averting existential risk.

As will become apparent, we are using demographic change to refer to a number of different phenomena including population growth and the changing nature of demographic profiles (age, education, wealth, etc.), both of which put pressure on the Earth's carrying capacity. These include urbanization, food security, the volatility of commodity prices, and other trends that are also being affected by climate change. Global warming will certainly influence demographic change. However, this influence is not a one-way process, and demographic change will affect what is feasible in the climate change context. One of the challenges for business will be to mediate between what makes sense from a climate change perspective and the logical choices for business given the risks and opportunities associated with demographic change. To reiterate our conclusion in Chapter 2, the model that has dominated business thinking for the past century is ill-suited to making such choices. Its core principle is that success equates with a constant increase in the amount of production and consumption, whereas climate change implies restraint. Demographic change is the temptress for business to carry on unreformed, and moreover to do so with a sense of righteousness because millions will be rescued from under-served markets. We believe that business can navigate between the temptation of demographic change and the restraints to do with climate change, but not by persisting with that model. We will make this case in later chapters, but in order to do so the true nature of demographic change needs to be understood.

Strands of demographic change

Demographic change can seem in turns energizing and enervating depending which facet of it one looks at. The central issue is population growth. Today there are about seven billion people on our planet. Fifty years ago that figure was three billion; forty years from now it is expected to be in excess of nine billion. Most of that increase will be in emerging and developing economies, and many of today's richest economies will have stagnant or negative population growth. In addition, most of that growth will happen in urban areas that, because of inward migration from rural areas and improvements in life expectancy and child morbidity, could account for 75 per cent of the total population worldwide. The emergence of mega cities with over ten million people (i.e. cities with populations larger than those of Israel or Sweden) and the rise in populations near the coast both bring new challenges with regards to pollution, transportation, housing, and waste management.

There is no real controversy about these figures and trends themselves but they have been interpreted in very different ways. On the one hand, demographic change is portrayed as a looming catastrophe which will leave swathes of people poor and dependent on broken ecosystems, while on the other population growth itself is applauded as a human achievement because people now live longer and more prosperous lives than their ancestors. History, it is argued, also shows that given the right conditions, poor people will benefit from population growth and wealthier people benefit from the rising prosperity of the poor. There is very little interplay between the demographic pessimists and optimists, and we do not intend to build those bridges here. But both interpretations affect what business is being asked to consider in the context of this crisis, and it is that we discuss below.

Demographic pessimism

In some people's minds, what is important about demographic change is that an unprecedentedly large global population puts an unbearable strain on the Earth's capacity to sustain current and future generations. In 1900, an individual had the equivalent of 7.91 global hectares at their disposal to supply the food, water, materials, housing, and other components of their well-being. Now, because of population increases and resource depletion that figure is about two global hectares per person, and by 2050 when the population exceeds nine billion, it could be 1.44 gha/person. Figure 3.8 shows that rising standards of living could drive an overall rise in energy demand of 40 per cent, in food of over 25 per cent, and in water of about 40 per cent. According to the

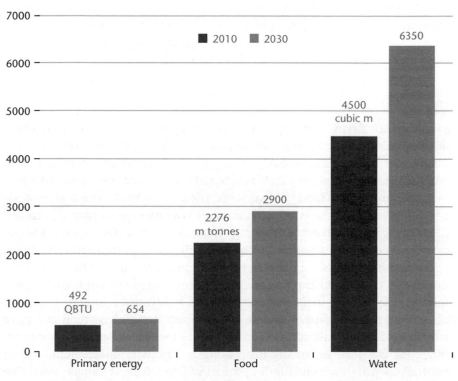

Figure 3.8: Predicted commodity demand growth 2010–2030

World Economic Forum, 'Unless the present link between growth and consumption of scarce resources is severed, our resource base, governance and policy structures are unlikely to sustain the standard of living societies have grown accustomed to and aspire to' (WEF, Accenture 2012).

Carrying capacity: uneven impacts

It is safe to assume that the consequences of population growth on carrying capacity will not be felt equally, and already it is apparent that the effects of climate change are being felt most acutely in poor countries such as Kenya. About 1.2 billion people, or one-fifth of the world's population, still live in 'extreme poverty' (less than US$1 a day). Half of the world's people lives on less than two dollars a day, and if we remove China from the equation, the total number of extremely poor increased by 28 million in the 1990s. Life expectancy, maternal health, child mortality, malnutrition, and disease not surprisingly reflect degrees of wealth and poverty. A woman has a 1-in-16 lifetime risk of dying from pregnancy-related illness in sub-Saharan Africa compared to 1-in-3,500 in North America. While life expectancy has increased from 47 to 65 years overall since 1950, asymmetrically in richer countries it is now 82 years. It is also worth noting that poverty is not the preserve of poor countries, and although a poor person in Bangladesh has a very different life experience compared to one in Missouri, USA, in both places it is different to be a poor man than a poor woman.[14]

Food

The issue of carrying capacity is highlighted by the current global food situation. Worldwide there are 925 million people who are hungry (i.e. who have insufficient carbohydrates, fats, and proteins), and two billion poor people who experience serious physical and mental impairment because of under- or over-consumption of food.[15] Historically, the price of food, as with other basic commodities, has declined in real terms and as a proportion of family expenditure. In the twentieth century, average commodity prices fell by almost 50 per cent even as demand boomed.[16] At first this seems counterintuitive but a combination of increased productivity and lower costs meant that Malthus's nightmare of a world that could not support a growing population never materialized. This situation has changed in recent years, raising questions once again about whether agriculture can produce sufficient food at a price at which people can afford to be fed. A century's worth of declining commodity prices was reversed in the first decade of the new millennium, and in contrast to what happened during much of capitalism, it can no longer be assumed that commodity prices will continue to fall as demand increases.

According to the Indexmundi Commodity Price Index, prices which in 2000 were as low as at any time since the Great Depression, had risen 160 points to an all-time high by 2010 with energy up 190 per cent and food up 135 per cent.[17] There is also evidence of a direct correlation between the rise in food prices and the number of food riots since 2000, so that in 2008 and 2011 when prices peaked there were over 220 riots compared to about 140 in each of the preceding years.[18]

Compounding the food crisis

This situation is complicated by increasing wealth in countries such as China, and the associated geo-political shifts that we discuss later in this chapter. China is increasingly reliant on imports to feed its 1.3 billion people and, according to some projections, over 66 per cent of current global grain supply could be consumed by China by 2030, a situation aggravated by the degradation of that country's traditional grain basket around the Yellow River.[19] At a global level, global food production must increase by 70 per cent by 2050 according to the Food and Agriculture Organisation in order to feed a population of more than nine billion free from hunger.[20] The real number could be more as diets change to include more animal protein and the estimated one billion obese adults continues to expand.

Equally, unless a more systematic approach to sustainable production is adopted,[21] the yields (i.e. the quantity of food produced per unit of land) to achieve that 70 per cent increase might have to rise by an even greater amount because of the competing pressures on land. Biofuel crops, for example, which are part of the climate change energy solution not just to run cars and trains but also to fuel the energy-intensive agricultural system, are competing for land with food crops. Land is also needed to create carbon sinks that, again, help combat climate change (e.g. through reforestation), and is being bought up as a commodity as countries and private sector companies hedge themselves against land degradation, water shortages, and other types of ecosystem damage. Indeed, speculation connected with food and land is one criticism of what some people regard as the financialization of the economy (Chapter 5). Even without that demand-side interference, there are additional supply-side constraints that will affect the Earth's capacity to provide food.

If climate change is the shark, water is the teeth

There are other factors affecting the carrying capacity of the Earth. In Chapter 2, we highlighted in Figure 2.3 how climate change will affect food commodity prices, and this is in part because of changes in rainfall. Agriculture consumes about 70 per cent of all freshwater (more in some countries

41

with rapidly growing populations), and aquifers for large cereal-producing areas in parts of the USA and Australia are already under stress. World wheat stocks hit a 30-year low in 2008, partly driven by the worst drought in Australia in 100 years which halved the winter wheat crop to12 million tonnes in 2007. Reports of drought and water shortages in north-west China, where most of that country's wheat is grown, have spurred international trading and overseas land investment by the government. There are claims that this could mark the end of large-scale production in such areas,[22] while elsewhere there are over a billion people without drinking water.

Technological plateau?

One of the struggles, then, is between providing enough water to drink and enough to meet the demands of agriculture. In the past, there have been technological leaps to overcome such problems. In recent years however global productivity has increased by little more than 1 per cent a year (1990–2007), and experts, such as the US Department of Agriculture, fear it will decline over the coming decade. Furthermore, there has been a lack of investment in agricultural research of the kind that gave birth to the Green Revolution. For example the budget of the Consultative Group on International Agricultural Research has fallen by half over the last 15 years.[23] So, although theoretically the agricultural component of the carrying capacity challenge could be resolved with technological breakthroughs a comprehensive study of the future of food concluded that *'any claims that a single or particular new technology is a panacea are foolish.'* (Government Office for Science 2011)

Demographic dividends

We warned against apocalyptaholics in Chapter 2, and demographic pessimism echoes that same mindset in many ways. Too much faith in what could go wrong often masks the emergence of the real challenges or the opportunities that arise from situations that are better than they might seem. Population growth is an example of this. There is good evidence, as we have shown, that the predicted rise in population will put pressure on the Earth's carrying capacity. However, exponential growth beyond 2050 seems unlikely, and Pearse and Rosling, both popular commentators on demographic trends, agree that the underlying factors causing population growth—large families, low mortality—have already changed, and we are entering a period when population will stabilize (Box 3.3).

Although we have framed the business challenge in terms of how to balance the temptation of growing markets with the restraint required by climate change, the longer term challenge for business could be how to succeed

Box 3.3 LIMITS TO POPULATION GROWTH

There is good evidence that we are doing quite well at defusing the perceived population time bomb.[24] World fertility has roughly halved since 1960, and women on average have half as many babies as their grandmothers did. For a period, the decline in child mortality rates because of vaccines and healthier environments meant that populations grew fourfold, but now higher survival rates mean women have fewer children. This trend is boosted by urbanization because children are less of an economic asset in cities than on farms.

The high and seemingly fast growing population figures seen today may therefore be an anomaly; the legacy of a population bulge caused by a lag between declining child mortality and the number of children born. It would be historically unprecedented for lower death rates not to reduce birth rates, yet the replacement rates used in some population projections assume that this will be the case. As one commentator puts it, 'the population bomb is being defused round the world. But the consumption bomb is still primed and ever more dangerous.'[25]

with a global population that for the last half of the twenty-first century may be fairly stable.

It will take two generations for this stabilization to work through, however, and in the meantime increased life expectancy and declining child mortality mean populations will increase at what appear to be alarming rates. Furthermore, linking back to the quadrilemma of crises, this period of rapid growth will occur during crucial times for the parallel crises of climate change, geopolitical shift, and the changing nature of governance.

Emerging opportunities

Yet the upshot is not a world without opportunity. Megacities, for example, are both the sites of immiseration in the form of slums and wealth represented by the growing prosperity of the new middle class. The booming middle class in emerging economies will account for a significant part of the anticipated 90 per cent rise in real global GDP from US$50 trillion today to US$95 trillion by 2030.[26] An estimated three billion people will have joined the middle class by 2030 in addition to the two billion middle-class people today. They will have expenditures of US$10–100 a day, and although in Earth carrying capacity terms the fear is their wealth will put yet more pressure on finite resources, their presence could also bring benefits. For instance, resource intensity stabilizes once people achieve middle-class status (and technological advances mean that resource intensity per capita should already be less than in the past), and certain economists argue that a strong middle class is essential to being able to afford proper climate change adaptation.

Even if one assumes that a Malthusian barrier is looming because the innovations to boost agricultural yields are currently missing, the consequences of this will vary from country to country depending on what stage they are at in their demographic shift, and how well placed they are to exploit what Bloom et al. (2003) call the 'demographic dividend.' They argue that population change means very different things depending on the relative size of different age groups and the institutional and infrastructural development of a country. A high proportion of young or old dependants can limit economic growth because of the resources devoted to their care (especially by women). Countries with more working age people may enjoy higher growth because of the number of people earning and saving, and reduced spending on dependants. They make up the kind of boom generation that stimulated economic growth in the USA after the Second World War, and who are now flourishing in some emerging economies.[27]

As Europe, Japan, and the USA are finding, population booms present different challenges as the boom generation moves through its lifecycle. Early on in the boom, the key concerns are health care and education; later they are job creation and capital accumulation; later still social security and retirement provision. The current debate in OECD countries about pension funds—should the younger generation support an increasingly elderly population through higher pension fund contributions? Should the retirement age be raised? How can individuals take more responsibility for their retirement?—is an inevitable result of demographic change and its economic consequences. Some predict that growth in household financial wealth in the richest nations will fall by more than two-thirds compared to historical rates, with knock-on effects around the world.[28] Even if that does not transpire, there is still a major question whether the type of economic growth open to earlier baby boomers is an option today given how some believe degraded ecosystems and climate change are becoming barriers to prosperity.

All of this points to the importance of having the right kinds of institutions and infrastructure in place to adapt to the shifting challenges of demographic change and increase society's overall well-being.

Implications for business

Any demographic change has implications for business, affecting decisions about what to produce, where to produce it, what capital is available, and how to market. Successful companies are well versed in managing these situations. What they are not used to addressing is moderation, and the possibility that meeting unprecedented demand will have serious consequences for business and society as a whole. At first glance, current demographic change is ideally suited to the business paradigm initiated by Henry Ford (Chapter 2) because it promises new and growing markets for decades to come. However, as soon as carrying capacity and climate change are taken into consideration, the weaknesses of that paradigm—especially in its current configuration—are exposed. Instead of vistas of opportunity, what are actually in place are structural drivers of price inflation due to a combination of long-run demand growth and permanent supply constraints. Inflation would moderate demand and thereby help resolve the temptation-constraint dichotomy, but if it damaged standards of living too much it would place business at a fork in the road: how much should companies focus on serving the thriving middle class and how much on the needs of the poor? Which market would be the most profitable, and which route is most feasible? To an extent, those decisions will be made for business as inflationary pressures begin to hurt free trade, and in response nations and regional blocs seek to defend their own interests.

This would deny business many of the benefits associated with the demographic dividend, but it could have even more severe consequences than forgone opportunities. The relationship between rising food prices and the uprisings of the Arab Spring has been well documented. In January 2010, in Rosarno, Italy, four migrant workers were shot and beaten and some 2,000 immigrants staged a protest against racially-motivated attacks. In Greece, immigration and austerity programmes have created an incendiary mix that has fuelled the rise of the right-wing Golden Dawn party. Political turmoil is one possible outcome of the current crises, and without claiming it is inevitable, we believe it is more likely because of the strains put on society by the dominant business model. There has been little serious thought given to how business will respond to the dichotomy of burgeoning markets and resource constraint. Attention is given to history instead and management theory tells us that demand growth is a fine thing for companies, investors, consumers, and workers alike. Yet this will only be true looking ahead if the negative feedback loops between climate change and demographic change are severed. The evidence, as we have seen, shows that decoupling emissions growth from economic growth is not happening at a fast enough rate, and this will not change under the current business paradigm. This is true of climate change, but similar arguments have been made by people such as Pavan Sukhdev in relation to biodiversity and Johan Rockstrom regarding planetary boundaries.[29]

Squandering the demographic dividend

Although population growth should therefore be a boon for business, the demographic dividend is currently being squandered because of dependence on a model that is proving dysfunctional. Increasing pressure on natural resources is in some respects an opportunity because it encourages investment in increasing crop yields and overall eco-efficiency. But the major leaps of the past, though, are noticeable by their absence. In the 1970s, the Green Revolution of higher yielding cereals as much as tripled food production in countries that had previously been at risk of famine.[30] Similar claims are now made for genetically modified crops, the latest rejoinder to Malthus's eighteenth-century prediction that the Earth's capacity to sustain human life was finite. However, the prospects for a new Green Revolution able to increase yields from a diminishing amount of arable land are dim, especially when one factors in the rising price of oil. Consequently, Malthusian predictions are relevant once more, not so much because they foretell the future, but because they depict a worst-case scenario that governments and others will respond to as the crisis of the geo-political shift shows.

The Economic Crisis and Geo-political Shift

Box 3.4 ECONOMIC CRISIS: THE BACKGROUND FOR BUSINESS

In addition to the environmental and social crises of climate change and demographic shift, there is an on-going economic crisis, which is far from resolution. It is a crisis to which multiple, often conflicting causes have been attributed, from the reliance on the false comforts of numerical models, to the spread of derivatives ('weapons of mass destruction'), to pro-poor Democratic housing policy. Our purpose here is to identify and link a number of structural factors that contributed to the crisis, and observe that some of them appear to remain.

• **Decline in manufacturing:** Since 1960, as we will explore further, there has been a decline in manufacturing among a number of OECD nations, driven in part by declining margins and the opportunities to lower costs through offshoring production to low wage manufacturing centres in China and elsewhere. The OECD share of global industrial value added dropped from 68.3% in 1971 to 51.9% in 2008, while the share of emerging economies rose substantially.

• **Credit-driven consumption:** Low interest rates, designed to stimulate economic growth, led to a sustained period of credit-not production-driven consumption and high levels of household debt.

• **Balance of payments deficits:** The same phenomenon of outsourced manufacturing led to mounting balance of payment imbalances, with 'producer' nations such as China accumulating current account surpluses and 'consumer' nations running ballooning deficits.

• **Emerging markets purchasing power:** The investment strategies of the new manufacturing giants sustained this growth model, placing money with 'safe havens' of asset classes such as collateralized debt obligations (CDOs) around the US sub-prime markets and the sovereign debt of highly indebted OECD nations. The result is an economic model, weakened but not delegitimized, that persists despite an unaddressed core crisis in productivity.

The economic crisis and geo-political shift: deeper dive

So far, we have highlighted the crises of demographic and climate change. Taken separately, they present business with a new environment that has significant consequences for success. Taken together, they throw up various dilemmas in which the obvious response to one crisis contradicts what is required by the other. Affecting this is a third crisis to do with economics and the global economy. China, for example, is the world's biggest importer of oil as well as its second largest economy. How it decides to meet its demand for oil will affect its industrial development, trade, investment decisions, standards of living, and its position in international negotiations. A China that reduces its reliance on oil will look very different to one with a foreign policy aimed at securing access to foreign energy. However, the point to make here is that because of the geo-political shift that is seeing power dispersed amongst more countries than in the past, China's decisions about climate change, poverty, quality of life, economic growth, etc. will have an impact on other countries in ways they did not in the past. Moreover, around the world, there are poor countries getting richer, rich people getting richer, middle class people in rich countries trying to stay middle class, poor people in poor countries rushing to become middle class, poor people in rich and poor countries left behind by the rich, and rich countries anxious about what will happen as emerging economies get wealthier and more influential. In short, this geo-political upheaval will have a profound effect on how other crises are addressed.

The changing face of wealth and power

We are entering into a period of transition, one that is so far relatively peaceful compared to previous eras of geo-political eruption. However, it is not without its tensions, many of which profoundly affect the turnaround challenge for business. For example, the increasing political strength of China and India has already had a significant influence on attempts to negotiate global climate change policy, and it would be a brave (or foolish) politician in countries such as Brazil or Vietnam who put the loosely defined interests of the planet ahead of the sharply enunciated aspirations of local constituents. There is a governance dimension to the geo-political shift which we will visit later on. For now, however, we want to focus on the economic dimension to that crisis because this is where the business implications are most immediately apparent.

Debt crises in various forms have been a recurring event identifiable from economic data dating back to the fourteenth century when England's Edward III defaulted on sovereign debt.[31] At first glance, there is nothing historically unusual about the financial crisis that hit OECD countries in 2007. The pattern of private debt surges, succeeded by banking crises, followed by massive public borrowing has a storied history dating back to the 1830s.[32] Likewise, the fact that large companies emerge with huge cash reserves they do not deploy even as recession hits national economies, is nothing unexpected.[33] However, for all its historical inevitability, the 2007 crisis was unique for two main reasons: its relationship to the bursting of the dot.com bubble in 2000, and its relationship to an ongoing geo-political shift.

The dot.com bubble was typical of the type of investment frenzy that happens during major technological upheavals (techno-economic paradigm shifts). As we discuss in detail in Chapter 5, financial bubbles on the back of technological innovation are nothing new, and had been witnessed by Arkwright, Stephenson, and Edison well before they had an impact on Gates, Moore, and Jobs.[34] However, this time around the implosion of the bubble occurred at the same time as two other important shifts were happening.

The decline of manufacturing

The first shift was the one in manufacturing from many of the original industrial countries to emerging ones. This resulted in OECD countries' share of global industrial added value dropping from 68.3 per cent to 51.9 per cent between 1971 and 2008 while emerging economies' share rose from 2.6 per cent to 16.5 per cent.[35] The decline in OECD manufacturing was masked by the rise in financial services which was a major beneficiary of the ICT paradigm shift. Indeed, as we will explain in the next chapter, financial services offered returns much better than conventional industrial investment, causing even manufacturing firms to behave more like financial ones (e.g. concentrating on financial transactions), and creating expectations about the wealth a financial service-driven economy could generate. Those expectations became increasingly relevant after the dot.com bubble burst because not only were politicians and the public in OECD countries unwilling to consider that their wealth was declining, demographic change and in particular the number of baby boomers approaching retirement meant that there was an eager 'hunt for yield,' i.e. financial returns sufficient to meet mounting pensions and insurance liabilities. This ultimately was a disaster for investors who in the USA since 2000, have found that for the first time since 1850 Treasuries offer a better return than Standard & Poor's equities. It was also bad news for many companies which had spent years trying to meet the engineered performance levels of the financial services sector (Chapter 5).

Geo-political shifts and the dispersal of power

The other important aspect of the dot.com frenzy was the international response. A feature of many recent economic crises such as the 1994 Mexican economic crisis and the 1997 Asian debt crisis is that the affected countries did not run a surplus—typically on the advice of the International Monetary Fund—and other countries were unwilling or unable to provide assistance. A chain of such crises eventually led emerging economies in Asia and Latin America to ignore such advice and, in the words of HSBC's chief economist, started to 'build war chests of foreign-exchange reserves to protect themselves against the risk of future balance-of-payments and currency crises' (King 2010: 75). Perhaps agreeing with Ha-Joon Chang that wealthy countries had not succeeded by following the strategies they now proposed for others,[36] emerging economies adopted a counter-cyclical stance and built up massive capital reserves (Figure 3.9) that acted as a buffer when the downturn came, and left them with huge surpluses.

This money has been used to buy the bonds of heavily indebted OECD countries in which private debt had been allowed to reach upwards of 170 per cent of GDP (USA) and up to 220 per cent (UK). Sovereign debt in the G7 countries reached almost 120 per cent of GDP in 2010, a figure not seen since those nations emerged from the Second World War.[37] A quarter of the value of one asset class alone—securitized mortgages—was written off. At two trillion dollars, this is more than the GDP of India.[38]

Debt crisis escalation

A private debt crisis became a banking crisis and in turn a sovereign debt crisis just as it had in the past.[39] Into the breach stepped emerging economies which in the past had normally been debtors but were now taking the role that Japan and West Germany had played in the 1980s. Now, they became creditors, adding a new momentum to their rise as economic powers since the late twentieth century. There is much talk about the demise of the West as a consequence of

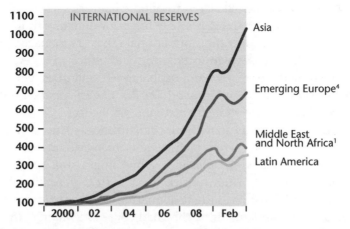

Figure 3.9: International financial reserve accumulation prior to 2008 financial crisis
Source: Fitzgerald, presentation at Queen Elizabeth House, Oxford, 2009

a flourishing Asia and Latin America, but this is neither accurate nor insightful. The global economy is not a zero-sum game, and the rise of one continent will not be at the expense of another. There will probably be localized crises as countries adapt to the new reality, but overall there should be a larger economic high table rather than fewer chairs. There will, however, be a shift in power and this is accelerated by emerging economies owning the debt of the rich.

Sovereign wealth funds have become important players in this shift. Although much smaller than countries' foreign-exchange reserves, they are important because they are interested in financial return whereas reserves are concerned with liquidity. Back in 2005, they were not significant enough to have a name; now they have assets approaching US$12 trillion.[40] Only one OECD country (Norway) is amongst the six countries with wealth funds in excess of US$100 billion. Thus, the funds represent a shift in wealth and financial power away from the USA and Europe, and an increasing role for overseas governments in managing that power. They have become market makers for government bonds and investors of last resort for some companies.[41]

New dynamics

There is anxiety in the West about such power being in the hands of new arrivals to the economic high table. This is probably overstated if we regard wealth funds as the ultimate 'universal investor' with an economic interest not only in the prosperity of individual countries but of the global economy as a whole.[42] Nonetheless, many of the largest sovereign wealth funds belong to countries looking to exert more influence in international politics. This was apparent in the last two climate summits in Copenhagen and Durban at which China and the USA were at loggerheads[43] and emerging economies as a whole undertook concerted action to oppose countries responsible for historical GHG emissions. It signifies a very different dynamic in international relations that will affect how transformational crises are managed politically, and which localized crises win international attention. However, whether different will be better or worse is impossible to tell, and titles such as *Civilization, Why the West Rules—For Now*, and *The Rise of China and the Future of the West*[44] may reflect anxiety more than reliable prediction.

The geo-political shift is something that business—especially the multinational corporation—is better placed than many to manage. Someone visiting the headquarters of Unilever or Shell might well think they have stumbled into a United Nations office, such is the international nature of the personnel; and a visitor to the headquarters of a company such as Manpower could understandably think they had come to a branch office because the vast majority of staff (and revenues) is not in the USA (and definitely not Milwaukee) but scattered around the world. Parts of the media and politicians persist in talking about large corporations as if they were national sports teams, but Holstein coined the term the *Stateless Corporation* in 1990,[45] and the relationship such businesses have with the many countries they are linked to through markets, production, financial arrangements, accounting, and capital adds complexity to the geo-political crisis.

However, companies should be aware of the potentially negative consequences of national responses to the new dynamic. Consider just one example, the negative balance of payments afflicting many OECD countries. This is increasing the size of national debt and related interest payments which in turn heightens bond market risk and the cost of sovereign debt. Governments normally respond to this with austerity programmes of the kind common throughout the European Union at present, and these result in removing support to business, for example, subsidies and government contracts, in price increases, loss of domestic and export markets, and a decline in production volumes that prevents products from moving down the price curve. These effects in turn impact the competitive environment: competitors with a strong foothold in more buoyant markets will be able to invest in weakened ones and entrench their market share. (This is what happened, for instance, when Vestas, the wind turbine company, closed its manufacturing facility on the Isle of Wight, UK, in 2009 in the face of Chinese competition.) This weakens the terms of trade and has knock-on effects for the national economy in reduced sales, lower employment, less consumption, weaker tax generation, and ultimately, an even worse balance of payments deficit.

Resource acquisition

Of course, companies can be instruments of government policy and vice versa. There are still many state-owned companies, and international companies with close ties to the state. The finger has been pointed at China for the conditions attached to its aid and investment in Africa (e.g. requiring that Chinese high-yielding rice varieties are used in agricultural projects). This kind of conditionality has long been a feature of USA and EU aid packages, and OECD countries are still far larger investors in Africa than China. What separates the policies is that China seems prepared to take a longer term perspective, and it is this willingness to think strategically and put less reliance on market-based interventions that irks policy-makers in the West.[46]

One area where this kind of long-term outlook is evident is in the buying up of resources as a hedge against resource scarcity. Land acquisition is an example of this wider trend. Increasing amounts of land and other resources are being bought up for security, private use, speculation, and to manage sustainability issues. The largest acquisitions have been by the private sector: almost 2.5 million hectares of land have been acquired in Ethiopia, Ghana, Mali, Sudan, and Madagascar since 2004, and similar trends can be witnessed in the developing economies of Africa, South and Central Asia, and Latin America. Russia, Ukraine, and Australia have also offered large tracts of farmland to foreign investors.[47] A 452500 ha biofuel project has been established in Madagascar, and a 100000 ha irrigation project in Mali. This trend is linked to the transformational crises of climate change and demographic change: some foreign investors are driven by food security concerns in their own countries due, for instance, to shortages of water and arable land; another driver is increased demand for biofuels and other non-food agricultural commodities. Some of the largest firms in the world such as Cargill and ADM are considering land acquisition as they pursue vertical integration strategies. However, land is not just being bought up because of its productive potential: as a United Nations briefing notes, 'It is no longer just the crops that are commodities: rather, it is the land and water for agriculture themselves that are increasingly becoming commodified, with a global market in land and water rights being created.'[48]

Governance Crisis

Box 3.5 BUSINESS BACKGROUND: THE GOVERNANCE CRISIS

The combined environmental, social, and economic crises represent a nexus of challenges that would stress-test the most robust systems of governance. The reality is that the governance framework that we have at our disposal falls far short of that model of robustness. A number of factors have weakened our capacity to act decisively at the moment of crisis.

- **Rise of nation state:** Increased complexity from break up of regional groups and rise in number of state actors

- **Privatization of regulation:** Increase in non-state actors, including civil society acting as informal regulator

- **Global problems:** Increase in transnational and wicked sets of problems, beyond remit of local, national, or regional governance systems, including global warming, biodiversity issues, and religious extremism

- **Competing governance traditions:** Shifts in economic power to new players with competing governance traditions

- **Business as representative institution:** Emergence of business as the representative institution for addressing societal challenges

- **Resource dependency:** risks of surface (policy level) or deep level (ideological) 'capture' by regulator dependent on corporate interests for funding and support

- **Challenges to legitimacy:** Erosion of funding for and reduction in operating scope and perceived legitimacy of international organizations

- **Threat rigidity:** risk of business focusing on maintaining status quo and challenging policy responses at moments of crisis

Governance crisis: deeper dive

In the past, it would have been easy to treat the geo-political shift as a governance crisis: the shift of state power from one bloc of countries to another. Government and governance have long been interchangeable: the nations with the most powerful economies historically have taken responsibility for keeping the sea lanes open. If the USA is in decline, as some people claim, the governance crisis should be about which country will keep the actual and virtual sea lanes of commerce open in the twenty-first century.

This was the situation during the early Industrial Revolution and, although government has grown more complicated and powerful since then, it remained essentially the same until very recently. Mass production has not only relied on centralized production and power generation, it has prospered in part because of a powerful, centralized government with a near monopoly on regulation. This was the assumption in Milton Friedman's famous definition of the duty of the firm as making profits for shareholders and abiding by the law.[49] It is something that has tended to get lost in the aforementioned tug of war between government intervention and government abstention when it comes to business, but it is still very central to debates about how to govern global crises.

However, it is too restricted a view of governance for the world we live in right now. Phenomena such as liquid democracy, civil governance, 'glocalism,' and transition resilience provide concrete examples of alternatives to the idea that government and governance are synonymous. There are people around the world who have nothing to do with traditional politics, but still keep an eye on what companies do and whether or not they are living up to society's expectations. Those people own a company's reputation, and have innumerable channels through which they can pass judgment that have nothing to do with governments. In addition, great swathes of the world including parts of Mumbai's slums and rural northwest India are beyond the control of formal government in any case,[50] and there are large and significant elements of society for which conventional notions of governance are irrelevant.

The Privatization of Regulation

The evolution of governance (or, as business might see it, risk) is depicted in Figure 3.10. For most of the era of mass, business was subject to a single main regulator, i.e. government. This was Phase 1. The number of de facto regulators increased, however, with economic globalization and we entered Phase 2, the 'death of distance.' Not only did companies operate in many more

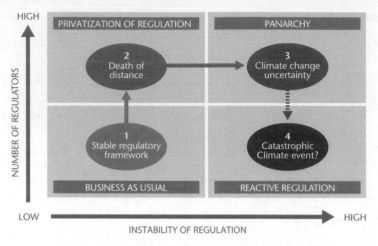

Figure 3.10: The evolution of governance and risk

jurisdictions, but they were subject to private as well as government regulation as civil society became better equipped to take on a regulatory role. This was still a reasonably stable system, with a pro-growth ideology and a manageable degree of risk for business. However, that has changed as conflicting crises have come to the fore (climate change included—Phase 3), each championed by a growing number of regulators or stakeholders. The regulators loosely agree that business has become part of an unsustainable social, economic, and environmental model, but have widely divergent views on why this is or how it can be resolved, other than a belief that business should do better. Consequently there is a regulatory free for all with a large number of regulators, a high degree of instability, and a much greater degree of business risk than in the past.

The final phase, possibly triggered by a catastrophic climate change event, is the return of a dominant regulator, this time reactive, trying to achieve a stable regulatory framework.

Conventional governance upheaval

Governance has changed throughout capitalism's history. Sometimes innovations such as the railways and the internet have enabled society to be governed differently; at other times, problems such as equity bubbles and monopolies have forced government to reconfigure capitalism. Anatole Kaletsky matches this governance evolution with four phases of capitalism.[51] Early on, the government's role was to protect the vested interests of the nation and its commerce; the economic collapse of the 1930s saw government become the manager of social welfare, and markets fell under the watchful eye of the state;

economic stagnation in the 1970s saw a resurgence of trust in free enterprise to the point where government came under the surveillance of the market. He argues that we are now entering a fourth phase (Capitalism 4.0 echoing Phase 4 in Figure 3.10) in which the excesses and failures of business will force governments to do more about regulation and macro-economic management than it has been inclined to do since the 1970s. At the same time, government is losing the will and the capacity to provide social safety nets in the way it once did, and this role will have to be taken up by the private sector.

The Governance Gap

One does not have to agree with Kaletsky to see that he is describing the evolution of national government. Furthermore, he is talking about a form of government that has evolved in conjunction with the rise of mass production. We have argued that that era has become a danger to society's future prosperity, and therefore the central question to do with conventional governance is whether or not it is able to govern a new era. For Joseph Stiglitz, the answer is 'no' because the real governance challenges are not sovereign ones as they once were. The issues for governments to tackle are ones such as global warming, world trade, biodiversity, world poverty, and religious wars, and these are not readily resolved by national governments even when they act together. According to Stiglitz, globalization has become a system of global governance without global government.[52]

The United Nations—a monumental achievement in its day—has been unable to solve this fundamental dilemma. A glance at the resolutions its General Assembly passes in a single year (Figure 3.11) reveals not just its ambition, but its commitment to a conventional top-down governance model typical of nation states. Yet, some argue it lacks the resources, authority, and legitimacy to behave as an effective global governance body. The same is true of other international governmental organizations. The International Monetary Fund, in terms of volume, if not influence, is a minor player in the world of global capital, its policies not always endorsed in the past by the countries it is meant to assist;[53] and the World Trade Organization, while not as humble as the Swiss Fleet, is no longer feared as the Royal Navy of economic globalization.

Part of the governance crisis, therefore, is the global governance vacuum. If Kaletsky is right, this will play out against a backdrop of financially weaker, but regulatorily emboldened national governments. There are two other factors however that need to be borne in mind. National governments, in OECD countries at least, started to abandon genuine nationalist economics in the 1970s. Although this has subsequently been blamed for opening the door to speculation and predatory capitalism, as Keynes predicted, changing

ILLUSTRATIVE EXAMPLES OF UN RESOLUTIONS	
Development cooperation with middle-income countries	Science and technology for development
Promotion of new and renewable sources of energy	Harmony with Nature
Convention on Biological Diversity	Protection of coral reefs for sustainable livelihoods and development
Addressing excessive price volatility in food and related financial and commodity markets	Information and communications technologies for development
The future we want	International Day of Happiness
Rights of the child	Women and political participation
Global health and foreign policy	The law of transboundary aquifers
International trade and development	Towards global partnerships

Figure 3.11: Selected United Nations General Assembly resolutions 2011

from being a protector of free trade to a defender against free finance would require a major shift in policy thinking that could take a generation or more to work through.[54]

Competing visions

The second factor is the nature of government itself, particularly as the geo-political shift unfolds and more countries are able to exert political influence. It is not just that more governments will be sitting at any negotiating table, but the new seats will often be occupied by people with very different governance traditions. The archetypal nation state model of good government promoted around the world by nations such as France, the UK, and the USA, may face competition from alternative models reflecting the values of emerging nations. As Martin Jacques notes, countries such as China not only fail to conform to this model, they have a centuries long tradition of a very different model, the 'civilization state,' based on a hierarchical structure from the family through to the central government, each level enforced by a sense of natural authority, legitimacy, and reverence.[55] Rather than an evangelical model, it is a tribute-based system that is built on respect rather than imitation. Remnants of such systems still exist in countries such as India and China, and the relationship between government and business often resembles a tribute-based system. If nothing else, accepting the possibility of these very different visions of government is a salutary reminder of the limitations of the current tendency to reduce political debate to a tug of war between protectionists and fervent believers in deregulated, integrated markets.[56]

Alternative governance

From a business perspective, the changing nature of formal governance is less intimidating than the appearance of entirely new types of governance. This is happening not only because in some areas conventional government is weak and inept: it has occurred because new types of governance are possible and allow entirely different issues and situations to be tackled. Pictures of Mohamed Bouazizi, the Tunisian street trader who set himself alight in 2010, were relayed by mobile devices around the world and became the inspiration for the 'Arab Spring.' Trafigura's attempts to cover up the alleged dumping of toxic waste in Côte d'Ivoire failed because every time it had a television documentary taken off air, or a gagging order imposed by a court on journalists, the story of 30000 deaths became ever-hotter news in tweets and blogs.[57]

Such cases cannot be dismissed as civil disobedience: they are part of a wider story about the rise in civil governance. Where once there were a few powerful regulators, now there is a large number of informal 'regulators' that individually have limited influence but collectively yield significant power. Civil governance is spawning new types of governance such as 'liquid democracy' whereby all manner of issues are put out for public vote and if individuals cannot get involved directly, they can choose to delegate their vote on certain issues to representatives who best reflect their views. This is one of the ways in which citizens can beat the cognitive dissonance they feel about conventional elections where they have to choose a single candidate even though on several issues s/he may hold views at odds with the voter's.

Local empowerment

Civil governance allows geographically separate people to govern together, but its rise coincides with an increase in local power. This is part of a long-running trend. There are 196 countries in the world today compared to 55 in 1900; the world's largest democracy, India, has over fifty state parties in addition to national parties; and the Tea Party in the USA is in some ways emblematic of a renewed interest in localized government around the world. Aspects of other crises lend themselves to local solutions rather than the grand-scale, homogenous ones favoured by central governments and large companies in recent times. For example, to reduce carbon emissions, countries may need to shift from standardized energy generation and distribution systems to ones where the type of energy generated is the one best suited to a location's natural advantage (e.g. wind in Scotland, solar in Egypt instead of oil in both). We will discuss this in detail in later chapters, but for now we only want to emphasize that heterogeneity will be an important element to governance and how society deals with the other transformational crises.

Implications for business

Companies are already well aware of the consequences of civil governance, and how it can affect their licence to operate.[58] This has been a major emphasis of contemporary corporate responsibility which has been embraced by nearly all of the world's largest companies.[59] With so many de facto regulators, the business risk today is enormous, and it is increasingly difficult for companies to be certain about what actions to take in particular circumstances. This is important when so shortly after the value of companies' intangible assets such as reputation have come to be recognized, their control of these assets is being yanked away by civil regulators, distant governments, social media, and other actors.[60] Moreover, it is especially important when, referring back to Figure 3.10, business finds itself operating in a period of turbulence and uncertainty, as is presently the case. Business risk as a consequence of conflicting regulators during such a period raises the real possibility that crises such as climate change will not be adequately addressed, and this could lead to catastrophic events. Historically, as Figure 3.10 suggests, these kinds of event, such as the aftermath of war and natural disaster, raise the possibility of authoritarian rule accompanied by protectionism, the collapse of democracy, state-control of capital, and so on. We do not want to make too much of this scenario, because the real challenge—that of unstable regulation resulting in a high degree of business risk—is already with us, and what happens next will depend on how society tackles this situation. But what we would stress is that the forces that will govern the way business can deal with climate change and demographic change are already in place, and cannot be ignored or wished away in the pursuit of idealized solutions.

Business and the governance gap

Some people blame business for the rise of civil governance, arguing that it has meddled with and undermined the credibility of government, forcing people to turn elsewhere for leadership.[61] The influence of business interests in some countries is real and often alarming, and has an impact on how crises are addressed as we will discuss in the next chapter. However, as noted earlier, governance is not a zero-sum game and the increase in civil governance marks a rise in what can be governed and how, rather than just a replacement of one type of governance with another. Consequently, for business in an age of turbulence, there are two dimensions to the governance crisis. One concerns how well conventional government is able to evolve to meet the demands of new crises, especially when these expose the limits of existing organizations and structures. The other concerns how new types of governance—both alternative governance and new formal models associated with emerging economic powers—affect the way crises are perceived and approached. If, for example, Western governments interpret the financial disasters post-2007 as something that can only be resolved through free markets, that will increase the likelihood that a crisis such as climate change is best dealt with through supply side rather than demand side interventions. Similarly, if civil governance insists that companies take a moral responsibility for the consequences of demographic change while governments reject the notion of companies

450 and 2	The global average temperature is expected to rise by 2°C if the amount of carbon dioxide in the atmosphere reaches 450 parts per million.
0.1%	Percentage of carbon dioxide and methane in the atmosphere
5.1%	Annual rate by which carbon emissions must be reduced to avoid temperature rises of more than 2°C. (Current rate is less than 1%)
20% 2030	Percentage of global energy currently estimated to be coming from renewable sources by 2030.
9 tonnes : 10 tonnes	Nine tonnes of carbon dioxide are emitted to produce every 10 tonnes of cement.
1.6 billion	Number of people worldwide without a reliable supply of electricity.
7.91 – 2 – 1.44	In 1900, individuals on average had the equivalent of 7.91 hectares of land from which to meet their needs. Today, that figure is 2 ha, and by 2030 it will be 1.44.
1 in 16; 1 in 3,500	A woman in sub-Saharan Africa has a one in 16 chance of dying from a pregnancy-related illness during her lifetime. In N America the figure is one in 3,500.
3.1 billion	The number of people in the world living on less than US$2 a day.
3 – 7 – 9 billion	In 1950, the total population was three billion; today it is seven billion; by 2050 it could be nine billion (some estimate 10 billion).
68.3% – 51.8%; 2.6% –16.5%	OECD countries' share of global industrial added value was 68.3% in 1970 and 51.8% in 2008. Developing countries' share was 2.6% in 1970 and 16.5% in 2008.
120%	In 2010, the sovereign debt of the G7 economies reached almost 120 per cent of GDP.
220%	Private debt in the UK is 220% of GDP.
55 in 1900; 196 in 2012	In 1900 there were 55 sovereign nations; now there are 196.

Figure 3.12: Mega-trends Quiz: Answers to Figure 3.2

being accountable for their social responsibilities, business will be torn between opposing agendas, neither of which it can entirely control.

Governance and the external crises

Ultimately, how the governance crisis unfolds will significantly affect the evolution of the other three crises. There are numerous examples of crisis-related problems being compounded by governance that conforms to its own logic irrespective of what a situation requires. The current situation is marked by incongruity: certain options for tackling lasting, fundamental changes are ruled out because they contradict what is thought to be true or what is believed to be more important. This incongruence is at the heart of the transformational crises, and it is the focus of the next two chapters. The governance crisis helps explain some of the reasons why society is responding to the crises in the way it is, but it is only part of the story. Although each crisis is powerful in its own right, we have suggested in this chapter that their real significance is in how they are entwined. The same is true of governance, and the idea that if governance is fixed everything else will fall into place is misguided. If business is to tackle the turnaround challenge it must take decisive action on each of the four crises, including the one of governance.

Notes

1. http://www.ifpri.org/sites/default/files/publications/pr21.pdf
2. http://necsi.edu/research/social/foodcrises.html, accessed 1/12/2012
3. (PwC 2011)
4. (Conn 2012)
5. (Stern 2008, Jackson 2009). Stern initially concluded that mitigating climate change would cost 1 per cent of GDP between 2008 and 2050. This was based on keeping emissions to 550 ppm, and he minimized the costs during the early years (0.3% by 2015), deferring them until nearer 2050 when the global economy was expected to be able to afford them. Since then, Stern has said we should focus on a target of 500 ppm, and this would increase the cost to 2 per cent of GDP. PwC economists, cited by Jackson, believe, however, that reducing emissions by 50% would cost 3 per cent of GDP, or as Jackson puts it, the difference between a growing and non-growing economy
6. (Jackson 2009)
7. (Shell 2011)
8. www.iata.org/SiteCollectionDocuments/Documents/Global_Approach_Reducing_Emissions_251109web.pdf, accessed 25 June 2011
9. (Blowfield 2012)
10. (Carbon Trust 2008)

11. (HSBC Global Research 2012)
12. For a fuller discussion of existential risk in comparison to other kinds of risk see (Tegmark, Bostrom 2005, Bostrom 2008)
13. (Prahalad, Hart 2002, Hammond et al. 2007, Hart 2010)
14. See (Ehrenreich 2001) for some interesting examples of what it is to be poor in rich countries
15. (Godfray et al. 2010)
16. (McKinsey Global Institute 2011)
17. www.indexmundi.com
18. (Lagi, Bertrand & Bar-Yam 2011)
19. See for instance reports of the Yellow River Conservation Commission/Committee and coverage at http://www.chinadaily.com.cn/china/2008-11/24/content_7232482.htm, accessed November 10, 2012
20. Introduction to the FAO World Expert Forum, *How to Feed the World*, Rome, October 12–13, 2009
21. (Godfray et al. 2010, Garnett, Godfray 2012)
22. (Intergovernmental Panel on Climate Change. Working Group III. 2007)
23. (Evans 2009)
24. (Pearce 2010, Bardi 2011, Pearce 2011)
25. authorsplace.co.uk/fred-pearce/blog/, accessed 4 January 2011
26. (WEF, Accenture 2012, McKinsey Global Institute 2011)
27. (Bloom, Canning & Sevilla 2003)
28. (McKinsey & Co 2005)
29. (Rockström et al. 2009, Sukhdev 2012)
30. (Conway 1997)
31. (Reinhart, Rogoff 2009)
32. (Reinhart, Rogoff 2010)
33. (Perez 2002, Freeman, Perez 1988)
34. (Perez 2002)
35. (King 2010: 63)
36. (Chang 2002)
37. Figures are from the IMF, presented in a series of lectures by Valpy Fitzgerald on Global Financial Crisis and Developing Countries, University of Oxford, 2010
38. Ibid
39. (Reinhart, Rogoff 2009)
40. (Truman, Peterson Institute for International Economics 2010)
41. (Clark, Monk 2010)
42. (Hawley, Williams 2000)
43. This book was completed before the Doha Conference of Parties in November 2012
44. (Ferguson 2011, Morris 2010, Ikenberry 2008)
45. (Holstein et al. 1990)
46. See the collection of essays in (Rotberg 2008)
47. (Cotula et al. 2009); www.un.org/esa/dsd/resources/res_pdfs/publications/ib/no8.pdf, accessed January 3, 2012

48. www.un.org/esa/dsd/resources/res_pdfs/publications/ib/no8.pdf, accessed 3 January 2012
49. (Friedman 1962)
50. (Boo 2012, Chakravarti 2008)
51. (Kaletsky 2010)
52. (Stiglitz 2002)
53. (King 2010): 39
54. (Palma 2009)
55. (Jacques 2009)
56. (Ghemawat 2011)
57. www.bbc.co.uk/news/world-africa-10735255;   www.guardian.co.uk/world/2009/
    sep/16/trafigura-african-pollution-disaster;   www.ft.com/cms/s/0/32634a10-a210-
    11de-81a6-00144feabdc0.html, accessed 20 April 2012
58. For an overview of civil governance see Blowfield 2012 Chapter 10
59. According to KPMG, 95% of the world's 250 largest companies report on corporate
    responsibility   activities.   http://www.kpmg.com/Global/en/IssuesAndInsights/
    ArticlesPublications/corporate-responsibility/Documents/2011-survey.pdf,
    accessed 7 November 2012
60. See contributions to (Barnett, Pollock 2012)
61. (Reich 2007)

4

Ways Out? The Oracles

IN THIS CHAPTER

Introducing the idea of congruence. Options for escaping the current challenges. Choosing which ideas are fit for purpose. How are they different, and how are they similar? Will they reestablish congruence? Do they help business face up to its turnaround challenge?

> 'It will take a hundred years to tell whether he helped us or hurt us, but he certainly didn't leave us where he found us.'
>
> Will Rogers on Henry Ford

Mass Production and the Technological Cycle

There has been no shortage of people jumping the gun to evaluate Ford. But now the twentieth century is up, it is a good time to see if Will Rogers was right and take an objective look at where the mass era has brought us. Ford helped us, transformatively so, but the era of fossil fuel-driven mass production and consumption he introduced is not the zenith and end-state of capitalism. What he and his peers brought society was a new general purpose technology that helped shape an era of technological, social, and economic life. As with any general purpose technology, the core of its adoption and ongoing legitimacy was the increases in productivity the model brought to people and business. Over time, as the technology matures, those productivity increases decline, but the genius of capitalism is its ability to cook up another productivity-enhancing general purpose technology to throw into the mix and deploy. If the GPT is a lime, it gets squeezed of its juices right until the pips squeak and the effort of squeezing exceeds the rewards. Then the invisible hand of the market reaches over the counter to grab a new lime, moving the old one to a new niche (and possible rebirth as e.g. candied lime peel). Think of it in James Bond terms. It's like Pierce Brosnan moving from 007 to a memorable role in the Abba Musical Mamma Mia. It's like DC power, in the battle between Tesla's alternating current and Edison's direct current, making way for Tesla's AC power, but surviving in useful niches from railway lines to telecoms and ICT. The Central Electricity Generating Board in the UK maintained a 200 volt DC generating station at Bankside Power Station on the River Thames in London right up till 1981. Its exclusive job was to power printing machinery for the UK's newspaper industry in Fleet Street. The last hotel in New York to convert to AC, ironically, was Tesla's favourite, the New Yorker Hotel. Constructed in 1929, with its own large direct-current power plant, it did not convert fully to AC until the 1960s. When Tesla died at the hotel in 1943, his deathbed was lit by DC power, the resistant technology he had worked so hard to marginalize.

Stalling productivity, emerging pathologies

Business is confronting a situation in which the productivity gains of the mass era have stagnated and the limits of the model that has dominated its thinking for a century are being exposed by simultaneous economic, social, environmental, and governance crises. We have shown in earlier chapters that the crises can individually involve downward spirals. On the economic side, we explored the downward spirals associated with the decline in productivity, with offshoring and job losses, with competitor growth, declining balance of payments, falling tax receipts and austerity restricting investment in productivity gains. On the social side we have seen the spiral of the instability of inequality leading to social unrest, political destabilization, business uncertainty, decreased foreign direct investment and reduced opportunities for local employment.

On the environmental side, a scientific consensus has emerged around an atmospheric 'tipping point' of 2°C of warming. At this point, corresponding to an estimated 450 parts per million of CO_2 equivalent in the atmosphere, we risk a runaway effect where warming accelerates beyond our control through a series of feedback loops. One of these is the albedo effect, where, as ice melts it becomes darker, absorbing more heat, melting more and becoming even darker. The Arctic is an example of this. Scientists estimate that there are hundreds of millions of tonnes of methane gas beneath the ice of the Arctic permafrost, which extends from the mainland into the seabed of the East Siberian Arctic Shelf. The volume of carbon locked up under ice is calculated to exceed the amount of carbon locked up in global coal reserves. With the polar region warming at a faster rate than other places on Earth, the risk is of releasing methane—a gas twenty times more potent as a greenhouse agent than carbon dioxide—at a scale that would dwarf decarbonization attempts. In December 2011, the eighth joint US-Russia cruise of the East Siberian Arctic seas found evidence of extensive methane leakage. Igor Semiletov of the International Arctic Research Centre commented, 'This is the first time that we've found continuous, powerful and impressive seeping structures more than 1,000 metres in diameter. . . . Over a relatively small area we found more than 100, but over a wider area there should be thousands of them.'

Finally, there is the risk of downward spirals on the governance side, where increased corporate influence leads to declining engagement and donation by party members, increased dependence on corporate donations, and a consequential increased risk of implicit or explicit regulatory capture where policy across the political spectrum accommodates the 'common sense' of business. This accommodation in turn reduces the perceived legitimacy of government, decreasing not just engagement in the political process but government's capacity to grab hold of the reins and redirect an economy towards a new wave of market-led growth at the crisis point in the economic cycle.

The threats of interdependency

Each of these cycles presents threats enough on its own. Recent scenario work by Shell has also shown that these crises are also interdependent, with one spiral accelerating another.[1] Along similar lines, *Global Risks 2013*, launched at Davos, the World Economic Forum's annual review of risk to the economic system, highlighted climate change as one of the top five risks most likely to have a global impact over the next decade. A group of 1000 global experts commented that the interdependencies between the top five risks of widening income gap between rich and poor, high government deficits, climate change, water shortages, and ageing populations could pose a threat for global economic and social stability.

Pinch points

While detailed discussion of these interdependencies is beyond the scope of this book, there appears to be an emerging set of potential pinch points for business to look out for:

Economic versus environmental
- Capital adequacy and environmental investment: the economic crisis and lack of capital prevents business investment in energy efficiency measures with long payback periods and in the longer-term high capex investment required to decarbonize.

- Lack of government capital to fund or subsidize the development of new approaches.

- Lack of government capital to roll out infrastructure enabling the acceleration of new technology.

- Austerity measures reduce the willingness of business to pass on costs to the consumer, blocking take up of new technologies higher up the learning curve.
- Volatility of climate commitments and instability of regulatory framework deters business from investing in long-term high capex technology.

Governance versus environmental
- Lack of government mandate reduces the capacity to direct and accelerate transition to new models through regulation (e.g. carbon taxation).

- Climate change impacts, either sudden or gradual, restrict economic development, decreasing government and business capital. While the immediate aftermath of natural catastrophe may strengthen the mandate for government, long-term failures to respond or adapt may erode legitimacy.

Environmental versus social
- The 'Arab Spring' in 2010 showed the potential for the environmental factor of climate change to impact the economic factor of food prices, and for this economic factor then to result in social unrest, political destabilization and reduced business investment.

Social versus economic
- Economists such as Joseph Stiglitz highlight the rising inequality within OECD countries, and this is cited as a factor behind the high rates of anxiety, depression, and other social disorders in those economies.[2]

- In the UK, as in the USA, a worsening current account deficit between the early 1970s and 2007 reflects a national rise in inequality. As the share of national income devoted to profits and top pay rose, real wages become squeezed. To sustain their living standards, workers borrow, aided by financial deregulation. Demand keeps on growing, but driven by the debt-fuelled consumption of imports. Finally, both debt and import levels become unsustainable. '[T]here is a very strong negative cross-country correlation, of almost −0.8, between changes in top income shares and changes in current account balances among OECD countries.'[3]

This last pinch point is worth highlighting because it is one that adds new insight into the body of claims that inequality has risen in the latter stages of the mass era. An increase of one percentage point of the top 5 per cent's share of income over the period concerned corresponds to a deterioration of the current-account-to-GDP ratio of 0.8 percentage points. The current crisis in

Britain—high levels of private sector debt and a record trade deficit—can thus be explained by the rise of inequality. As Kumhof's IMF working paper sums up, 'greater income inequality, with or without added financial liberalization, creates pressures for the current account to deteriorate.'[4] The magnitude of the effect is sufficient to roughly explain the UK's entire current account deterioration experienced between the late 1970s and 2007. 'In the long run, there is therefore simply no way around addressing the income inequality problem itself. Financial liberalization in surplus countries only buys time, but at the expense of an eventually much larger debt problem.'[5]

Critical to this restoration of incomes for the working poor is to address the underlying issue of the long-term decline in productivity as shown by the *Shift Index* analysis of the diminishing return on assets at the later stages of the mass era. As Will Hutton comments, 'The paradox is that the chief reason capitalism is in crisis is that... it has undermined its own dynamism and capacity for innovation. Instead, it merely offers enormous and unjustified self-enrichment for those at the top.'[6]

Exit from Petropolis?

The transformational crises, in short, are complex, interdependent, and not going away. They also appear to be well known and yet resistant to attempts to address them, with a number of potential drivers of lock-in. In other words, without a compelling alternative, they are taking us on our current trajectory towards what in Chapter 1 we called the Petropolis. To reply more fully then to Will Rogers's query; Ford helped society, but there is also a possibility that he could hurt it. He could hurt it if, despite its emerging weaknesses, the mass era continues to be championed as the only feasible way of tackling those crises and achieving advances in human well-being. He could hurt society, in other words, if we maintain a stance of techno-economic monoculturism and make the assumption that 'There is no alternative.'

The difficulty for any alternatives is that the bar is high and has become both higher and harder to dislodge as the market has grown in size and complexity over the evolution of capitalism. It is no mean feat that new options have to pull off to gain acceptance. If we are looking for alternative approaches, they have to meet a twin test. They have to meet the external challenges of addressing the social, environmental, and economic threats that confront us. This is an adequacy test. They also have to meet the internal governance challenge of being do-able at the scale and speed required. This is an achievability test.

Defining a viable way out

So what are the criteria for adequacy that the alternatives we are looking for have to meet? The heart of it is 'fit'. What does this external fit look like? The behaviour, strategy, actions, and other discernible practices of an institution or organization must fit or be congruent with what external circumstances demand. This means that any element of society—social, legal, economic, political, and technological (SLEPT)—must fit the needs of the world it finds itself part of, because to be otherwise is to jeopardize society's well-being and erode the social operating licence that society grants. High carbon emissions from business fitted an external environment where there was no known carbon constraint and threat of global warming. Mass production of the automobile fitted with an external social condition of rural communities unconnected to the market. But this need for fit is ongoing: if external circumstances change—a carbon constraint, for example, becoming the scientific consensus—the organization, to remain healthy from society's point of view, must adapt.

External fit: the challenge of adequacy

What we are describing here is 'congruence': the mutually supportive relationship between an institution and its environment (Chapter 5). An alternative approach to the current model passes the adequacy test if it offers something that strengthens society's congruence with the external environment. In a capitalist society, special emphasis is put on the congruence of business as what Drucker called the 'representative social institution.'[7] He was referring to the wide array of functions business has to perform in society, and the fact that business has become central to society's prosperity. Even if, as some claim it should, it attends to its own narrow needs such as profitability, business still has to satisfy the needs of others such as consumers and employees, and contribute to stability, prosperity, and peace for its own longevity. Conversely, although other people argue it is overly-powerful, the reality is that business has become so embedded in modern life that removing it from the social system would be an unfeasible task. What is more, for all of its weaknesses and pathologies, an enfeebled business could be more damaging to society at the present time than one that is strong and prosperous.

Internal fit: the challenge of achievability

However, external congruence is not the only aspect that is important. Veblen refers to the pattern of social and economic institutions aligning around a technology. The alternative economic model must not just be adequate, it must be achievable in the context of the path dependency and resistance which the vested interests of political, social, legal, and economic institutions and norms will offer. These institutions are vital, both to block new entrants and approaches that have the capacity to destabilize a techno-economic paradigm that is about to or is in the middle of delivering prosperity, and to drop their guard and cautiously allow the next potential dominant technology to put down roots and grow when the previous era is past its prime.

The main argument for maintaining the Petropolis is that up to now it has functioned as an internally and externally congruent system in which the SLEPT elements interact to benefit society as a whole. Thus, historically it has allowed business to make a profit, and companies are supported in this by other institutions and general social expectations. For example, the legal framework has given business the certainty it needs to make investments that will be to citizens' overall benefit, and politicians have supported this through such measures as social safety provision and favourable economic and trade policy. This internal congruence is no longer present. For example, the fall out of the dot.com bubble and the financial crisis a few years later weakened social safety nets, damaged manufacturing, lowered standards of living, and (paradoxically) strengthened banks across the OECD, and there has been a resurgence of fear about the effects of capitalism in many countries. In Chapter 5, we will argue that there is indeed internal incongruence, and this is a major hindrance when it comes to creating a new prosperity. However, for the time being, we want to concentrate on external congruence, and the idea that even an internally congruent system is only truly congruent if it is consistent with the wider environment it is part of. If we have a model that is taking us towards Petropolis, are there 'Oracles' with visions of how to extract us from the mess we are in?

Market Moderation, Market Solutions, or Market Exit?

There are three broad types of option currently on offer to tackle the problems we have described. These are:

a) *Market moderation*: To moderate the market, maintaining the current core growth model, while mitigating features of it to adapt to the external environment.

b) *Market exit*: To abandon the market as an economic model incompatible with societal challenges.

c) *Market solutions*: To unleash the market, allowing it to come up with the technological breakthrough that removes carbon from the atmosphere, removing the need for systematic decarbonization from industry.

Each option has its own Oracles, as we will explain. But what is the proper test of an Oracle's wisdom? Are their ideas both adequate to the challenges we face, and achievable? Do their ideas increase external congruence without requiring internal incongruence to the point of instability?

The Oracles

Figure 4.1 sums up the three main branches of Oracle wisdom.

The first, Market moderation, hinges on the conclusion that free market capitalism, as it has evolved since industrialization, is the best hope for addressing its crises: not only is it the best route for business, it is the best way for society as a whole and business should be allowed to take on as big a role as possible. It includes those who want little or no market moderation, but it also includes people who think the market is imperfect but the existing model can be adapted to deliver more favourable outcomes. The first group believes in 'business as usual'; the second advocates 'green business as usual' based on the belief that free markets have tended to treat the negative social and environmental consequences of commercial activity as externalities, and now is the time to recalibrate elements of capitalism so that business internalizes its negative impacts and at the same time is incentivized to treat the crises as major opportunities for growth.

The second branch has no such faith in the market to deliver sustained prosperity. They want to see the market radically constrained, if not done away with entirely. The most developed of these ideas adhere to what Tim Jackson calls 'prosperity without growth.' Its basic argument is that the pursuit of economic growth has caused numerous environmental problems that threaten the sustainability of current and future generations as well as the sustainability of the Earth's ecosystems overall. Its Oracles therefore propose alternatives to conventional economic models built on ideas such as steady state growth and the stationary state.

The third branch wants to unleash the power of the market to foment technological innovation that will restore external congruence. Unlike our other Oracles, they do not use conventional economics as their starting point; instead, they offer technological options that will facilitate fundamentally different ways of responding to the crises. Geo-engineering, agricultural innovation, and nuclear fusion are examples of technological leaps that would significantly affect the impact of demographic and climate change for society as a whole. Another option, though, is a form of social triaging, with these innovations used selectively to protect certain groups from catastrophic change. 'Plutonomy', as we discussed earlier, refers to a type of economic development that is powered by and offers most benefits to the richest members of society. It

ORACLE	ORACLE PHILOSOPHY
MARKET MODERATION	
Business as usual	• Markets allocate resources rationally (Efficient markets hypothesis) • The role for government should be limited • Social well-being follows from and equates to economic well-being • Change is gradual and guided by market interactions • Environmental and social resources are externalities, not to be factored into decision making • The business of business is business. • Universal economic laws exist akin to the laws of physics
Green business as usual	• Market failure occurs in the context of some environmental resources • Change is gradual but can be accelerated through incentives and government intervention • The business of business is sustainable business • Change is largely technology-driven but benefits from government action • Transformation is something that can be managed by governments and the private sector
Green plutonomy	• Challenges can best be met by serving the needs of the wealthiest members of society • Influential members of society should shape the activities of government and the private sector • 'Things must change to stay the way they are'—concessions on environmental or social terms may be needed to maintain the status quo
MARKET EXIT	
Prosperity without growth	• Current economic system is irrational and 'uneconomic' • Unlimited growth not possible on finite planet • Prosperity is not synonymous with economic growth • Economic growth needs to be constrained to establish equilibrium between society and the environment • There are many dimensions to a prosperous society including fairness, equality, spirituality and opportunity
MARKET SOLUTION	
Geo-engineering (techno-optimism)	• Major challenges are best met through major technological innovation • Technological breakthroughs will allow us to remove carbon, avoiding the need for industrywide decarbonization. • Investment should comes from both the private and public sectors, with state intervention to secure funding of geo-engineering as a public good project

Figure 4.1: Overview of the Oracles

is often used by social protest movements such as Occupy to rally support against social inequality, but a techno-plutonomy variant, linked to radical techno-optimism, and legitimized by the promise of breakthrough technologies for all, could also be seen as a legitimate response to catastrophic change.

Market Moderation

The first of our Oracles are those who argue that incongruence and threats to prosperity do not require structural change. On the contrary, crises are best addressed if private enterprise is allowed to do what it does best: create wealth by providing the goods and services people need. The business as usual (BAU) Oracles are a broad church, normally represented by economists but with numerous adherents amongst politicians. They include past and present UK chancellors of the exchequer Nigel Lawson and George Osborne, economics professors William Nordhaus and Richard Tol, statistician Bjørn Lomborg, and scientists Claude Allegre and Richard Lindzen. Some of those mentioned would be horrified to see their names linked together, and their motivations for advocating BAU as an approach are often quite different.[8] For example, Nordhaus has been critical of the economics underlying green business as usual, but has been even more vocal in his criticism of those who doubt the very concept of anthropogenic climate change such as Allegre and Lindzen.[9] Likewise, Lomborg has been heavily criticized for his early remarks questioning the severity of climate change, but one of his aims was to draw attention to the needs of an expanding population of the poor, something that is missing from some global warming analysis.[10]

The logic of Business as Usual

Although the BAU Oracles might be awkward dinner companions, their common ground is that the free market capitalist business model is the best available to allocate scarce resources and deliver human well-being. They accept, for instance, that gross domestic product (GDP) is a valid measure of economic performance, and that economic performance is the primary indicator of social progress. Over time, progress is experienced by everyone as the economy grows thanks to investment, productivity, and consumption, and benefits are shared through wages, investment returns, and the availability of goods and services. This is the ideal model of free market capitalism that has evolved since the early Industrial Revolution, and it is one built on the strengths of private enterprise as a creator and distributor of wealth. At its centre is the conviction that prosperity equates with economic growth, and the amount of growth in GDP a country enjoys is now shorthand for how well it is doing. A second and compelling notion, linked to the interdependency of environmental and economic challenges, is that this is a moment of economic crisis and time to focus on growth, not on environmental and social concerns that might restrict it.

While some advocates of BAU are outright sceptics about the reality of crises such as climate change, others say that it is exactly because the crises require serious action that we should use the most effective tools to address them, and that means putting more effort than ever into economic growth. Since the early Industrial Revolution, world GDP has gone from about US$180 per person to its current level of US$6,600. To a BAU Oracle, 97 per cent of human wealth has been created during 0.01 per cent of human history,[11] and it is only this sort of growth that will generate the wealth needed to deal with the transformational crises: meeting the basic needs of over nine billion people and the aspirations of the three billion new members of the middle class; producing surplus capital to invest in new energy infrastructure and flood protection; creating the returns sovereign wealth funds expect on corporate and government bonds.

Moreover, growth needs to happen now, a) in order that companies can flourish and invest more in creating a prosperous society, and b) because the higher the level of GDP at any moment in time, the greater the potential for economic expansion in the long term. From an ethical perspective, they argue, the needs of future generations are best served by maximizing the prosperity of the current one because this will equip our descendants with greater wealth to address whatever challenges they confront.

GREEN BUSINESS AS USUAL

The essence of the green growth position is that there is a carbon constraint and capitalism can handle it. Climate change represents a market failure—an environmental 'externality'—which needs to be addressed by means of carbon taxation or cap and trade. The moment this economically logical step is taken, the argument goes, the market will in theory correct and investment will flow towards low carbon opportunities, helping us to decarbonize some 80 per cent by 2050. The issue of current versus future wealth has been the main bone of contention between BAU Oracles and their Green Business as Usual (GBAU) counterparts. The latter are not opposed to economic growth, but economists such as Nicholas Stern and Carlo Jaeger insist that the markets by themselves will not channel capital in a timely, optimal way, and this will increase the cost for future generations of taking crisis-related action. Therefore, rather than allow growth to continue unabated, a better path is to tackle in particular existential risks as soon as possible on the premise this will ultimately be less costly than deferred expenditures.

In Stern's initial analysis, the cost of mitigating climate change was estimated to be 1 per cent of GDP between 2008 and 2050.[12] He has subsequently adjusted this to 2 per cent of GDP, while PwC economists cited by Jackson estimate a 50 per cent reduction in greenhouse gas emissions will cost 3 per cent of GDP.[13] Each of these numbers is a significant portion of global wealth over a prolonged period, and they are very different from the figures associated with a BAU response to crises. Stern's analysis, which was the first of its kind, claimed that the costs of unmitigated climate change would be anything between 5 and 20 per cent of global GDP annually. In stark contrast, BAU economists such as Nordhaus contend that the damage from climate change would be 0.5 to 2 per cent of global GDP per annum.

At the heart of this discrepancy is a disagreement about discount rates: i.e. how much importance is attached to the relative welfare of future generations compared to present ones. According to GBAU Oracles, it is unethical and economically damaging to ignore the consequences of phenomena such as climate change for future generations. If they were with us now, it is argued, they would ask us to do what we could to avoid putting the Earth's future carrying capacity at risk. If that means diverting current investments into areas such as climate change mitigation, then that is the right thing to do.

This is the kind of prescriptive approach to discounts used by Stern in his analysis of how to combat climate change. It is also evident in the green economic stimulus packages adopted by countries such as South Korea, the European Union, and China in the aftermath of the 2007 financial melt-down,[14] and it is a recurring theme in climate change policy debates in the USA and the UK. Stern used a very low discount rate (0.1 per cent), thereby giving almost equal importance to the welfare of current and future generations. This was justified by the high estimated damage global warming would cause to global economic production: the social cost of carbon, as it is known, was put at US$310 of damage per tonne of carbon emissions.[15] By contrast, BAU economists such as Nordhaus and Tol use much lower estimates of social cost (US$40–120 per tonne of carbon), highlighting the difficulty of applying cost–benefit analysis to the long term. They also employ a higher discount rate (in the range of 4 per cent per annum), in part because history says that future generations will be much richer than today's, and therefore will have greater wealth to cope with what crises have to throw at them. Consequently, the BAU argument goes, people today should not stifle the creation of that wealth by prescribing spending on climate change mitigation or any other action in which the costs will be borne by the current generation and the benefits reaped by future ones.

The logic of Green Business as Usual

The GBAU argument to spend today to prevent much higher costs tomorrow has been largely developed in the context of climate change. The Economics of Ecosystems and Biodiversity programme (TEEB) has developed a similar approach for valuing biodiversity, helping government to make economic decisions about species and ecosystems. As the then British Prime Minister famously put it, the economic benefits of early action outweigh the costs: 'It proves tackling climate change is the pro-growth strategy.'[16] BAU Oracles disagree: today's wealth that is diverted into mitigation efforts deprives the poor of the opportunity for greater economic growth, and will ultimately leave their descendants in a weaker position to defend themselves against any negative consequences relating to population growth, ecosystem change, or even shifts in power.

GREEN PLUTONOMY

A second form of green business as usual is what could be termed green plutonomy. Stella McCartney, for example, an outstanding British designer, has built her career as a high end fashion designer partly on ethical principles about animals and materials. Her £610 Mock Croc Lauren Pump and her £855 Faux Python Tote are made from synthetic materials, and her brand's website tells visitors about its commitment to recycling, reuse, and avoiding materials from animals.[17] Philippe Briand, the superyacht designer, has built his brand on the principles of 'efficiency, sustainability and robustness,' and his US$100 million vessels are promoted as the least polluting in their class.[18] Bentley, famous for fast, luxury, and fuel hungry cars, is committed to reducing CO_2 emissions by 40 per cent and giving owners the option of running on renewable fuels.[19] Tiffany & Co, whose off-the-shelf jewellery can sell for over £20 000, is committed to sustainable sourcing of raw materials.[20]

Alongside brands for the wealthy, there are companies that serve this market's wider needs in areas such as housing, security, and leisure. There are also many innovators who use this market segment—which in the USA, for instance, accounts for over 40 per cent of income[21]—to introduce new ideas that could one day become household items. BAE Systems uses extensive social and environmental criteria in designing products such as its ICOP battlespace workstation, the type of technology being deployed in the flourishing anti-piracy security industry which serves private yachts as well as commercial shipping.

The logic of Green Plutonomy

Focusing on the rich has an economic logic, and even if its impact is not quantified, McCartney's commitment to recycling, reuse, and avoiding materials from animals is rooted in environmental values.[22] As noted, the rich have often been the pioneer consumers of new innovations that later benefited a mass market. Furthermore, with the right tax regime, non-productive

Figure 4.2: Bentley and Electric Car

consumption of this kind could be used to generate revenues for congruence-creating productive investment, as proposed by Robert H. Frank.[23]

But what is not clear is that green plutonomy, of the type on display in the Notting Hill driveway in Figure 4.2—the family G-whizz electric vehicle parked beside the family Bentley—addresses the social or environmental challenges head on.

In Chapter 3, we talked about the private acquisition of large swathes of land as a hedge against the consequences of climate change and overpopulation. Gated communities have become a worldwide phenomenon and are an example of how something that began with the very wealthy has trickled down to the richer middle classes, whether they be in Johannesburg or the USA's largest gated community, Hot Springs Village, Arkansas. For those who worry gated communities are not safe enough, 'seasteading' on floating cities is now proposed as a way to help people escape what they see as dysfunctional political systems.[24] If that is too expensive, Microsoft captured media attention when it patented a mobile phone app to help pedestrians avoid ghettoes.[25] Meanwhile, a company in Colombia has launched a range of designer bullet proof vests and rucksacks for schoolchildren.[26] Green plutonomy may readily pass the achievability test, but in so far as it fails to address the environmental challenge of mass production, and leaves unmet the needs of the many, it risks failing the adequacy test and instead increasing environmental and social instability.

Prosperity Without Growth

Arguments over discount rates, the social cost of carbon, and what percentage of GDP should be diverted to particular activities are an economists' parlour game, according to one group of Oracles. For them, the market itself is the problem. As another economist, Dieter Helm, states, 'The easy compatibility between economic growth and climate change which lies at the heart of the Stern Report is an illusion. The truth is that there is as yet no credible, socially just, ecologically sustainable scenario of continually growing economies for a world of nine billion people.'[27] Prosperity Without Growth Oracles (PWG) hold that the relentless pursuit of economic growth—the central plank of BAU and GBAU thinking—is flawed. Although brought to prominence in recent decades in books such as *The Limits to Growth*,[28] *Beyond Growth*,[29] and *Prosperity Without Growth*,[30] it boasts an ancestry in the works of classical economists such as Mill and Malthus who recognized economic growth could not continue indefinitely if the resources an economy could draw on were finite. This is alarming to the politicians and business leaders baptized and raised in a tradition that equates growth with prosperity and absence of growth with decline and poverty.

The logic of Prosperity without Growth

For PWG Oracles, it is a fundamental truth that an economy cannot be so large that it disrupts the environment it is a subsystem of. For them, this is the essence of incongruence. The key challenge for economics is not to maximize growth, they say, but how to maintain growth at an optimal level so that it ensures human well-being without the benefits being outweighed by the cumulative social, financial, and environmental costs. Greenhouse gas emissions are an example of what happens when economic activity exceeds the Earth's carrying capacity resulting in an unsustainable level of economic growth. Daly calls this 'uneconomic growth' because the benefits are increasingly outweighed by the costs as human economic activity uses up more natural capital than can be absorbed or replaced.[31] Uneconomic growth is exemplified by 'overshoot' when a population needs more resources than it can acquire. Peak oil—used to describe the decline in availability of conventional oil—is an example of overshoot, but with the increasing availability of non-conventional oil from deep offshore sources, tight oil, and shale oil, it has been used by critics as a case of unjustified pessimism on the part of PWG Oracles.

In reply, it is argued that new sources of oil are a curse because they will lead to even greater emissions overshoot and divert investment from sustainable energy. As Jackson points out, innovation and ingenuity have made some areas of production more efficient (e.g. since the 1960s tailpipe emissions from USA cars have fallen from a hundred grams per mile driven to two grams), but economic growth means that any efficiency gains have been ultimately offset by the extra resources used, the pollution, and other harmful effects of ever-greater consumption. Thus, although humans have to an extent weakened the historical link between greater productivity and greater resource use—what Jackson calls 'relative decoupling' (see Box 4.1)—the figures presented in Chapter 3 show that there has been little progress in 'absolute decoupling,' i.e. severing the links between overall economic growth and resource use or ecosystem degradation.

It is the failure of GBAU and BAU Oracles to solve the problems of over-shoot, absolute decoupling, and uneconomic growth that has led the PWG counterparts to look for an alternative to conventional growth. They draw a distinction between economic growth and sustainable development, and argue that it is quite possible to lead prosperous lives in a low- or even no-growth society. This is a world of 'steady state growth' or the 'stationary state,' and it is one in which poverty is solved through population control, wealth redistribution, and advances in resource productivity.

Some people apply a strong ideological gloss to the PWG philosophy, singling out how avarice drives unsustainable consumption, or how pride and vanity fire immoral capitalism. Equally, some of PWG's opponents high-light sloth and despondency as sins associated with those who are cynical about conventional growth. However, PWG is not necessarily a morality

---

Box 4.1 RELATIVE AND ABSOLUTE DECOUPLING

RELATIVE DECOUPLING: Historically, carbon emissions and resource usage have increased in line with economic growth. A major challenge in the sustainability context is decoupling these two phenomena so that economies can grow without increasing material throughput. The reductions in material and energy intensity in OECD countries in recent years have strengthened belief that decoupling can be achieved. This is an example of relative decoupling where resource intensity for every unit of production/ output is reduced.

ABSOLUTE DECOUPLING: However, the greater challenge is absolute decoupling, i.e. reducing the total carbon emissions or other resource use without affecting economic growth. According to the IPCC, absolute decoupling would need to reduce carbon emissions by 50–80 per cent by 2050 to avoid dangerous climate change. Changes of this magnitude are unlikely to be achieved by relative decoupling which can lead to greater eficiency but does not prevent a net increase in inputs to the overall economy.

project. Oracles such as Randers and Daly accept that economic growth has probably led to a better standard of human well-being than would otherwise have been the case, but humanity is now at a point when the marginal benefits of continuing to pursue that model are offset by the marginal costs: 'No one is against being richer.... But I think economic growth has already ended in the sense that the growth that continues now is **uneconomic**; it costs more than it is worth at the margins and makes us poorer rather than richer.'[32]

Market Solutions

Techno-optimists

THE LOGIC OF THE TECHNO-OPTIMISTS
Each of our Oracles has his own form of optimism: the market moderators believe in conventional economic wisdom; the PWG Oracles have faith in the human capacity to change. Our last group are techno-optimists who, instead of focusing on the hard yards of decarbonizing, believe that the market, with some support from the state, will produce a technological breakthrough that addresses the carbon challenge.

State support will be needed and warranted, they argue, to deliver a complex and high cost technological challenge crossing national boundaries. But the grounds for optimism are the genius of capitalism and the capacity of the market to innovate. Some in this camp are looking at geo-engineering involving deliberate, large-scale interventions in the Earth's climate system as set out in Box 4.2. Their aim is to moderate global warming either by removing greenhouse gases from the atmosphere or by shielding the Earth from increased solar radiation.[33]

Box 4.2 TYPES OF GEO-ENGINEERING

There are two types of geo-engineering technology:

- *Carbon Dioxide Removal (CDR) Technologies* that address the root cause of climate change by removing greenhouse gases from the atmosphere. Examples:
  - Fertilizing the seas with plankton to absorb and lock away carbon
  - Reforestation with natural and artificial trees to absorb carbon

- Solar radiation management (SRM) techniques that attempt to offset the effects of heightened greenhouse gas concentrations by shielding the Earth from increased solar radiation. Examples:
  - Cloud-whitening using salt sprayed from the oceans to reflect the sun
  - Painting roofs and roads white to reflect the sun
  - Space mirrors to reduce the sun entering the stratosphere

---

The current difficulty with geo-engineering technologies is that none has been shown to be both effective at an affordable cost and with acceptable side-effects. In theory, CO_2 Removal Technologies are more attractive because they permanently return the climate system to something like its natural state. However, they can be costly, and their impact is slow, measured in decades. Solar radiation management techniques, although involving radically new technologies, are probably less expensive, and could have an effect within a few years. They can be thought of as a performance enhancer that could be introduced for a limited period if efficiency and substitution technologies are not delivering emissions reductions at the necessary rate. However, not only are they a long way from realization, they create an artificial balance between increased greenhouse gas concentrations (e.g. from conventional manufacturing emissions) and reduced solar radiation, and this would need to be managed and maintained, potentially for centuries. Depending on one's viewpoint, this represents an exhilarating challenge or a terrible threat to the idea of the Earth as a self-regulating system of the kind described in the works of James Lovelock.[34] It also poses unprecedented challenges for global governance because interventions at a national or corporate level have international consequences that are well beyond the competence of current governance mechanisms.

Evaluating the Oracles

Those, in sum, are the views of the current Oracles. Do any of them pass the twin test we set out earlier: are they both adequate to the crises confronting us, and achievable given society's path dependency and the crisis of governance? They need to be ambitious because of the size of the present challenges, but they must be plausible given the timeframe for action which in many cases is a handful of decades. The ultimate test is whether they reestablish external congruence so that the well-being of business is consistent with that of the wider environment it is part of.

In order to evaluate the Oracles properly, let us in Figure 4.3 map out four scenarios from now to 2050. The vertical axis is CO_2 use per person; the horizontal, per capita GDP. Historically, as GDP increases, so individual CO_2 use rises, from Ethiopia in the bottom left corner, to China in the middle, and the USA in the top right corner. The dashed line represents the environmental constraint on growth imposed by climate change. As we have discussed, scientists do not know the exact tipping point, but agree it is somewhere between 350 and 450 parts per million of CO_2 or equivalent gases. At present, the figure is about 400 ppm. Therefore, any Oracle that takes us over that threshold is increasing existential risk, even if they increase economic wealth;

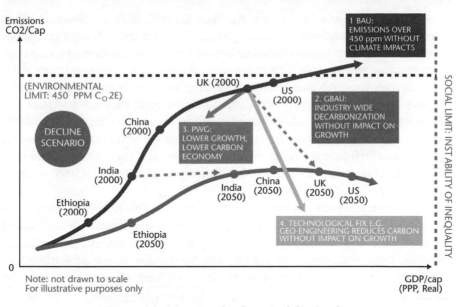

Figure 4.3: Mapping the dreams of the Oracles

whereas an Oracle that pulls society away from the dashed line but at the expense of economic growth is risking instability from inequality, plutonomy, and social breakdown.

All four of the scenarios, depending on one's viewpoint, are optimistic. They correspond, broadly, with the options on offer from the Oracles discussed so far. Let us get a sense based on these scenarios of where we think— not hope—society is going to be by 2050.

EVALUATING BAU

BAU is Scenario 1 in Figure 4.3. It promises to enhance well-being around the world through economic growth, and in some people's minds this will be accompanied by other improvements such as liberty, democracy, and opportunity. BAU is synonymous with free-market capitalism which has raised average global financial wealth to unprecedented levels, and brought benefits that even some critics of economic growth recognize as outweighing its disadvantages.[35] Those benefits have not been equally shared, either within or between economies; but there is no empirical evidence of an alternative system achieving sustained long-term well-being on the scale achieved through BAU. Moreover, BAU has the appeal of the familiar, and is an option that many emerging economies feel comfortable with because it is not a threat to their claim for a bigger share of global prosperity.

BAU, because it represents the status quo, is comforting in numerous other ways as well. It shares, for instance, a way of thinking about the future similar to the one common in the discipline of business finance. It employs a descriptive discount rate that uses historical data to predict the future, in a similar way that Net Present Value is used in business to evaluate the value over time of investments made today. Nordhaus' disagreement with GBAU Oracles is not because he disputes the climate change science, but because the benefits of immediate action do not in his view justify the economic cost (page 74). In both cases, the future is a function of the present, and there is an assumption that to think of the future as anything fundamentally different from today is folly.

The unprecedented nature of the current crises means, however, that a good outcome for future generations requires interventions that cannot be justified by following past trends. This is most apparent in the context of climate change. The consequences of climate change are already being felt and are expected to become more severe over time. Therefore, *when* an investment is made is vital: deferring it for twenty years for purely economic reasons makes no sense if during that period land is lost to desertification, factories have to be relocated because of rising water levels, and the rural poor in sub-Saharan Africa suffer from drought and unpredictable weather patterns. At present, BAU experts argue that the cost of dealing with these kinds of changes is too expensive, and the world should focus on building its economy so we have adequate wealth in the future to afford the huge costs associated with climate change adaptation. In response, there are strong scientific claims that the costs of plausible effective action that could be taken now are much lower than BAU economists reckon.[36] However, assuming these do not meet the cost–benefit test, the reality is that a BAU trajectory is highly likely to take us beyond the dashed line in our graph and hence into a zone of climate unpredictability that will make conventional analysis worthless. Indeed, although Scenario 1 promises economic growth, it ignores the strong possibility that once the dashed line is breached, climate change events will damage the economy and trigger downward spirals. Therefore, although we have optimistically associated BAU with Scenario 1, it could equally be linked to climate change driven reductions in economic growth.

The critical flaw of BAU: the economic costs of climate change

It is BAU's failure to assimilate what science says about how the climate change crisis will unfold that makes it dangerous. BAU, no matter what its form, never really accepts that climate change is an existential risk. It is so inflexibly wedded to economic growth as the benchmark of prosperity, and so accepting of the power of economic theory to interpret the world accurately, that it ends up trying to justify implausible ideas that are ambitious only in their fancifulness. Take, for example, demographic change, aspects of which are an important element of BAU thinking. Nobody would deny that the poor would benefit from being wealthier, and historically this has come about through economic growth. But if poor regions will be most adversely affected by climate change as BAU economists such as Tol say, failure to factor in the time dimension and potential irreversibility of global warming will increase the risk that the poor will be denied the opportunity to prosper as the ecosystems they depend on deteriorate. In ways already discernible in parts of Africa and South Asia—the cradles of global poverty—they will become increasingly dependent for their survival not on growth but on aid and the creation of the kind of state-backed safety net that the more libertarian BAU proponents find abhorrent.

EVALUATING GBAU

Green Business as Usual and Business as Usual have much in common in that they both believe in the power of the markets to address social and environmental challenges. However, while BAU treats economic growth as the primary way to address the consequences of demographic change and climate change, GBAU treats climate change as something unique and deserving of a different approach. A practical consequence of a GBAU-based policy of the kind proposed by Stern or Jaeger is that it would deliberately reallocate a portion of economic growth now, in order to reduce climate change later on. In China, for instance, several generations of citizens would be less wealthy than they might have expected in order that their descendants could be wealthier and more secure. The question is, how much less wealthy (would they be impoverished, for example?), how much more secure, and would the cost to China be more or less than the cost of climate change (i.e. the social cost of carbon)? GBAU Oracles tend to think that the effects of unmitigated climate change will be catastrophic before the end of this century, and take seriously the consensus of the Intergovernmental Panel on Climate Change that human activity (especially economic activity) is responsible for unprecedented warming. Therefore, the question of 'how much less wealthy' is a secondary one because if the security/mitigation one is not tackled, the subsequent harm could destroy the prosperity prospects for future generations.

GBAU is therefore Scenario 2 in our graph, associated with lower emissions but minimal long-term impacts on GDP. At first glance, this might make GBAU ideas implausible, not least because the changes in geopolitics and governance would create a resistance to actions that seem to make the poor even poorer. Part of GBAU's appeal is, however, that it treats climate change as a pro-growth strategy and, as noted earlier, it formed part of green stimulus packages around the world. Germany's anti-nuclear, pro-renewables energy policy shows that some countries are willing to gamble on the GBAU logic proving right, but in the UK, the USA, Canada, and parts of the Eurozone, prolonged sluggish growth is making it less and less acceptable to talk of green growth as an alternative to conventional growth.

The critical flaw of GBAU: rates of decarbonization

The effort of stimulating green growth should not be underestimated. Building enough onshore and offshore wind farms to meet just Britain's projected needs would require 60 million tonnes of concrete and steel, equivalent to 5 per cent of global steel production, and a level of effort matched only by the manufacture of Liberty ships during the Second World War.[37] There are few companies that do not pay attention to eco-efficiency nowadays, and even heavy industry has made significant progress (e.g. the steel industry has reduced its energy consumption per unit by 29 per cent since 1990).[38] But for all of the opportunities to invest in low carbon productivity, many of them fall foul of the decoupling dilemma exemplified by the air transport industry (Chapter 3).

What is more, many of the opportunities are unattractive to investors. It has been calculated that over half of energy-related investments connected to climate change, for instance, offer an internal rate of return of less than 10 per cent.[39] In other words, at a time when in order to stabilize the climate an additional US$370 billion needs to be raised annually to invest in low-carbon energy, the rate of return for a potentially high risk investment is little higher than for a lower risk Indian government bond.[40]

In addition, as we have seen, the governance crisis and capital constraints have undercut business confidence in the long-term regulatory frameworks needed to underpin high capex investments in decarbonization technologies such as carbon capture and storage. Renewable energy supply has risen by nearly 50 per cent since 1973, but has barely shifted as a percentage of total energy production, and global renewable energy investment fell by 11 per cent in 2012.[41]

As we saw from PwC's Low Carbon Economy Index (Figure 3.4 in the previous chapter), the rate for improving carbon intensity in order for emissions not to breach the dashed line in our graph has gone from 2.0 per cent annually in 2000 to 5.1 per cent in 2012. Even if the current decarbonization rates were quadrupled, society would still be on track for 1200 ppm of CO_2e by 2050.[42] The risk is that GBAU does more to give the illusion of action than address the structural environmental, social, and economic challenges. Consequently, GBAU today is associated with a failure to decarbonize and to grow the economy. Instead of Scenario 2, it might, in the long run, be more accurate to link GBAU with the same outcomes as BAU, that is, climate change driven reductions in economic growth. In this scenario, the allocation of capital to high cost centralized decarbonization projects fails to generate increases in productivity. Moreover, this capital allocation does little to alleviate social challenges. At the same time, partly for cost reasons, it is not carried out at a volume sufficient to avert the climate crisis.

Technological wild cards?

There are technological wild cards. They include nuclear fusion which, although a long way off as a commercial proposition, if successful would solve energy emissions and security problems by using readily available fuels such as deuterium to produce zero-carbon energy without long-life nuclear waste. There are, nevertheless, genuine issues about the plausibility of the GBAU alternative given the current geo-political and governance situation. In terms of the reallocation of capital, regulation, and incentivization, GBAU implies massive government interventions that are not universally politically acceptable. Opponents of government intervention have jumped on poor investment decisions such as the Obama Administration's support of the Solyndra solar energy company,[43] and allegations of government subsidy to green technology industries have led to the threat of trade wars as proved the case with the alleged dumping of Chinese manufactured solar panels on the USA and EU markets in 2012.[44] These kinds of examples show that there is a plausibility gap between the ambitions of GBAU policy and what can realistically be achieved.

This is not simply a case of political muscle flexing as new alliances are created. For as long as GBAU being the 'pro-growth strategy' of the twenty-first century remains a slogan rather than an empirically verifiable fact, politicians, civil leaders, and communities will ask why the prosperity promised them is not being delivered. It would be surprising if people who feel disadvantaged could overcome their preference for what they have long been told will help them, in order to back an untested theory.

EVALUATING PWG

Both of our market moderation ideas, BAU and GBAU, have flaws that seem to put society on a trajectory towards higher emissions in the short run, low GDP in the medium term, and a long-term state of external incongruence. The PWG Oracles offer an ambitious plan to avoid that situation by abandoning conventional free markets, and replacing them with mechanisms for managing steady state growth. Their ideas are compelling insofar as they treat existential risk as a unique crisis that requires a departure from established wisdom. If GBAU is a blood transfusion, then PWG is a change of blood type.

PWG requires people to set aside the belief that neoliberal economic theory represents universal truths about growth, productivity, and the umbilical link between economic performance and prosperity. This is not as huge a leap as it might sound. Throughout human history and in different cultures, very different economic systems have existed, and they flourished not because they were a universal truth but because they suited society's purpose (and equally faded away when they did not). Mainstream economists are reluctant to admit to this and treat economics—especially neoliberal/neoclassical theories of the kind underpinning GBAU and BAU—as a universal truth, as immutable as the laws of physics with which they consciously draw parallels.[45]

Of course, the laws of physics are not immutable and theories are continually being challenged and overthrown: they are true until they are not. This is what the PWG Oracles claim about conventional economics: a model that was suited to its time is no longer fit for purpose, and will actually damage human well-being. One of the strengths of neoliberal economics was that it offered efficient ways of allocating scarce resources; the evidence now is that it is no longer able to achieve this and is permitting the unsustainable extraction of materials, pollution, and unbalanced ecosystems to continue unabated.

The PWG critique of economic growth is ambitious and builds on over four decades of analysis. It has been dismissed or largely ignored by mainstream economists and consequently has been championed by environmental groups but marginalized from business strategy and public sector policy. For some people it is the guerilla in the room, especially in the context of climate change; for others it contributes to an unhelpful white noise that is contingent upon implausible types of change.

The debate between advocates of economic growth and prosperity without growth has become a dialogue of the deaf, and there is little objective comparison of the opposing schools of thought. However, the fact that PWG is an alternative to and exposes certain shortcomings of the market moderation Oracles, does not mean it is satisfactory. In our view, adherence to PWG ideas for all its appeal, may lead society towards Scenario 3 with worsened instability and without lasting social or environmental benefit. There are two reasons for this. First, the transformation involved to develop a PWG economy is enormous and ultimately implausible. It may or may not be true that economies can survive with low or no growth, and that the fascination with growth is a relatively new obsession.[46] However, growth is now king, and although unrelenting pursuit of it without taking into account the social or environmental consequences could prove disastrous, replacing it is not going to happen quickly any more than feudal economies were suddenly exchanged for a capitalist model, and is certainly not going to happen in the required timeframe. In terms of economic management, the institutions and tools for turning off, slowing down, or redirecting markets, competition, and growth still need to be developed, and then defended against opposition from the status quo. Even if they were in place, they would need to ensure sufficient growth for investment into adaptation and mitigation, and to protect the most vulnerable from low growth and climate change. They would also need to find ways to counterbalance the compounding of interest that is already in the system, and to meet the challenges of health, education, and immigration without the normal levers of economic control. This would be a real-time experiment, and to argue it is feasible within the very clear timeframes of our crises is a brave, if not hubristic, statement.

The critical flaw of PWG: getting there from here

In practice, society today needs growth to keep schools open, match the rising interest on national debt, and sustain hospitals and pension plans. Rising populations of elderly people, increasing medical costs, and the impact of economic stagnation on tax revenues make it all the more urgent; and on top of this there is the cost of climate change adaptation, not least for the poorest in low-level seaboard megacities that face disproportionate climate threats.

Even if this were not the case, the kind of ideological shift PWG requires is not simply about institutions and tools. Growth is the dominant ideology of contemporary society, and it affects not only the economic system, but wider society. As PWG economists such as Jackson recognize, a sustainable economy would require different sets of values.[47] He highlights the problems of over-consumption which brings to people's minds fast cars, over-sized houses, and bedrooms full of Hello Kitty paraphernalia. However, there is a deeper history to how growth became an ideology. Since the Enlightenment, work and virtue have gone hand in hand to the degree where work, according to Max Weber, became a religious vocation (*beruf*). While some people who question growth regard over-consumption as a kind of false consciousness in which humans seek happiness in what they buy, the consumption economic growth allows us also facilitates innumerable socially valuable interactions such as gift giving, family occasions, social networking, bonding with friends, and philanthropy. When one looks at shopping malls, it is tempting to conclude consumption is valued for itself (and this is true to a degree), but that is only part of the story of why it matters and the alternatives necessary to replace it.

Growth also equates with things we value at the level of society such as material well-being, security, and even democracy. Over time, society has come to accept the morality behind growth such as the right to make a profit, the rights of capital, the rights of labour, the legitimacy of self-interest, and the justice of making almost anything a saleable commodity. At different times in the past, all of these have been seen as immoral or inconceivable but, as anthropologists such as Geertz and Lévi-Strauss have shown, value change is one of the most complex processes societies can undergo.[48]

BAU and GBAU Oracles do not need to consider this because they accept the current economic system as it is. Their PWG counterparts, however, cannot ignore it because they are proposing something quite different; but for the most part they talk about the shift from economic growth to sustainable development as if it is a case of switching engines rather than building a new car.

Transition pathway

The final failing of PWG is that it offers no clear transition pathway, which makes any action to implement it highly unlikely and potentially very dangerous. The immediate transition problem—an acute one in a period of austerity—is to do with mathematics. Debt compounds, and Western nations are deeply indebted. If PWG theory does not offer ways to grow that at least keep up with compounding debt payments, society is going to end up shutting schools, libraries, and hospitals.

In the longer term, there is the issue of prosperity and population growth. PWG Oracles recognize that development has to meet the needs of the poor, and that population growth will largely occur where the poor live. They do not offer, however, a convincing explanation of how the different needs and aspirations of poor, middle class, or rich people can be met in a plausible fashion. It can be argued that the term 'prosperity without growth' is misleading because some of its Oracles acknowledge that the limits to growth should be applied only where there is already a sufficient surplus of wealth to make growth unnecessary. In these cases, steady state growth could be achieved without reducing human well-being. In poorer societies where there is an insufficient surplus, conventional growth is an option to raise people to a level where steady state growth is acceptable. The difficulty here is that given the current state of knowledge and general acceptance, this is little more than a hypothesis that is radically optimistic about what sort of change can be enacted over what period of time.

Furthermore, before the hypotheses could be tested in any rigorous way, it is possible that conditions will have changed such that PWG's purpose becomes redundant. For example, it may be that economic growth over the next forty years is not as great as descriptive analysis would suggest. Rising commodity prices, smaller populations in richer countries, pollution, climate change, and opposition to widening wealth gaps could put a dampener on growth even in emerging economies. In wealthier economies, productivity growth could slow because it is harder to increase productivity in service-oriented economies. In poorer countries, lower fertility rates associated with increasing wealth and urbanization could lead to a smaller workforce than projected. In both rich and poor countries, erratic weather could make agriculture output less predictable. Taking these and similar factors into account, Randers estimates that instead of the expected tripling in size of the global economy by the mid-century, the actual increase will be about 2.2.[49] His calculations are sure to be controversial, and will certainly draw a strong reaction from those wedded to growth. However, even if they prove only partially true, they highlight the possibility that PWG, rather than being too slow and cumbersome, offers too much too late, and growth that is slowing of its own accord opens up the opportunity for less radical alternatives.

EVALUATING THE TECHNO-OPTIMISTS

There is one more group of Oracles that we need to evaluate: the strand of techno-optimists focused on geo-engineering. However, before we do, we want to spend a little more time on economic growth itself, a concept that has been at the heart of our Oracles so far. Techno-optimists also believe in the power of economic growth, but only because it unleashes innovation. If there were other ways of acquiring capital, that would be fine as well: the main thing is to do what it takes to achieve technological advances. This is a very different position to the one shared by our previous Oracles who all treat innovation as a consequence of properly functioning economies. They have different ideas about what 'proper' means in that context, but they all agree that economics is key to understanding prosperity.

The ideology of growth

Oracles' ideas are strongly rooted in specific ideologies, and nowhere is this more apparent than in relation to economic growth, which across the political spectrum is a shibboleth of modern political and economic thought as we were reminded in Figure 4.1. Growth is no longer synonymous with prosperity in the way neoliberal economists pretend, and it may in part be 'uneconomic' as PWG Oracle Herman Daly claims. However, it is too deeply embedded into society to be yanked out and discarded. Growth is the dominant ideology of modern life in the sense meant by Boltanski and Thévenot, i.e. it is embedded in the organizational, institutional, and legal mechanisms that control society.[50] It reflects the equation of virtue with work that has dominated Western thought since the Enlightenment, and it is linked through social norms and individual psychology with things we value such as democracy, material well-being, and security. Furthermore, we accept the morality behind growth such as the right to make a profit, and the rights of capital. Growth equates with virtues such as entrepreneurship, innovation, independence, and freedom. It is also a concept that is embedded in economic science and management studies, and is therefore drilled into people's minds on a routine basis.

There is, of course, dissent and disagreement about growth, but alternative models raise as many questions as they answer, and taken at face value do not convincingly address problems of inequality, privilege, and deprivation. On the contrary, in some ways they seem to exacerbate them. At the same time, these alternatives do not offer the promises of emancipation, political freedom, and economic independence often associated with growth.

None of this is to say that economic growth as an ideology is better or worse than its alternatives. Given how embedded it is as an ideology, and given the time periods over which the challenges are unfolding, questions about better or worse are irrelevant. Even if mainstream economists banded together today to denounce the logic of the growth model (as a few have), it would be a sideshow. Economic growth is no longer the domain of economists; it is a social construct that informs people's beliefs, values, and ideals. As such, it cannot be readily replaced even if there were a consensus that it was wrong or harmful.

Paying the bills

The majority of Oracles approach growth as a problem of economics, but at least since the mid-twentieth century it has become much more than that. Portraying the crises as ones of economics rather than ones of society in a much wider sense, gives rise to all manner of misguided suggestions. However, that is exactly what continues to happen, and is one of the key reasons the Oracles are of limited use to companies that want to take on the turnaround challenge. Economic logic alone will not provide business with the answers it needs for future prosperity, and yet this is where its focus lies at present even as the environment it is operating in grows increasingly hazardous. It is no help to a company to be told that it cannot grow when it has dividends and salaries to pay, and needs profits to recruit and retain the best employees, to acquire capital at advantageous rates, and to invest in research and development. What is more, retained income is increasingly essential for investment and expansion as established companies face up to competition from ones in emerging markets.

PWG Oracles are right to say that there are problems with their BAU and GBAU counterparts' ideas when it comes to understanding climate change, but they are wrong to treat the engineering of growth as a trivial problem. Accelerating growth, modifying it, or eradicating it ultimately increase the risk that society will end up without growth and with an unstable climate, creating in the process a society that is externally incongruent with its environment and riddled with internal tensions. What we hoped for from Oracles was that they would offer a genuine alternative to the mass era that is now a danger to prosperity. What we have discovered are alternative ideas that fall short of their goals and in different ways end up in the same place, i.e. a situation in which existential risk increases, human well-being is endangered, and incongruence persists. This leaves us with the option of techno-optimists unleashing the power of the markets. Is their vision a more viable one?

EVALUATING TECHNO-OPTIMISM

There is plenty of interest in geo-engineering, comprising CO_2 removal technologies and solar radiation management techniques (page 79). The difficulty with both, as we have seen, is that none has been shown to be effective at an affordable cost and with acceptable side-effects.[51] History tells us that these kinds of technology are not without their consequences—Arkwright's Mill in the eighteenth century changed not only production but a centuries old tradition of labour relations;[52] high yield varieties of rice triggered the Green Revolution that on the one hand helped prevent famine and on the other led many small farmers to lose their land[53]—and even if in many cases the advantages of a technology are accepted as outweighing any negative effects, techno-optimists have a poor track-record of considering the inevitable social upheaval that follows technological breakthroughs.

The critical flaw of geo-engineering: moral hazard

The Green Revolution had profound repercussions for rural communities in Asia and Africa that are felt to this day, but these were localized and the benefits tangible (e.g. more plentiful and cheaper food). Geo-engineering technologies, in contrast, will have localized as well as global impact (e.g. converting arable land to forests; altering micro-climates) but without necessarily palpable local benefits. In 2009, the British Royal Society concluded that the main challenge with geo-engineering was the governance issues it raised at national, regional, and global levels. Without the right governance mechanisms, the technologies are a threat as much as a solution.

In summary, without evidence of major technological leaps in the pipeline that would alleviate the consequences of climate and demographic change, and given the trend for innovations to worsen incongruence, we cannot agree with techno-optimists who envisage they will reach Scenario 4. On the contrary, the risk is that geo-engineering projects will create moral hazard, substituting for rather than complementing decarbonization efforts, and accelerating the move towards the decline scenario, the common destination of all our Oracles, despite what they may have wished.

Reviewing the Oracles

So far, we have made the case that society is locked into a social and economic model that for a long period served large numbers of people very well and understandably became an almost universal aspiration. Business is the representative institution in that model, and its licence to operate is based on the model's success at delivering increased and more widespread prosperity. That success is now open to doubt. One can see this, for instance, by looking at the relationship between performance and productivity. One of the chief goals of modern management is to increase productivity in order to improve company performance. An immediate effect of this might be unemployment, but in the long run business, and therefore society, should be more prosperous. But as we have seen from Deloitte's Shift Index in Chapter 2, since 1965 despite a 2.5 times increase in labour productivity, there has been a long-term decline in performance as measured by return on assets. Ironically, the response to this, especially during economic hard times, has been to lay off workers rather than cut back on profits or productivity. In other words, companies are resorting to measures that are only effective in the short run, and which erode their licence to operate in the long run. As the Deloitte report states, 'There continues to be a profound cognitive dissonance around this point: on the one hand, we all acknowledge experiencing increasing stress as performance pressures mount; on the other hand, we seem unwilling to accept that all of our efforts continue to produce deteriorating results.'[54]

Mapping the dreams of the Oracles against long-term trends

Deteriorating results of one kind or another have become common. Companies seem to have run out of ways of making major technological breakthroughs, and so are reliant on tweaking the business model along the lines Piepenbrock and others have documented.[55] In the absence of technological leaps, the only genuine area of innovation has been in finance, but not only did this lead to economic disaster, it coopted and ultimately corrupted ICT, the one area of innovation with the potential to displace the mass era paradigm. Consequently, society is reliant on a business paradigm riddled with symptoms of enervation. However, the rotten beams, falling tiles, and dry rot of bank collapse are not the real dangers. The economic edifice society built and which served it well is now situated in an inhospitable environment. To keep itself safe from real and metaphorical rising waters it relies on growth when growth poses an existential risk, and it is producing inequality when decline in prosperity is a threat to social stability, business success, and human justice.

The Oracles propose different ways of resolving this situation. If BAU Oracles were the homeowner, they would want to rent out the house and generate as much income as possible to make repairs down the line. If GBAU Oracles owned the house, they would raise the rent and use the income to make it more resilient to floods. Their PWG neighbours on the other hand would tear down their house, and build afresh, although what they would do for shelter in the meantime is unclear. Geo-engineering focused techno-optimists, on the other hand, would invest in a mixture of flood protection and rebuilding, but only once the materials they needed were invented at some stage in the future.

The trouble with our Oracles is that their ideas, despite having various strengths, will not resolve the external incongruence confronting business and society as whole, and in some cases rely on internal incongruence on the part of society's institutions. The distributional outcomes of the different Oracles are portrayed in Figure 4.4.

The square boxes show what is intended to happen in terms of economic growth and prosperity distribution: for example, PWG ideas are associated with low growth and high equality. The cluster in the oval, though, shows likely longer-term outcomes, if the Oracles' models were implemented in the face of today's crisis. For all of the optimism surrounding their different ideas,

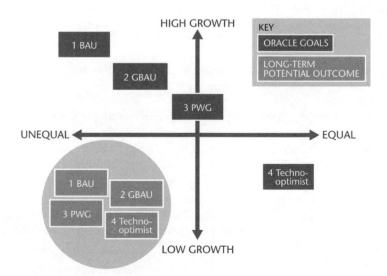

Figure 4.4: Oracle goals versus the long-term potential outcomes

the Oracles end up in a situation almost identical to the one we hoped they could help society avoid. They do not offer a convincing alternative to the Petropolis that society is struggling under, and in some cases they offer the worst of all worlds: a period of low growth that does nothing to tackle social and environmental problems, and leaves economies unable to afford anything other than the polluting technologies that created this situation. At one extreme, they invite business to ignore the crises of the real world, and concentrate instead on bringing to life a model of economic growth that was always theoretical. At the other end, they invite society to abandon capitalism, and gamble instead on an ideological dream. In both cases, business is hostage to implausibility.

What we hoped to get from the Oracles were plausible ideas about how to achieve prosperity while addressing the social and environmental issues embedded in a fossil fuel, mass production economy. What we found was that none of the models appears both internally congruent in the sense of being do-able by business, and externally congruent in that they align society's institutions with the main social and environmental challenges. Though they seem to be opposing views, because of how they treat incongruence, they are different routes to a single destination that neither business nor society wants to reach.

Notes

1. (Shell 2011)
2. (Stiglitz 2012; Wilkinson 2010)
3. (Kumhof 2012). See in particular Figure 3 in that working paper
4. Ibid
5. Ibid
6. http://www.guardian.co.uk/commentisfree/2013/jan/20/davos-world-economic-forum-bad-capitalism, accessed January 27, 2013
7. (Drucker 1946)
8. E.g. (Carter 2006; Tol 2009; Nordhaus 2007; Lomborg 2007)
9. Nordhaus 2012; Allegre 2012
10. (Lomborg 2007; Howard 2011; Lomborg 2010)
11. (Beinhocker 2007)
12. (Stern 2008)
13. (Jackson 2009)
14. Korea, the European Union, and China allocated 81 per cent, 59 per cent, and 31 per cent of their respective stimulus packages to green investment ($31 billion, $23 billion, and $221 billion)
15. (Jackson 2009)

16. http://www.standard.co.uk/news/blair-world-needs-to-act-on-climate-change-now-7248241.html, accessed September 20, 2012

17. http://www.stellamccartney.co.uk/en/, accessed September 25, 2012. Stella McCartney brand is part of the PPR group

18. (Howorth 2012)

19. (Bentley unknown)

20. http://www.tiffany.co.uk/csr/, accessed September 25, 2012

21. (Kapur 2005)

22. http://www.stellamccartney.co.uk/en/, accessed September 25, 2012. Stella McCartney brand is part of the PPR group

23. (Frank 2000, 1999)

24. (White 2012)

25. http://news.cnet.com/8301-17852_3-57354445-71/the-joy-of-microsofts-avoid-ghetto-gps-patent/?tag=cnetiosapp, accessed December 2, 2012

26. http://www.google.com/gwt/x?u=http://www.dailymail.co.uk/news/article-2255064/Colombian-company-makes-child-size-bulletproof-vests-Sandy-Hook-shooting.html&ei=fSviUKb4KtCH_QbxjoHQBQ&wsc=fa, accessed December 31, 2012

27. (Helm 2008)

28. (Club of Rome 1974)

29. (Daly 1996)

30. (Jackson 2009)

31. (Daly 1996)

32. Daly in Randers, J. 2012: 73–4 (emphasis in the original).

33. (Royal Society 2009)

34. (Lovelock 2010, Lovelock 2006, Lovelock 2000)

35. E.g. (Daly 1996; Randers 2012)

36. (Intergovernmental Panel on Climate Change, Working Group III 2007)

37. (MacKay 2009)

38. (HSBC 2011)

39. (McKinsey Global Institute 2011)

40. Indian government bonds yielded 8–8.66 per cent depending on duration (July 2012)

41. (see FT, January 14th, 2013)

42. (PwC 2012)

43. http://abcnews.go.com/Blotter/solyndra-report-obama-admin-restructured-loan-pr-concerns/story?id=16912518#.UGMwu66mEgo, accessed September 26, 2012

44. http://abcnews.go.com/Blotter/solyndra-report-obama-admin-restructured-loan-pr-concerns/story?id=16912518#.UGMwu66mEgo; http://www.ft.com/cms/s/0/36 23df3a-d254-11e1-abe7-00144feabdc0.html#axzz27ay86Jj2, both accessed September 26, 2012

45. (Beinhocker 2007)

46. (Victor 2008)

47. (Jackson 2009)

48. (Geertz 1963; Levi-Strauss 2001)

49. (Randers 2012)
50. (Boltanski 2006)
51. (Royal Society 2009)
52. (Thompson 1963)
53. (Cleaver 1972; White 1991)
54. Hagel III, J. 2011: 6
55. (Piepenbrock 2010)

5

The Dynamics of Transition: Techno-economic Paradigms

IN THIS CHAPTER

The importance of congruence and how to recognize it. How congruence is established. Why incongruence flourishes. The importance of techno-economic paradigms and the way they evolve. The failed ICT paradigm shift. Plausible options for a prosperous future.

> *'Do not put too much faith in the end of the world.'*
>
> Polish proverb

Waiting for the Wave to Break

'More than any other time in history,' Woody Allen commented, 'man stands at a crossroads. One path leads to despair and utter hopelessness, the other to total extinction.' In the Introduction, we said this book is about the rights to optimism. Stress-test the optimism of the Oracles in Chapter 4 against the reality of the challenges we face, and it is hard not to agree with Woody. However, for a group of social scientists who trace their origins back to the 'creative destruction' ideas of Josef Schumpeter, the picture is less bleak. For them, the problem and its solution are simple. The genius of capitalism, as we have mentioned in Chapter 2, is its capacity to hunt out and bring to life the new general purpose technology that has the potential to deliver a new surge in development. As Schumpeter put it, 'The [...] same process of industrial mutation [...] incessantly revolutionizes the economic structure from within, incessantly destroying the old one, incessantly creating a new one. This process of Creative Destruction is the essential fact about capitalism.' (1942, p. 80–4). For Schumpeterians there is one conclusion to draw from the economy-wide declines in productivity that have set in. The darkest hour comes before the dawn. The stage is then set for a new techno-economic paradigm to emerge. *The Economist* has described the twenty-first century as Schumpeter's century. Are they right? Is a new wave about to break, one that will replace the Fordist model of fossil fuel-driven mass production and consumption? And if so, where is it? Does it give us the right to be optimistic?

Revisiting the Information and Communications Technology (ICT) revolution

We propose to look for this wave in the most unexpected quarter, the revolution in information and communications technology (ICT). That may seem an uninspired choice; after all, ICT companies from Apple to Google have ridden the mass era hard, and yet, as Robert Solow notes, its vaunted contributions to productivity have shown up 'everywhere but the statistics.' Just look at 2012's crop of inventions. As well as the iPhone 5, ICT has given the world Popify, a voice activated popcorn dispenser that at your word launches a piece of salted or caramelized popcorn right into your mouth. It gave us, courtesy of adidas, the high performance athletics shoe with a live Twitter feed on it. It gave us Memmento, an online site that replaces the inconvenience of graveyards for remembering loved ones by giving them a permanent home in cyberspace. Memmento provides you with 100 complimentary credits you can use to purchase virtual flowers and candles. Thomas Zempliner, Memmento's founder, hopes the site will all but replace regular visits to the cemetery. 'People today in their busy lives rarely find the time to visit the cemetery because they spend more and more time by their computers, but the human need for remembering the departed loved ones remains', he said in a press release.

ICT and the productivity gap

ICT has brought sushi slicing robots and luxury cars such as the Mercedes C series which, instead of a dipstick to check the oil, sends an email and the coordinates of the nearest mechanic who can replace the oil for you. ICT has also enriched our lives with the global online marketing of Leaf, the world's first eco-vibrator, both phallus and phthalate free. Gary Kasparov, former world chess champion, speaks eloquently on the subject of the innovation gap, the absence of breakthrough innovations in the last fifty years. There is a YouTube video of Kasparov getting interrupted mid-speech by an object flying through the air in the room just above the heads of the small crowd. It transpires that it is a radio-controlled, airborne dildo, and although Russian security men ultimately remove it from airspace, they should have let it hover.

As an artefact, it illustrates Kasparov's point. Is this as good as innovation gets? As Gordon (2012) comments 'invention since 2000 has centered on entertainment and communication devices that are smaller, smarter and more capable, but do not fundamentally change labor productivity or the standard of living in the way that electric light, motor cars, or indoor plumbing changed it... The iPod replaced the CD Walkman; the Smartphone replaced the garden-variety 'dumb' cell phone... these innovations were enthusiastically adopted but they provided new opportunities for consumption on the job and in leisure hours rather than a continuation of the historical tradition of replacing human labor with machines.'

ICT as life support for mass

There has been another use of ICT, though, where it appears not just to have failed to deliver real innovation and the acceleration of a new techno-economic paradigm, but to have held it back. While the explanations for the subprime crisis are multiple, we have already seen in Chapter 2 that innovations in finance played a part in triggering the economic crisis that resulted. As Michael Lewis, amongst others, explains in *The Big Short*, advances in ICT in the early 1990s allowed massive amounts of data to be mined and analysed within microseconds. Wall Street started hiring Ph.D. mathematicians for a new category of job: the Quantitative Analyst, known as the 'quant'. Their computerized financial models, known often as 'black boxes', underpinned the pricing and international distribution of the complex set of mortgage-backed securities and associated derivatives around the subprime market. With leverage multiplying the exposure of global financial institutions far beyond the value of the assets, as early as 2003, US investment guru Warren Buffet had referred to quant instruments as 'financial weapons of mass destruction.' The toll on the interlinked financial system led France's *Le Monde* to point the finger in one direction. Its 29 March 2012 issue featured an article entitled 'Crise financière: la faute aux mathématiques?' (The financial crisis: is it the fault of mathematics?).[1]

The story also notes the alarming downside of high-frequency trading. As shown by the recent erasure of US$440 million of Knight Capital's funds with a glitch in the software programme for their high-frequency trades, the role of ICT in finance has by no means diminished. In an article called 'The Rising Cost of Faster Trades', The New York Times reports that 'the time it takes to execute a trade on the New York Stock Exchange's most popular platform has dropped from 3.2 seconds to 48 milliseconds, but that the costs for investors of trading a share, partly as a result of the ICT investments efforts, have increased 10% in the past two years from 3.5 cents to 3.8 cents.'

ICT and energy

As well as propping up a financialized economy focused less on value creation than value transfer, ICT may also be playing a critical role in the sphere of energy. Advances in computer processing power now enable geologists to interpret seismic data at depths of 15 000 feet or more, penetrating thick ocean floor layers of salt to reveal untapped reservoirs with three-dimensional imaging and seismic mapping. Advances in nanotechnology and alloys allow drill bits to go into previously inaccessible high temperature and high-pressure fields. Driven by these technological advances, recent finds include vast amounts of natural gas found deep under Israel's Mediterranean waters, finds in the high Arctic waters north of Norway, a shale field in Argentine Patagonia, the oil sands of western Canada, and deepwater oil prospects off the shores of Angola. In each case, giant new oil and gas fields will be mined, steamed, and drilled with new technologies.

We have already highlighted research suggesting that there are more reserves incorporated into the valuation of energy companies than could ever be exploited without serious climate change consequences. ICT advances will enable an additional hundreds of billions of barrels of recoverable reserves to be brought to market in coming decades and shift geopolitical and economic calculations around the world. The new drilling boom is expected to diversify global sources away from the Middle East, just as the growth in consumption of fuels shifts from the United States and Europe to China, India, and the rest of the developing world. 'We are just at the beginning of this story,' said William Colton, Exxon Mobil's vice president for strategic planning. 'It's only likely we will find more deepwater resources.' 'The fossil fuel age will be extended for decades,' said Ivan Sandrea, president of the Energy Intelligence Group, a research publisher. 'Unconventional oil and gas are at the beginning of a technological cycle that can last 60 years. They are really in their infancy.'

Reclaiming the ICT Revolution

The ICT revolution divides Schumpeter's followers. Amongst those interested in short-term cycles of creative destruction, ICT advances further proof of how one technology displaces another, evident in the rise of Epson and the decline of Olivetti, or YouTube's boom and Kodak's bankruptcy. Others focused on longer-term waves are more cautious, arguing, for instance, that instead of ushering in a new era of capitalism, ICT innovation kept alive the paradigm of fossil fuel-driven mass production and consumption.[2]

We will examine that argument in detail later but there is good reason to doubt the lasting social benefits of what was meant to be a revolution. As Kentaro Toyama, co-founder of Microsoft Research India, puts it, 'Since 1970, we've also had a boom in digital technologies from the PC to the iPhone, from Google to Facebook. If these technologies are solving social ills as social-media cheerleaders would have us believe, then we'd hope at the very least that in the golden age of innovation in the world's most technically advanced country, all this technology would have put some dent in poverty. It hasn't.... As a society, we haven't been so intent on eradicating poverty, as much as perhaps, on ever cleverer ways to guide us to the nearest cup of coffee.'

Like Kentaro Toyama, we believe in the potential of ICT to do much more than steer people to coffee shops without entering ghettoes, but it has not yet been fully explored. We have already highlighted the failings of the first wave of ICT innovation which had little impact on productivity and helped prolong the mass era. It is the next waves where the promise begins. However, to understand how this can be realized, we need to understand how it got locked up in the first place.

Look again at the picture of New Orleans we used in Chapter 2 to highlight the crises affecting business and society. We saw degraded ecosystems and the potential havoc climate change-related storms can produce. We saw the precarious situation of poor people faced with the consequences of climate change. Many of those people could have lost homes bought with sub-prime mortgages that helped accelerate the geo-political shift. The presence of Wal-Mart lorries, rather than government officials, bringing emergency relief showed shifts in governance. We saw something out of keeping with a society at the zenith of its wealth, influence, and power.

Take another look at that picture, though, and a further story emerges. This time it is the story of Incongruence that, as we mentioned in Chapter 4, is one of the main challenges for anyone proposing alternatives to the current dominant business model. The first attempt at an ICT revolution did not fail because of the technology, but the way the technology was used. This was because of society's institutions and ultimately their incongruence with each other and the external environment. Our discussion of Oracles showed that they all fell short when it came to rebuilding external congruence because they were either fixated on breathing new life into economic models that were incongruent with social or environmental well-being, or demanded changes that were implausible given the nature of major global crises and the current state of key institutions. The Katrina picture says a lot about those institutions and their organizations. Why is it, for instance, that Wal-Mart is there and the government is absent? Why were poor people encouraged to take out mortgages they could not afford? How was it possible to turn natural storm barriers such as mangrove swamps into prime real estate? Given what is known about the links between storms, rising sea temperatures, rising sea levels, and climate change,[3] why is it that events from Katrina in 2005 and Cyclone Nargis (the cause of over 130 000 deaths in Burma in 2008) to the impact of 2012's Hurricane Sandy on Staten Island, New York, have not led to major policy or behavioural changes? How is it that Incongruence has been allowed to flourish?

We will answer that question in the following pages. In doing so we will also identify alternative models that are congruent with the needs of business and the wider environment it is part of. They are also models that are plausible, given where society stands today. Whether or not they are equally desirable, though, is something we will address in later chapters.

Internal and External Congruence

There are many types of congruence. The one most familiar to business students is the one least relevant here. It refers to the strategic fit (or lack of it) between a company's capabilities and the demands or opportunities of its business environment. In organizational behaviour studies, incongruence also occurs when a company's vision is at odds with the way it conducts itself (goal incongruence). In both cases, incongruence refers to a disparity between what is being done and what needs to be done, or as Tushman & Nadler describe it, the cultural, work, human resource, and structural constraints on improved performance.[4]

However, strategic fit and goal incongruence are about company management in its narrowest sense: identifying opportunities and delivering on them at the level of the firm.

As we will turn to later, that may entail encouraging a very different type of business than the one that dominates today. But there is also a need for congruence at the level of the model of growth. If ICT as a GPT is to define prosperity, it must be externally congruent with the megatrends confronting society, and internally congruent with what is achievable. What does this look like?

Internal congruence

As Veblen showed, the key institutions that order a society, such as its laws, customs, and practices, align around the requirements of the dominant technology. If business, as the representative social institution, is in contention with these, then there is a considerable risk of tension and fissures that will ultimately undermine its prosperity. These institutions can be grouped under five main elements—social, legal, economic, political, and technological (SLEPT)—and they are discernible in the actions of a continually changing

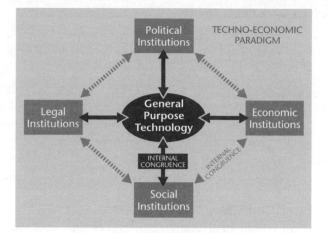

Figure 5.1: The techno-economic paradigm: Internal congruence of GPT and institutions

cast of organizations such as companies, political parties, the markets, and the courts (Figure 5.1).

Tension is an intrinsic and probably essential characteristic of such a society, and is certainly central to much of political theory. However, societies do not prosper if there is so much internal conflict that institutions and organizations are constantly at odds with each other (e.g. the judiciary versus the legislature), or that there is no consensus about the common good. How such a consensus is achieved may well involve exhibitions of power rather than just good will, and as Foucault and others have analysed in depth, there are many ways that a society is disciplined, not just by laws and enforcement organizations, but by the way it formulates or responds to a problem.[5] An example of this is the way theories associated with conventional economics of the kind described in the last chapter are regarded as universal laws even though they result in incongruent actions by institutions, and prevent alternative ideas from receiving any serious consideration.

We are not arguing that congruence is a utopian state in which everyone is content; nor is it a fixed equilibrium that cannot be changed. Individuals and organizations have differing degrees and types of power that they can use in overt, covert, and undetectable ways.[6] Furthermore, history accounts for various kinds of path dependency that prescribe and proscribe different courses of action. (We discussed in Chapter 3 how examples of path dependence accounted for some of the crises.) Power and path dependence mean that there is always disagreement and dispute, and this in turn helps foment change. However, this does not mean that some groups are permanently suppressed by others. In a congruent society, there has to be a consensus that the institutions are working towards what is acceptable as the common good.

The business requirement for profit

In modern society, business is essential to achieving that common good. One can agree or disagree with the desirability of this, and whether or not the private sector is always a responsible custodian of the power it wields. However, in a capitalist society of the kind that has expanded around the world since industrialization, there is no doubt that business is crucial to society's prosperity. Therefore, in these societies the law must be broadly amenable to business making a profit and using it for its own interests because, without profit, business cannot function. Likewise, the political system must recognize the legitimacy of business, and not seize its assets for political ends.

THE SOCIAL REQUIREMENT FOR BUSINESS UTILITY
Communities and individuals must also accept this legitimacy. Political theory from Machiavelli to Marx and from Hegel to Derrida has stressed the value of suppression to win legitimacy, but the endurance of capitalism, despite the rise in the number of educated, healthy, enfranchised people who are not truly capitalists (i.e. able to invest their capital assets for profit), suggests the need for an alternative explanation. Boltanski and Thévenot describe what they call 'orders of worth,' referring to the ways the majority of people who are not capitalists justify capitalism.[7] They describe six orders of worth or justifications, shown along the top of Figure 5.2. These are most easily understood if one thinks of the chronological progress of industrialization, although Boltanski and Thévenot are at pains to explain the orders of worth are not time specific.

Capitalism and the evolving vision of the good life

In the early industrial era when water power, Arkwright's mill, and the mania for building canals were the emerging features of technology, creativity, and

Cities of capitalism/ Justifications	Inspired	Domestic	Civic	Opinion	Market	Industrial
Mode of evaluation (worth)	Grace, nonconformity, creativeness	Esteem, reputation	Collective interest	Renown	Price	Productivity, efficiency
Format of relevant information	Emotional	Oral, exemplary, anecdotal	Formal, official	Semiotic	Monetary	Measurable: criteria, statistics
Elementary relation	Passion	Trust	Solidarity	Recognition	Exchange	Functional link
Human qualification	Creativity, ingenuity	Authority	Equality	Celebrity	Desire, purchasing power	Professional competency, expertise

Figure 5.2: Justifications of capitalism
Source: Adapted from Boltanski and Thévenot 2006

non-conformity were amongst the most esteemed values, and capitalism was congruent with a mood in society that human ingenuity, free labour, and innovation were economically and socially virtuous. Capitalism was justified by what Boltanski and Thévenot term an 'inspired order of worth.' Politicians at the time fought fiercely over the rights and wrongs of the new social order that was emerging, and a mass movement to fight slavery and support the principle of free labour was created. By 1788, two-thirds of enfranchised men, including some factory-workers, had signed anti-slavery petitions, and by 1833 1.3 million people, a third of them women, had signed petitions across England.[8]

However, as industrialization became more complex and was embodied more by captains of industry than artisanal entrepreneurs, a different justification—the domestic order of worth—was needed. The inspired order of worth was appearing more and more at odds with the new world that was evolving. People sought out new justifications. Technological innovations such as the railways, new laws to create limited liability companies, financial innovation, the growth in towns, and the ascendancy of coal as the main source of energy, undermined the idea that capitalism valued creativity and inspiration above all else. In order to make the growth in industrial towns, manufacturing, and pollution of the natural landscape congruent with society's sense of well-being, an order emerged based on the family. This is the world captured in Dickens's novels in which industrialization causes injustice and exploitation (*Hard Times*), the artisanal innovator struggles against the financier (*Little Dorrit*), there is a battle between immoral and virtuous wealth (*Our Mutual Friend*), and sorry situations are put right by a benevolent head of family or society (*Oliver Twist*). Dickens described both incongruence (e.g. the outdated legal system that caused misery rather than security) and an emergent congruence (e.g. the creation of a meritocracy). In the domestic order of worth, congruence is achieved by putting trust in leaders who exhibit esteem and reputation. Queen Victoria and Prince Albert were the exemplars of this order, but it was also reflected in scions of principled capitalism such as the Cadbury brothers and Titus Salt (creator of the Saltaire model community).

The good life of industrial capitalism

As noted above, orders of worth are not specific to particular eras in capitalism's evolution, and at any given time more than one order may be evident. For example, the mass era is justified by features of both the market and industrial orders of worth. Social relationships based on market exchange (buying and selling) and business function (e.g. management, worker, customer) are fundamental to human interaction. Consistent with the declining productivity of late-stage mass, we also see an increasing focus on efficiency, productivity, and price that Boltanski and Thévenot link to their industrial order of worth.

We have argued that this era is no longer sustainable, but a cause of incongruence is that the orders of worth used to justify it remain robust. When some of our Oracles reduce humans to rational economic actors, they are reinforcing certain orders of worth. Other Oracles who have a more radical economic vision overlook the importance of orders of worth in justifying capitalism to the majority of society, and in doing so trivialize the process of transformation to the point where their alternative visions are implausible. Since the original work on orders of worth, Boltanski and Chiapello have added another justification that they claim captures a new consensus emerging today. This is based on networks and individual creativity, and in a number of ways resembles the artisan-based, inspired capitalism of the late eighteenth century.[9] For reasons that will become clear in later chapters, this new order of worth is important for developing a plausible alternative for business success.

MASS PRODUCTION AND ITS INCONGRUENCE

The special position of business in the capitalist system means that it has consistently been singled out in relation to congruence. Durkheim, often called the father of sociology, said for instance there were two main causes of social incongruence: first, the division of labour that makes people cogs in a wheel rather than creators in their own right, and second, anomie (the separation of people from each other, typically due to population growth), and both of these were exacerbated by industrialization.[10] Our Oracles display pro and contra positions about the role of business in relation to the current crises. In daily life, the interests of business and the wisdom of business leaders are routinely paraded as being specially important.

From time to time—and throughout the history of capitalism—business has been accused of being too powerful, and of unduly influencing society's institutions for its own interests. Thomas Quinn, for instance, bemoaned 'the highest degree of concentrated economic power in our history' that led to excessive salaries, bonuses, pensions, and stock options.[11] For all of his resonance with a modern audience, however, he was writing about the 'monster businesses' he blamed for the Great Depression of the 1930s, just as Adam Smith had complained about collusion in the eighteenth century, and William Taft had taken on trust and monopolies in the early twentieth. However, to say business has too much, or indeed too little, power is to use the term in a particular way, i.e. a collective noun for organizations engaged in commercial activity. If this meaning is used, then parts of business can be said to be too powerful (e.g. the banks that were criticized for being too big to fail in 2007–2008), and others may be too weak (e.g. local firms in competition with multinational companies on the high street).

The Evolving Norms of Business

This is an important distinction when it comes to the turnaround challenge because although companies can be powerful, exerting influence over politicians through lobbying and consumers through advertising, business as an activity has no innate power; it is simply a set of practices (e.g. commercial transactions, engagements, and undertakings) designed to serve society in the same way that the law or politics does. We want to stress this point because it is often missed by people who say they are opposed to or are in favour of 'business.' They claim, for instance, that business is good or bad because it makes investors rich, but there is nothing inherent in business as an activity that demands a particular type of capital–company relationship. They also claim that business is good or bad because it encourages consumption, but again there is nothing that says companies have to produce anything there is a market for.

What we are highlighting here is that business is not configured by immutable laws. The form it takes is the result of choices and it has the potential to be a highly flexible institution. The fact that it is not perceived in this way is itself a result of incongruence, and the fact that throughout the era of mass a particular model of business was confirmed by political, legal, technological, and economic institutions. It is this model that has reached the end of its useful life, and yet it is the one many of our Oracles want to maintain. However, there are other forms that would allow business (the organization) to be successful in business (the activity). In particular, given the current crises and business turnaround challenge, there are two options (cités in Boltanski and Thévenot's language) we will explore. Neither of these is the cité of today—the one embodied in the Petropolis. But both can be realized if a new internal congruence is created. Only one of these options, though, is externally congruent with society's challenges. It is to this challenge of external congruence that we now turn.

There may be much debate about what well-being means (e.g. the ethics of Kant versus those of Mill) and how to achieve it (e.g. the role of competition and innovation); but these are signs of vibrancy, not societal incongruence. Societal incongruence is more likely to resemble a logjam in which debate is stymied and innovation stagnates or is directed in ways that will ultimately damage society's prosperity. There are many reasons societal incongruence occurs, and we will explore the ones most relevant to the current situation. But the main significance of the current societal incongruence is its relationship to external incongruence.

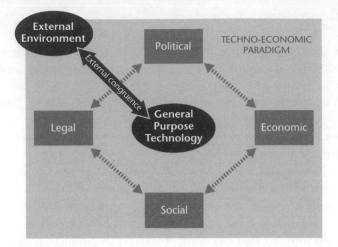

Figure 5.3: External congruence of TEP and external environment

External congruence

External congruence refers to a state where the consensus that a given society has created about its purpose and well-being is congruent with the needs of any larger system that society is a subset of (see Figure 5.3). Specifically the SLEPT institutions are aligned to support the rollout of a dominant GPT that addresses the challenges and opportunities of the external environment.

Uncurtailed greenhouse gas emissions due to industrial activity, or pressure on land and water due to demographic change, are symptomatic of external incongruence because the needs of human society are at odds with the sustainability of the larger ecosystem it shares. Jared Diamond's depiction of the collapse of Easter Island is an example of this type of incongruence; he describes a society that destroys itself by environmental over-exploitation.[12] Diamond's examples are interesting for two reasons. Firstly, he argues that societies are not self-regulating when it comes to the environment, and contrary to what some economists in particular claim, environmental catastrophe is always an option. Secondly, however, he argues that this is a choice and societies are not predestined to suffer environmental destruction.

Talk of incongruence often leads to mention of collapse, although the two are not inherently linked. Incongruence (internal and external) often results in turmoil, but that is a far cry from the collapse that afflicted the Easter Islanders, Nordic Greenlanders, or the Mayan civilization. Nor does collapse have to be environmental. According to Toynbee, it comes as the result of loss of creativity and the onset of inertia; for Tainter it happens when people feel the effort involved in sustaining a society is no longer justified by the benefits. Niall Ferguson argues that collapse is sudden, and the result of fiscal failures.[13]

Furthermore, collapse can have positive and negative consequences. Ottoman Istanbul at the end of the First World War was a society that fell into chaos in a matter of days,[14] but the collapse of the Western Roman Empire in the fifth century was welcomed by many at the time who saw their standards of living improve.[15]

Incongruence and its Impacts on Transition

Our interest, however, is not in predictions about what will happen as the crises play out. Libraries are littered with grand theories applying the lessons of history to the future; most become redundant as soon as they are published.[16] But they shed light on what can happen when incongruence is ignored. For example, different elements of society can come into conflict with each other leading to disruption. A critical mass of the pillars of society remain mutually supportive but refuse to reinvent themselves to meet new challenges. This results in stagnation and entropy. Equally, important institutions become vassals of particular ideologies, and are either radicalized themselves or provoke revolution. Disruption, entropy, and radicalization are all evident in the incongruence affecting society today. Business can contribute to this and can also be its victim. Business figures such as the Koch brothers, for example, have supported organizations seeking to disrupt the debate about climate change; but equally companies such as adidas and Vodafone have spoken out about stagnation and government inaction on climate change.[17]

There is plenty of evidence for this in the way business and society has dealt with the issues of climate and demographic change over the last decade or more. The 2000s were a lost decade in terms of stabilizing the climate (Chapter 3), but they were squandered as well in terms of addressing demographic change. Trends that were already apparent in the 1990s such as job insecurity, the wealth divide, wage stagnation, and an underserved ageing population continued throughout the 2000s. If, on the surface, emerging economies seemed to be booming, most of them had adopted the economic model of the OECD, and were exhibiting some of the same symptoms affecting developed economies. We explain how this happened in the section on the Strange Life of the ICT Era (page 118). The upshot, though, is already clear from Chapter 2: the current external incongruence afflicting business and society as a whole arises from the need to rein-in on resource utilization at the same time as economic development and justice demands we use more, and the need to deploy solutions to global-scale problems at a time of geopolitical shift and governance crisis.

How Congruence Happens: the Schumpeterian Approach

There is no such thing as perfect congruence. Sociologists such as Parsons and Habermas, economists such as Schumpeter and Solow, and management theorists like Lewin and Kotter all acknowledge that there needs to be some kind of disharmony, imbalance, and disequilibrium in order for change and progress to happen. Therefore, when we talk about congruence happening, we are referring to a broadly discernible state in which the well-being of society is being served over a period of time. It is not a static state, and it is a temporary period. It is probably most readily observed in its opposite, i.e. the periods of incongruence when institutions are severely disrupted and society is at odds with its external environment.

We have discussed the features of congruence: but how do congruence and incongruence come about? There are various explanations. Incongruence can take the form of collapse as noted in the previous section. It can be a protracted ideological struggle as happened with the worldwide movement to abolish slavery in the eighteenth and nineteenth centuries. Either of these could be relevant to the future of business *if* the challenges of climate change and demographic change are not addressed. Our interest, though, is in addressing those challenges and with that in mind we want to examine another model of change.

During capitalism's two century reign as the dominant social system, its dynamism has been described in several ways. Ironically, Marx was the first economist to talk about what Schumpeter later called 'creative destruction,' a concept that has become central to neoliberal economic thinking.[18] Schumpeter described the progress of capitalism through a series of S-curves in which the technology of one era is displaced by the next, destroying the value in old industries but replacing it with increased value from new ones. This journey, propelled by creative destruction, broadly complements Kondratiev's waves of economic growth and depression he claimed characterized the capitalist economy.[19] Polanyi described similar waves in which economic activity became highly incongruent (disembedded) with society, and then shifted to congruence (embeddedness) as the negative consequences of economic booms became clear.[20] More recently, Solow and Romer have built on this legacy to develop models of how improvements in technology drive economic growth, and in particular how this is an endogenous process affected by human decisions rather than a consequence of natural economic cycles.[21]

Carlota Perez has drawn on this heritage to develop a model of technological and financial innovation that explains the dynamics of a capitalist society. Using a 40–70 year timeframe similar to Kondratiev's, she identifies five major techno-economic paradigm shifts between the early industrial era and today.

Figure 5.4 sets out her five technological revolutions, beginning with the Industrial Revolution that began in Britain in the second half of the eighteenth century and ending with the Information and Communications Revolution which began in the 1970s and presents the new products and industries and new infrastructures associated with each of them.

Figure 5.5 shows how each of her revolutions broadly follows the path of a Schumpeter S-curve, sharing the following features. There is an initial gestation period during which the paradigm-shifting technologies are being invented. Not every technological breakthrough has this capacity. For

TECHNOLOGICAL REVOLUTION	NEW TECHNOLOGIES & NEW OR REDEFINED INDUSTRIES	NEW OR REDEFINED INFRASTRUCTURES
FIRST: **The 'Industrial Revolution'** Britain. From 1771	Mechanized cotton industry Wrought iron Machinery	Canals and waterways Turnpike roads Water power (highly improved water wheels)
SECOND: **Age of Steam and railways** In Britain and spreading to Continent: and USA. From 1829	Steam engines and machinery (made in iron; fuelled by coal) Iron and coal mining (now playing a central role in growth) Railway construction Rolling stock production Steam power for many industries (including textiles)	Railways (Use of steam engine) Universal postal service Telegraph (mainly nationally along railway lines) Great ports, great depots and worldwide sailing ships City gas
THIRD: **Age of Steel, Electricity and Heavy Engineering** USA and Germany overtaking Britain. From 1875	Cheap steel (especially Bessemer) Full development of steam engine for steel ships Heavy chemistry and civil engineering Electrical equipment industry Copper and cables Canned and bottled food Paper and packaging	Worldwide shipping in rapid steel steamships (use of Suez Canal) Worldwide railways (use of cheap steel rails and bolts in standard sizes). Great bridges and tunnels Worldwide Telegraph Telephone (mainly nationally) Electrical networks (for illumination and industrial use)
FOURTH: **Age of Oil, the Automobile and Mass production** In USA and spreading to Europe. From 1908	Mass-produced automobiles Cheap oil and oil fuels Petrochemicals (symthetics) Internal combuston engine for automobiles, transport, tractors, airplanes, war tanks, and electricity Home electrical appliances Refrigerated and frozen foods	Networks of roads, highways, ports, and airports Networks of oil ducts Universal electricity (industry and homes) Worldwide analogue telecommunications (telephone, telex, and cablegram) wire and wireless
FIFTH: **Age of Information and Telecommunications** In USA, spreading to Europe and Asia From 1971	The information revolution Cheap microelectronics Computers, software Telecommunications Control instruments Computer-aided biotechnology and new materials	World digital telecommunication (cable, fibre optics, radio, and satellite) Internet/ Electronic mail and other e-services Multiple source, flexible use, electricity networks High-speed physical transport links (by land, air and water)

Figure 5.4: The five techno-economic paradigm shifts of the capitalist era
Source: Perez 2002

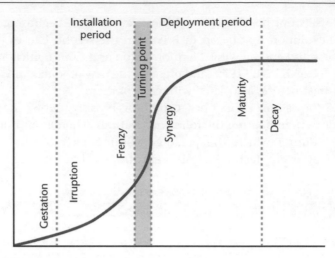

Figure 5.5: Phases in a techno-economic paradigm
Source: Perez 2002

example, mobile phones have been revolutionary in many ways and have been the cause of creative destruction in telephony, but they are part of the much larger information and communications technology shift that began with the invention of the microprocessor. In other eras, this paradigm-shifting role has been attributed to Arkwright's water-powered cotton mill, Stephenson's railway engine, Carnegie's adaptation of the Bessemer steel-manufacturing process, and the Model T Ford.

Installation Period

Irruption

Successful inventions emerge from gestation then burst into society in a phase Perez calls 'irruption'. They spawn new products and new industries during an explosive period of growth. They are also closely associated with new types of energy so that Arkwright's mill harnessed water, the steam engine turned coal from a peripheral to a primary energy source, and the internal combustion engine turned oil into a source of wealth and power. Thus, for instance, Carnegie's steel mills, coinciding with electricity generation, spurred an unprecedented increase in patented inventions such as the electric streetlight, the electric motor, the roll film camera, the cigarette machine, and the linotype printer. New industries sprang up, costs fell (the price of steel dropped from £40 to £7 a long ton), and productivity increased (production rose from 200 to 120 000 units a day in Buck Duke's cigarette factory).

Frenzy

This and declining previous GPT returns in turn prompts an investment frenzy that funds the installation of the new technologies to the point where they are commonly available. This could be seen with the growth in the internet in the 1990s—the frenzy phase of the ICT era—and Britain's railways between 1830 and 1850 when about 36 per cent of GDP was invested in expanding the network.[22] In Britain, and later in the USA as well, invest-ment mania resulted in financial collapse, causing one commentator to remark, 'our railroad system has cost more than $1 000 000 and has brought ruin upon nearly everyone connected with it, the nation included.'[23]

Indeed, this kind of frenzy always ends in financial collapse, precisely because the new technology confronts a set of social, legal, and political institutions that are aligned against it, and congruent instead with the old. In the mass era it famously took the form of the Great Depression, just as the frenzy of foreign investment in transcontinental railways and global markets for meat, wheat, and copper had ended with the Panic of (18)93, the worst depression the USA had ever experienced up to that point. (Its consequences were worse still in Argentina and Australia.)

Turning Point

The end of frenzy marks the end of speculation but not the end of the techno-economic era. After the railway mania of the 1850s, the USA's railway network grew from 30 000 to 253 000 miles over a fifty year period;[24] the internet has continued to expand as a global phenomenon even though telecommunica-tions investment halved in some OECD countries after the dot.com bubble of 2000. The share value of Yahoo! might have fallen from US$475 to US$8 a share between 2000 and 2001, and Bernie Ebbers was in prison after his accounting fraud contributed to the bankruptcy of Worldcom, then the second largest telecoms company in the USA. Yet, the number of internet hosts worldwide grew from 100 000 000 to one billion between 2001 and 2009.[25]

According to Perez, the financial collapse that follows investment frenzy is the trigger for a turning point. Prior to that, innovators, and then speculators, have the greatest influence. They are portrayed as heroes whose genius earns them celebrity status. Indeed, referring back to Boltanski and Thévenot's orders of worth, this is likely to be a period when capitalism is justified by the high opinion society has of its entrepreneurs and financiers. As has happened during the ICT era, government sees its role as removing the barriers to trade and free enterprise, allowing markets to be self-regulating. This was as true of Gladstone as it was of Hoover and Thatcher. Over time this creates incongruence as the damage of the frenzy makes society reconsider the justification for capitalism. Some politicians continue to defend their hands-off approach, but the real life experiences of others make them amenable once again to greater government economic intervention, tougher regulation of finance, and more investment in social welfare. One should be wary of too many convenient correlations, and, as historian Asa Briggs points out, stories of social reform resemble serials rather than novellas.[26] Nonetheless, laws to redistribute national wealth to improve overall well-being have often coincided with post-frenzy periods (e.g. the British Factory and Workshop Act 1895; the USA's 1935 Social Security Act; Sweden's accident compensation scheme, 1901).

Deployment Period

Following the installation period and its turning point comes a period of deployment when internal congruence is reestablished. There is no fixed pattern to this, and as Geels has identified through numerous micro-level examples of the change process, society's institutions react at different speeds and often in unpredictable ways.[27] Just as chaos theory in the natural sciences describes the complex array of interactions that affect any natural events, Geels shows how the reaction of individuals and organizations to events creates 'complex adaptive systems' the exact outcomes of which are less predictable than a lottery. Therefore, civil society may be the driving force for change as it was in the case of slavery, but equally farsighted politicians might preempt social revolution with reforms as Briggs argues happened repeatedly in Victorian Britain.

Synergy

Perez divides the deployment period between synergy, maturity, and ultimately decay. Synergy is when the full social potential of the new era is realized in terms of expansion and market potential. The innovations are no longer attractive to speculators who in any case have squandered much of their capital and are subject to greater regulatory constraint. Investment takes the form of what Solow calls industrial rather than financial capital, and instead of high returns on investment, companies deliver less spectacular but steadier returns; it is a time for dividend investors rather than equity ones.

The synergy phase is often looked back on as a Golden Age, not just in terms of economic prosperity, but also social progress. Early nineteenth-century

Britain might be remembered for its inhumane treatment of children, brutal factories, and reaction to the revolutions in France and the USA, but it was also a period of reflection and reform exemplified by the first Factory Acts, the 1815 Corn Law, and the 1823 Prison Act. As already mentioned, the Belle Époque followed the financial collapse of the 1890s, and the New Deal that came out of the Great Depression of the 1930s laid the ground for the USA's post-Second World War prosperity. External events can affect this evolution from incongruence to synergy, notably major wars that act as a brake and a stimulus. The early industrial revolution was affected by the revolutionary wars in France and the USA, and the Napoleonic wars; the Belle Époque ended with the First World War; and the Second World War made synergy and the deployment period as a whole a very different experience in Germany and Japan, or the UK and France, compared to the USA and Australia. Nonetheless, over the course of the 30–40 years of deployment, the pattern is consistent for all capitalist economies.

Maturity

Synergy is followed by maturity, by which time the new status quo is firmly established. Carnegie, whose steel mills played a huge part in the creative destruction of the steel, electricity, and heavy engineering techno-economic paradigm, had transformed himself from the personification of the rapacious businessman to an icon of progressive philanthropy in the early 1900s. From Lever's Port Sunlight, to Nobel's endowment of the Peace Prize, and Bill Gates' funding of disease eradication, the revolutionaries of one period become the good citizens of maturity. The old common sense is replaced by a new common sense that is treated as being universally true. The new order is now taken for granted as Žižek observes, 'once [an] order is installed, its contingent origins are erased. Once it IS here, it was ALWAYS ALREADY HERE.'[28] In Polanyi's terms, the economy is embedded once again in society; in Schumpeter's terms, 'monetary capital' has been usurped by 'real capital', and for economists such as Galbraith, predatory capital that had held business hostage to unsustainably high returns is displaced by productive capital that enables the potential benefits of the new technologies to be fully deployed.

It is at this time that the 'virtuous circle' described by Romer results in net wealth creation rather than wealth redistribution as investment in technology leads to technological advances enabling more investment, and producing better technology.[29] There are still disputes and friction between and amongst the different elements of society, and the next generation of creative destroyers will be starting to gestate, out of sight and unnoticed. But overall this is a period of congruence in which capitalism is easily justified by whatever orders of worth society values at that time.

But as the deployment period matures, it is associated more and more with satiation, languor, and eventually stagnation. Politically, it is a time when the new status quo is focused on maintaining the order it has helped build, evident for instance in the nationalist De Gaulle's return to power in 1958, and the initial protectionism of the European Economic Community. Socially, it has been associated with leisure and consumption (e.g. Veblen's theory of the leisure class), and the dominance of corporations (e.g. Galbraith's corporate republic).[30] In economic terms, maturity has been linked to stagflation, the period in the 1970s when inflation spiralled despite the lack of growth and high rates of unemployment. It also coincided with Britain's return to the gold standard to protect the economy from growth-oriented but destabilizing monetary policies in the 1820s.[31]

The Uses of Techno-economic Paradigms: Mapping an Economy on the S Curve

Not every event in a particular era can be neatly mapped against the phases of a techno-economic paradigm. The space race and the youth revolution of the 1960s, for example, occurred during the latter stages of the mass era, and are remembered for their vibrancy and upheaval. Britain's return to the gold standard was not fully completed until the 1840s by which time the disruptive effects of the railway age were proceeding apace. The evolutionary model of techno-economic paradigms is a schema for understanding the underlying dynamics of major changes: it reveals the currents that force change, but does not predict or account for every eddy and whirlpool that will appear along the way; it explains why ships will move and erosion occur, but it cannot forecast what will happen to every vessel or groyne.

What it does present, however, is a pattern of events that are a recurring feature of capitalism since the early industrial revolution. When we consider our four crises (Chapter 3), we might hope that some of these behaviours are absent this time round, or that we could deal with the crises in some other way than capitalism. That, though, seems like wishful thinking. The crises are already upon us, and around the world social, legal, economic, political, and technological elements largely take for granted the desirability of some sort of capitalist system. Perhaps there are useful lessons to draw from socialism, biomimicry, systems thinking, and other alternative frameworks for thinking about the crises. But they are only worthwhile if they can be made to work within a society that is ordered around capitalism because for all of the shifts in geo-politics, the changes in governance, the impacts of demographic change, and implications of climate change, if it is to shape practical consequences, the debate today must focus on how to make capitalism better not how to replace it with something new.

The schema we have outlined is not a comprehensive theory of change, but in the context of business's turnaround challenge, it can be used in two ways. It identifies the recurring periods and phases common to different eras, and sheds light on what is likely to happen during each one. It helps identify where society is situated on the paradigm's evolutionary journey, and therefore what events may affect or be affected by the different transformational crises. There is plenty of room for interpretation here and not everyone will agree about where on the S-curve society is, nor how institutions will react.

... and defining the boundaries of the possible

The schema's second function is to help explain the force and momentum of the paradigm at different phases. How does a new GPT evolve and gain traction? What are the boundaries of the possible at different phases? This is important because the options for addressing the different crises currently on offer require different degrees of change, and there needs to be a basis for assessing their feasibility. This is not something that Perez, Schumpeter, or the other techno-economic thinkers on whose work we have drawn in this chapter have paid attention to. Their starting point is that, although it might end up destroying itself, capitalism is able to rejuvenate itself, and certainly does not suffer from external incongruence. They depict societal incongruence as an inherent feature of capitalist progress, while in our view, for that progress to be durable, the rejuvenated model must be congruent with the wider ecosystem. Chapter 3 highlights that in important areas this can no longer be taken for granted. Hence, the schema's second function is to shed light on the type and degree of effort necessary to break down external incongruence even as the dynamics of societal incongruence continue to play out.

Decay

No matter how one uses the schema, the final phase is always disarray and decay. This is a metaphor that has gained increasing approval in economic, political, and social thinking, thanks in large measure because it echoes developments in physics showing how nature moves from order to disorder (i.e. entropy). By this time, there are no more genuine technological innovations to be squeezed out, the key breakthroughs of the era have been fully deployed, and what economic progress there is comes from incremental efficiencies rather than leaps in productivity.[32] The effects of this are felt throughout society, exemplified in the high unemployment of the 1970s as the oil-car-mass production era stagnated, and in the parliamentary and workplace battles of

117

1910 Britain. In both cases, this was not the result of financial collapse (unlike the end of frenzy), but rather a confusion and malaise that historian George Dangerfield captured in his book title, *The Strange Death of Liberal England*.[33]

The Strange Life of the ICT Era

The recurrence of techno-economic paradigm shifts throughout capitalism is one of the main reasons for the reluctant optimism that characterizes our attitude to tackling the quadrilemma of crises. However, there are two immediate problems with it. First, it does not explain how to achieve external congruence, and it certainly offers no evidence that this would be the inevitable outcome of any future shift. Second, thinking back to our earlier discussion of how the mass era has endured, it seems to have identified an era that we have overlooked.

These two problems are interrelated, as will become clear, and they are not problems with the techno-economic paradigm model, but rather relate to a series of strange events affecting the final stage of the mass era's deployment period and the information and computing technology's installation period. Instead of decay of the old and a genuine irruption of the new, ICT innovation ended up being used to prolong the life of the mass era and the Petropolis. Instead of technological and financial innovation being harnessed to build external congruence, it has wound up supporting incongruence. This was not inevitable; it was the consequence of many choices.

Installation

The mass era reached maturity in the 1960s, and by the 1970s the countries at its vanguard, notably the USA, were suffering from stagflation and the onset of decay. At about the same time, there was a flurry of innovation in the ICT arena, and in 1971 the Intel 4004, the first commercially-produced microprocessor, was launched. Its first commercial use, according to one of ICT's more famous offspring, Wikipedia, was in a calculator, the Busicom 141-PF, but its real significance was to spur the development of increasingly powerful microchips that were the basis for IBM and Apple personal computers and operating systems such as DOS. Computers themselves improved with innovations in hard disk drives, graphics, and the graphical user interface. The technology also opened the door to networking systems that in turn enabled, amongst other things, the global value chain revolution in business. Riding on the wave of increasingly powerful processors, new ways of production, management, consumption, and leisure have become the norm. From web browsers, to online social networks, to automated check-outs, none of this existed when

Kim Kardashian was born in 1980, but by the time Bill Clinton was impeached following the Lewinsky affair in 1998, the infrastructure that would enable these developments was firmly installed.

And yet until the start of the new millennium there was nothing unusual about the ICT era. Jobs and Gates had emerged blinking from the gestation phase to experience the same kind of irruption enjoyed by Arkwright or Stephenson. As had happened with the introduction of revolving credit and joint stock in the nineteenth century, or hire purchase in the early twentieth, the new technology demanded a new type of investor and new investment vehicles. Kleiner Perkins was an early innovator in the venture capital model that became the lifeblood of hi-tech pioneers. Two months after Kim Kardashian was born, Apple Inc. heralded a long series of huge ICT IPOs when it went public for US$1.3 billion. There was the typical frenzy of investment in companies from the successes of Cisco and Genentech to the failures of Pets.com and eToys.com which respectively lost US$82.5 million in nine months and suffered a share price collapse from US$84 a share to US$0.09 in two years. In 2 000, the NASDAQ Composite Index rose to a few points shy of 5 000: a year later it was less than 2 000 points. The dot.com bubble had burst.

In techno-economic paradigm terms, this was a case of so far so good, but all that was about to change. Throughout the ICT era's installation period, the mass commercial model struggled to retain its preeminence. Facing saturated domestic markets, companies in industrial economies turned to international trade. The high price of oil drove their costs up but also meant there was ample capital available for investment from resource-rich countries. Instead of being associated with a few industrialized economies that were accused of exploiting others, the mass era started to be seen as an engine of international economic development through an agenda of trade and investment. There was a considerable rise in the percentage of manufactured goods that were traded internationally, from less than 55 per cent in 1980 to over 70 per cent when the dot.com bubble burst.[34] In a few short years, the world went from an age of smuggling Swiss watches to one where they were the staple of shopping malls. Economic globalization was truly underway.

ICT and the decoupling of asset values from real sector profitability

There were two ongoing trends as the ICT era reached its frenzy period. On the one hand, there was the opportunity to invest in ICT technologies and the companies they spawned. On the other hand, there were opportunities to deploy ICT in incumbent industries to make them more efficient and profitable. At a time when many national governments had converted to a belief that markets were the best arbiters of social well-being, it did not matter what was manufactured provided that investors were content. Indeed, the very idea

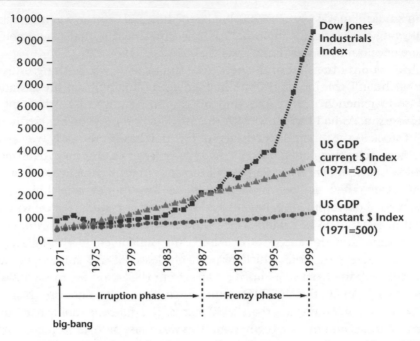

Figure 5.6: Changing relationship between the real economy and asset values, 1971–1999

Source: Perez 2002 10.1 p 112

that production and well-being were related started to seem odd. Figure 5.6 shows the correlation between major stock indices and GDP that had existed for decades starting to unravel in the 1990s until the dot.com collapse.

Investors were now primarily interested in returns of the kind associated with the ICT successes. They ploughed money into ICT companies that could be portrayed as generating those returns regardless of their role in the real economy as measured by GDP (e.g. Yahoo! and AOL). They also invested in companies from established industries that deployed ICT innovation to bolster their bottom line. Thus companies such as Nike and Wal-Mart used ICT advances to build global supply chains, and thereby generated returns that other companies had to imitate or face being cut off from cheap capital. Enron became the poster child of a company in an established industry that lost its way by using ICT innovation to create the illusion of prosperity.

The financialization of the economy

However it was not alone. Referring back to the problem of energy return on investment in Chapter 4, ICT innovation is what has made otherwise unusable fossil fuel resources technologically and economically viable.

Moreover, actual sustainable profitability became increasingly less important as the finance industry deployed the technology to develop ever more complex financial instruments. It enabled a debt-based economy to be portrayed as prosperous so that as early as 1995, the USA's 'derivative economy' (i.e. the paper wealth that is created to keep the debt-system afloat) was valued at US$64 trillion, almost equal to the bonds, equity, and bank assets of the 17 strongest economies in the world.[35] By 2009, credit market debt in the USA was valued at US$52 trillion compared to US$10 trillion in 1987.[36]

The real achievement of the ICT era, therefore, was not personal computers and mobile phones, but how it enabled the 'financialization of the economy'.[37] This idea has been around in different forms for a long time. Ruskin distinguished wellth (*sic*) from illth, and the same moral overtones were present in Nazi theory which talked of creative capital (*schaffendes*) and predatory capital (*raffendes*). Galbraith distinguishes predators from prey, *Financial Times* journalist Roger Bootle laments the dominance of distribution over production,[38] and Schumpeter divides monetary from real capital. Nonetheless, the separation of the real economy (what Solow calls the industrial economy) from the financial economy is crucial to understanding the incongruence that has worsened since the dot.com bubble. The technological revolution is not just financed through financial innovation, at some stage it is hijacked by it so that technologies are deployed to sustain the increase in financial wealth. In the ICT era this has meant that managerial efficiency has been taken to unimagined levels; manufacturing jobs have been relocated in the creation of global value chains; share trading has become faster and cheaper, and in some people's eyes has fundamentally altered the nature of company ownership; and there has been a surge in new financial instruments based largely on unprecedented computing power. ICT innovation enabled a frenzy of wealth creation and financial innovation allowed it to continue even when there were no longer sound investments to back up the high returns investors had become used to. Not only was ICT innovation coopted to prolong the mass era, the mass era itself was redefined by the financial economy.

A turning point...

In hindsight it is obvious that the financialization of the economy would lead to disaster. Based on previous techno-economic paradigm shifts, this should have happened at the end of the installation period at the turn of the millennium. By that time, the stock of global financial assets as a multiple of global GDP had reached 4.4 (approximately US$200 trillion) compared to 1.2 when Kim Kardashian was born.[39] In the USA, the ratio of financial assets to GDP was over 320 per cent, in the European Union it was over 400 per cent, and in

Asia it was over 500 per cent. At the same time, the income share of the top 1 per cent in the USA reached roughly 20 per cent (including capital gains) compared to less than 10 per cent at Kardashian's birth. Thus, during the phases of irruption and frenzy up to the expected turning point, the average income of the lowest earning 90 per cent of the population in the USA fell 0.1 per cent, the gap between median earnings and those of the top 10 per cent increased by 4 per cent in the UK, and similar instances of a growing wealth divide were observed in various OECD economies.[40] Moreover, this reversed the trend until the 1980s when income inequality was being reduced.[41]

However, it is at this stage in the ICT story that events took an unusual turn. Put simply, the transition towards synergy observed in previous eras did not take place. Perhaps the web of social safety nets in OECD economies prevented a damaging social collapse of the kind felt in the 1890s and 1930s, even though losses on the stock markets were broadly similar. Equally evident, though, is that the incongruence that had grown during the frenzy, but which on historical evidence should have been healed during synergy, continued apace in defiance of any turning point. Instead of institutions converging around a new common sense as had happened in the past, many of them suffered a failure of imagination and ambition. For example, the reform of UK company law, which had started in the late 1990s with the intention of strengthening social responsibility and accountability, was almost abandoned at the insistence of the Treasury, and eventually came onto the statute books in a diluted form.[42] Elsewhere in Europe, companies in Germany started to incorporate as *Societas Europaea* which have less strict requirements on employee representation.[43] In the USA, the 2002 Sarbanes-Oxley Act, passed in the aftermath of the ICT frenzy to reform accounting, protect investors, and strengthen the position of owners, was praised and ridiculed in equal measure, but in the end did nothing to prevent the financial crisis of 2007–2008.[44]

... that never happened

Following the 2000 dot.com crash, the reality was that the trend towards light-touch regulation with a bias against tougher laws and in favour of directives and industry self-governance continued unabated. Not only in finance, but on seemingly far-removed issues such as ethical trade, sustainable forestry, and corruption in oil, gas, and mining, 'voluntary regulation' was preferred to government intervention. Furthermore, a knock-on effect of ICT innovation was that energy remained cheaper than predicted during the 2000s, easing the burden on consumers, and reducing the incentive for governments and the public to consider alternative energy sources seriously. However, it was the financial economy rather than the real economy that benefited the most. Advances in computing power, infrastructure, and software made the financial services sector the main market for ICT applications by the time of the 2007–2008 crisis.[45] Technological innovation in turn enabled financial innovation such as credit default swaps and collateralized debt obligations, both of which came to the fore in the early 2000s, and which were a major factor in the 2007 debt crisis.

The technology, therefore, made possible the financial innovation that resulted in a second financial collapse seven years after what should have been a turning point. Instead of technology being deployed to rebuild the real economy, it was used to continue the financialization of the economy— the deepening of Schumpeter's monetary economy or Solow's financial economy. It created a period of gilded prosperity that reinvigorated the frenzy of the installation period but did nothing to help society reach synergy and maturity. Instead, when the second bubble burst, government prerogatives in the most indebted countries were to save the financial economy. In the wake of the 2007–2008 financial crisis, while countries such as China and South Korea put together stimulus packages to invest in the industrial economy, in the UK the £1.162 trillion cost of salvaging financial institutions (a sum greater than the national debt which in 2011 stood at £0.91 trillion) meant that there was little left to spend on helping the real economy.[46]

Prolonging the pathologies of mass

However, this was a decision, not an inevitability. At previous turning points, actions were taken by individuals, organizations, and institutions to rejuvenate the 'real economy.' The reasons why that did not happen this time around are attributable to decisions (and non-decisions) across the spectrum of society that left particular orders of worth in place, perpetuated certain values and notions of prosperity, and worsened the potential negative consequences of the crises. From the point of view of business, the worst effect of the choices made is that it is ill-equipped to face the crises it is in the midst of now. The decisions that were taken favoured a model of business that is demonstrably redundant, one that prolongs the pathologies of the mass era (e.g. dependence on fossil fuels, decreasing return on assets, capture by the financial economy, reliance on consumption) without actually succeeding in terms of its own goals (e.g. delivering sufficient growth, enhancing human well-being), or establishing external congruence. Those decisions included the ones taken by politicians to favour business over other instruments for achieving well-being, and of treating business as synonymous with finance. It also included the decision by economists to treat growth as the main signifier of performance, and to marginalize non-conventional economic thinking.

It is hard to overstate the failure of the economic status quo either in predicting what would happen if their theoretical models were unleashed on the real world, or in accepting responsibility for how their ideas influenced and continue to influence business and politicians. Minsky may have foreseen, as early as the 1980s, the fragility of financial systems that during what we have called the installation period attract a flood of new investors with a growing appetite for risk, and are then left bereft of capital once the size of the risks becomes apparent and investors flee.[47] However, such voices were given scant attention until after the second financial crash. And even after the dot.com bubble, the conditions for a second crash were still allowed to build.

The crisis of economics, the failure of economists and their role in the current incongruence are the subject for a book in its own right, but it is not this book. If we were to try to explain incongruence using the norms and tools of an economist's perspective here, we would fall into the trap of giving the impression that society can only be understood through that lens. The decision to turn away from what should have been full deployment, and repeat a period of financial frenzy that prolonged the mass era may have been guided by economic principles to a degree, but there were many other factors.

From Producers to Consumers

We have touched on the political dimension, but we should also look at the social one. As we have shown, people have justified capitalism in many ways, not just monetary ones (page 104). Since the mass era, OECD populations have identified themselves as consumers at least as much as producers, either with the regret of Putnam's *Bowling Alone*, or the celebration of a 'shop til you drop' attitude in game shows and popular culture.[48] There is something morally unnerving about levels of consumption that at times seem driven by the urge to own more Hello Kitty paraphernalia, and which are touted by politicians as essential to economic growth. However, it is easy to get judgemental about consumption (especially other people's). It is not an unfortunate by-product of techno-economic paradigms; it is an essential element of them for three interrelated reasons.

First, government economic policies are now highly dependent on increased worldwide consumption around the world, and when, after the dot.com bubble, President George Bush urged USA citizens to 'get down to Disney World in Florida. Take your families and enjoy life, the way we want it to be enjoyed',[49] he was speaking for policy-makers across the OECD who want people to set aside their worries about job security and debt and spend more. Second, decades of what marketers call the 'manufacturing of desire'[50] have caused people to associate consumption with prosperity as was clear from a disillusioned voter in the 2012 USA election who lamented that his family could 'only afford to buy the things we need'.[51] That desire had different implications in the 1950s and 1960s when wages rose and productivity gains drove down prices (the period Galbraith called 'affluenza'), than it has had in recent years when real wages amongst those used to high levels of consumption were only improving slightly or had stagnated entirely. Lower cost imported goods went some way to reduce the cost of living, but what really enabled a mood of prosperity to be preserved was cheap credit that stimulated a housing boom enabling more people to buy homes or release the equity in their property—decisions that were made all the more possible by the use of ICT advances in financial innovation.

Third, that kind of consumption is exactly what came to be vaunted as progress during the mass era. The manufacturing of desire may have encouraged seemingly frivolous consumption such as the Hello Kitty or the sushi-slicing robot of Chapter 4, but what consumption really became was an expression of values, affinity, and culture. Consumers act out of need, self-gratification, desire, obligation, generosity, and all manner of motivations that are cultural, psychological, and social. They do not buy just for the sake of it: on top of any basic needs, they consume to express their feelings toward others, to express status, to entertain, and to fulfil many of the other acts involved in being a human. For them, it is a highly congruent thing to do and one so deeply embedded in ideas of society's well-being that it is hard to imagine it not existing (certainly not during the period some of our crises will play out). Yet consumption, along with a commitment to economic growth, locked into political, economic, and legal institutions are not only failing in their own narrow measures of human well-being, they are now at the core of external incongruence. Perhaps the single biggest reason for us being reluctant rather than exhilarated optimists is the intensity and complexity of this quandary. We *are* optimists, however, and in the last section of this chapter we will start to explain why.

Plausible Options

Heading towards Petropolis

Business could find itself operating within three environments in future. The first is the one we labelled the Petropolis in Chapter 2, built on a protraction of the mass era by the continued cooption of ICT innovation and replication of the OECD model of development even further afield. This promises economic growth and does not depend on actions that contradict path dependency or people's justifications for capitalism. It would see a restoration of the real economy and the continued decline of financial capital and the financialized economy. Economic growth would largely come from deploying the general purpose technologies of the mass era (including ICT) amongst more people in what might be called a period of global synergy. There do not appear to be imminent breakthrough technologies that would disturb the course from synergy to maturity, and hopefully during the thirty to forty years one might expect this to happen over, the kind of growth BAU Oracles predict would generate the surplus wealth necessary to launch the next techno-economic paradigm.

But we have already explained the trouble with the Petropolis. It is a model that threatens the Earth's carrying capacity unless there are unimaginable technological advances ready for installation very soon. It requires huge advances in energy production that are unlikely to be achieved without the use of fossil fuels at rates that endanger the climate and other ecosystems. Much of that energy will be costly to produce in both financial and energy return on investment terms, making improvements in carbon intensity to lower GHG emissions even more important than they are already. We showed the size of that challenge in Figure 2.1. If it is not met, then it would either lead to a period of synergy and maturity that was haunted by climate change, or one characterized by unbalanced growth that ignored demographic and geo-political changes. In both cases, the result would be incongruence and a failure to deliver prosperity.

Paradoxically, a reason for optimism about the Petropolis is the likelihood that its problems will accelerate the next wave of creative destruction. Capitalism as a model, and the citizens who justify it, are too smart to allow otherwise. Rising energy prices, worsening balance of payment deficits, lower incomes, and commodity price inflation would all be a brake on economic growth that would help address external incongruence. It would also require society at some stage to reconsider what it means by prosperity, but the journey to that point would be highly precarious and gives little reason for cheer.

Are there alternative cities of the future?

The Petropolis is now governed by a belief that there is no alternative, and the pervasiveness of that conviction is what tempers our optimism. This chapter has shown, though, that great change is not only possible, it has happened as a norm at the maturity of successive technological cycles of capitalism. That is what makes us optimists, and in the final chapters we will see if that optimism is justified.

This is not to say either is unambitious or easy. They will both require, for instance, a different type of business than the one that was fit for purpose in the mass era, and it will take more than a leap of imagination to make this possible.

In the next two chapters, we will explore two other options that are feasible and appear to take the crisis of external congruence seriously. They are very different in terms of the kind of world they promise and what they mean for human well-being. They offer clear alternatives to the Petropolis and mass era, but unlike the ideas of some of our Oracles they pass the tests of plausibility given the quadrilemma of crises.

Notes

1. http://rocketscienceofwallstreet.blogspot.co.uk/2012/07/did-mathematics-caused-financial-crisis.html
2. (Palma 2009)
3. For the most recent overview, see (IPCC 2012)
4. (Tushman, Nadler 1978)
5. See for instance Foucault's use of the panopticon as a metaphor for how society is disciplined (Foucault 1979)
6. (Lukes 1974)
7. (Boltanski, Thévenot 2006)
8. (Drescher 2009)
9. (Boltanski, Chiapello 2005)
10. (Durkheim 1893)
11. (Quinn 1962)
12. (Diamond, Diamond 2005)
13. (Toynbee 1946, Tainter 1987, Ferguson 2005)
14. (CASSON 1937)
15. (Tainter 1987)
16. For an overview of the trouble with predicting the future, see (Gardner 2010)
17. http://www.2degreecommunique.com/, accessed 11 November 2012
18. (Marx 1973, Schumpeter 1942)
19. (Barnett 1998)
20. (Polanyi 1944)
21. (Solow 1956, Romer 1991)
22. (Kostal 1994, Reed 1975)
23. Henry Carey Baird cited at http://www.caslon.com.au/boomprofile3.htm#railway, accessed 5 November 2012
24. http://www.caslon.com.au/boomprofile3.htm#railway, accessed 5 November 2012
25. Figures from the Internet Systems Consortium
26. (Briggs 1959)
27. (Geels 2002)
28. (Žižek 2011, emphasis in the original)
29. (Romer 1991)
30. (Veblen 1899, Galbraith 2008)
31. (Scott 1903)

32. (Piepenbrock 2010)
33. (Dangerfield 1936)
34. (Melchior 2012)
35. (Martenson 2011)
36. Palma 2000 cited in (Perez 2002); (Martenson 2011)
37. (Krippner 2005)
38. (Bootle 2009)
39. (Palma 2009)
40. (Palma 2009); Office of National Statistics Data; (Alderson, Nielsen)
41. (Palma 2009, Alderson, Nielsen)
42. (MacNeil 2006; Sealy 2007; Williamson 2008)
43. (MacNeil 2006; Sealy 2007; Williamson 2008)
44. (Adams 2012)
45. (Gartner 2010). The banking and securities industry had an ICT spend of US$358.2 billion in 2009
46. Office of National Statistics figures and (NAO 2011)
47. (Minsky 1982); (McCulley 2008)
48. (Putnam 2000)
49. http://www.nytimes.com/2012/01/15/business/consumer-spending-as-an-american-virtue.html, accessed 1 November 2012
50. (Berger 1996)
51. This phrase comes from someone interviewed during the 2012 USA presidential elections who, complaining about the state of the economy, said, 'Things have gotten so bad, we can only afford to buy the things we need.'

6

Cyburbia

IN THIS CHAPTER

The Smart City. The logic of mass revisited. Redirecting ICT innovation to build the sensored city of the future. Sliding from sensored to censored. Is Cyburbia a way out of or a way back to the Petropolis?

'*I am your Destiny*'

Slogan for Florida eco-city

Songdo: 'Everything one could possibly want'

At the entrance is a sign saying 'Welcome: we will change the face of business.' Pass through that gate, and you are in Songdo, 'everything one could possibly want, need and dream of in a world-class city.'[1] South Korea's New Songdo City, about 55 kilometres from Seoul, is said to be the largest private real estate development in history. Once Songdo is completed in about 2015, it will be a free economic zone with 80 000 apartments, over five million square metres of office space, and over 900 000 square metres of retail space. It is part of Incheon free economic zone with international and national transport connections.[2]

Songdo's aim is to overcome the problems caused by modern urban life. Its publicity points to the environmental damage, undereducated workforce, and lack of space in Asia's major business centres. 'It would seem a city that enjoys clean air...and a superior quality of life just doesn't exist anymore.' Songdo addresses that problem by starting from scratch. In contrast with the Petropolis typical of Asia's economies, 40 per cent of Songdo is designated green space including a 40 hectare park. The main car park is in a sunken courtyard to reduce heat and emissions, but reliance on the car is reduced by a public transport system that includes underground trains linked to Seoul and a network of electric water taxis plying the city's salt-water canals. There is also a high-speed rail link to Seoul and Incheon International Airport. All told, Songdo should be one of the cleanest international cities in the world. In 2012, the United Nations' Global Climate Fund chose Songdo as the permanent home for its secretariat.

All apartments have Telepresence, with 52-inch LCD monitors and multi-directional microphones allow for seamless video-communication. Beneath a central console that controls the apartment's heating/cooling and other settings is a medical device that can take blood pressure and read blood samples, and relay them digitally to a local clinic.

Through Telepresence in every home, office, and school, the city's carbon intensity improves because people have less need to travel. Some of Songdo's designers go further and say that Telepresence is a critical technology for the city. It will offer residents and the workforce access to a host of innovative services that allow people to 'meet' without the inconvenience of travelling. One of the city's designers points out that this will reduce the anxiety associated with figuring out where to meet and when: in Songdo 'You're always there.'[3] With its ubiquitous network built into houses, streets, and offices, Songdo has been called a digital commune. As architect of Songdo's master plan, Kohn Pedersen Fox, describes it, this is 'the project of a lifetime.'[4]

A model for the future?

The vision for Songdo and other smart cities is largely technological, driven by an engineering and planning perspective. One of the companies that sees the potential of Songdo is Cisco, which has called it a 'model for smart cities around the globe.' It has a multibillion-dollar contract to provide network technologies to the new city. According to the company, the network will connect all of the components in the city: residences, offices, schools, and all of the buildings. 'In this networked community, residents will be able to control the functions of their homes remotely, and everyone will be able to interact through video from anywhere. New and old technology working together will create a truly sustainable city.'[5] Therefore, the power and fire alarm systems, and other facets of the built environment are linked together to reduce maintenance costs as well as increase efficiency. Residents can manage their home's energy use remotely, and adjust everything from lights to air conditioning. Just by touching a screen, the system seeks out areas of energy use and makes them more efficient, reducing inhabitants' carbon footprints in the process.

Cisco's publicity material summarizes the central idea behind them: 'the foundation for the city of the future will be the network and the information it carries.'[6] In these cities, a steady flow of information will link the physical with the social world and the data cloud. Songdo's IT specialists are experimenting with Telepresence systems to deliver education, health care, and government services directly into the homes, with lampposts equipped with public wi-fi, CCTV, and information services set up all over the city.

Cisco is not the only company to have recognized the apparently huge potential for modern information technologies to transform the cityscape. IBM has launched its Smarter Planet initiative, for example, while Siemens has established a new company sector focusing on infrastructure and cities. IBM is forecasting US$10 billion of revenues from its Smarter Planet initiative by 2015. GE is investing US$200 million in what it calls the 'industrial internet' which connects different sorts of industrial machinery with each other as well as with users over the internet to increase productivity and reduce costs. Duke Energy in the USA is partnering with Cisco to develop the 'energy internet,' a smart grid communications architecture that Cisco says has the potential to be 10000 times larger than the conventional internet if deployed around the world.[7]

Songdo is one of over a hundred smart cities currently being constructed around the world. It has been hailed as the city of the future and an experimental prototype community of tomorrow. Stanley Gale, Chairman of Gale International, one of the companies at the heart of Songdo, says, 'There's a pattern here, repeatable.' He plans to roll out cities across China, using Songdo as his template, starting with Meixi Lake, to be built in China's Hunan Province. Each will be built faster, better, and more cheaply than the ones that came before. 'It's going to be a cool city, a smart city! China alone needs five hundred cities the size of New Songdo'.

Destiny: 'America's first eco-sustainable city'

In the USA, the new city of Destiny promises to be 'America's first eco-sustainable city.' As its developers, the Pugliese Company, put it, 'I will be Florida's greatest city... I am your Destiny.'[8] The City of Destiny is to be built on a tract of land 20 per cent larger than the City of Miami, and about the same size as Disney World, that will offer a new kind of living environment, complete with advanced health care, for Florida's growing population. Moreover, it says it is at the heart of a 'new American dream.' Pugliese describes Destiny as a 'forward-thinking Environmentally Planned Community of Today' and has already trademarked that term. 'Destiny,' it adds, 'is the right place and at the right time.'[9]

The reality is that Destiny aims to be built within a twenty to forty year time frame. Its last progress report was in 2009. The Asian market is operating not just at a different speed, but on a different scale. Of the 500 new cities Gale cites as being needed by China, his one company has plans for involvement in twenty.[10] As Gale adds of his Asian rollout plans, 'We start from here and then we are going to build twenty new cities like this one, using this blueprint. Green! Growth! Export!'

The logic of Cyburbia

By 2025 there are expected to be thirty-seven megacities with populations greater than ten million; twenty-two of those will be in Asia. A number of push and pull factors support the drive towards the smart city, not least elements of our quadrilemma of crises, population growth, the rise in the global middle class and the pressure such trends place on energy prices, as we show in Figure 6.1.

A critical pull factor is capital. Two numbers sum it up: US$204 trillion vs US$ 465 trillion. The first number is China's positive current account war chest. Another pull factor is the national current account deficits of some of the major OECD economies, the UK, most of Europe, and above all, the second number above, the USA, displayed in Figure 6.2. The US$465 trillion negative number is the USA's current account deficit and represents in part the legacy of outsourcing production to emerging economies. It has a fundamental impact on the capacity to escape the model of Petropolis.

In summary, the contours of the smart city are emerging in the sand as the possible successor to the Petropolis. It occupies a physical space, but also exists in cyberspace thanks to its connectivity and automation. Suburbia exemplified the good life of the Petropolis; the smart city is Cyburbia, it is the new citadel with a core client base that includes the cash-rich emerging market giants that made their fortunes manufacturing, and who have now got the cash to build cities that escape the air and water degradation that resulted. But let's go back to the challenge that began this book. Does this city and the way of life it embodies represent a cause for optimism? Does it meet the test of adequacy and achievability in relation to the quadrilemma we identified in

PUSH FACTORS	PROBLEMS	PULL FACTORS
Urbanization		Capital available
Population growth	**Environment:** Disposable city	Carbon reduction targets
Rise of the middle class	**Social:** Gated city	Smart building systems
Energy cost rises	**Economic:** Product in,	
Grid instability	trash out city	
Decline in urban liveability	(PITO)	

Figure 6.1: Push and pull factors affecting the shift to Cyburbia

International Ranking (out of 194)	Country	Current account	Date
1	Germany	$ 204,300,000,000	2011 est.
2	China	$ 201,700,000,000	2011 est.
185	Europe	$ -32,720,000,000	2011 est.
186	UK	$ -46,040,000,000	2011 est.
194	US	$ -465,900,000,000	2011 est.

Figure 6.2: Current account situation of major economies, 2011

Source: CIA World factbook, retrieved 20 January 2013 https://www.cia.gov/library/publications/the-world-factbook/rankorder/2187rank.html

Chapter 2? If Petropolis, in short, runs the risk of failing our neighbour, does Cyburbia in fact serve him or her better?

The Benefits of Cyburbia

Yours for twenty-five million Dirhams. A recent real estate development in Dubai is a tower with four rotating penthouses and a rotating villa that has its own car lift. The rotating units can revolve 360 degrees and residents can choose if they want the rotation to occur over three, six, 12, or 24 hours. It is the brainchild of Faisal Ali Moosa, inspired by a series of rotating villas in Germany, and deciding to create his own version in Dubai. A Saudi prince is said to have placed a DH 25 million bid on the villa at the peak of the tower which has its own car lift with three parking spaces.

Recognition of environmental constraints

Cyburbia on many levels marks a constructive step away from this model. Unlike the planning embodied by the Dubai car lift, it shows an awareness of the environmental crisis society is dealing with, an awareness that will be vital for urban China. The World Bank estimates the economic costs of environmental degradation in China to have reached 8.1 per cent of Gross National Income. The ongoing Beijing air quality crisis illustrates these costs. PM2.5 are minute particles of air pollution capable of penetrating into the lungs, with a safe level of 25 microgrammes PM2.5 per cubic metre, designated by the World Health Organization. In January 2013, according to an official monitoring centre in Beijing, levels of PM2.5 were well above 600 microgrammes per cubic metre in several places, and may even have hit 900. Hospitals reported increases of up to 30 per cent in the number of patients reporting breathing problems. Cyburbia offers a compelling vision of a better lifestyle for the growing middle class.

It is not the city per se that Cyburbia is an alternative to. On the contrary, smart cities reflect the belief that dense cities are less environmentally harmful than sprawling ones even without the benefits of ICT innovation such as that planned for Songdo. Glaesner, for instance, has argued a household living in a community with more than 10000 people per square mile uses about 1 800 less litres of petrol than if they were in a community with less than 1 000 people per square mile[11] (2 600 litres compared to 4 406 litres).

Construction and jobs

Investments in Cyburbia are justified not just by improvements in the quality of life: there is also the dimension of growth. Keynes famously described just how simple it can be to use state stimulus to boost employment and create wealth. 'If the Treasury were to fill old bottles with bank-notes, bury them at suitable depths in disused coal-mines which are then filled up to the surface with town rubbish, and leave it to private enterprise on well-tried principles of laissez-faire to dig the notes up again . . . the real income of the community, and its capital wealth, would probably become a good deal greater than it actually is.' The smart city is a clear upgrade on the Keynesian stimulus plan. As a high capex and long-term infrastructure plan, it also has the virtue of generating growth that might lift us out of the 'great stagnation' described by Cowan.

Technological fit

The Cyburbia option is also achievable, not just in terms of capital and local governance, but in terms of technology. It focuses on the deployment of existing technologies where there are strong corporate partners with the commitment and capacity to deliver. It is also appealing because not only does it appear to address the four crises that comprise business's turnaround challenge, it offers plenty of commercial opportunities. Design, infrastructure development, construction, utilities, engineering, environmental consulting, finance, software and hardware, and real estate are just some of the industries already involved in smart city projects around the world. As already mentioned, some in the industry estimate a market for 500 such cities in China alone, and the problems they are trying to resolve are common throughout Asia in some of the most densely populated countries in the world. Similar projects are getting attention elsewhere. Rio de Janeiro is taking on smart city principles in constructing the 2016 Olympic site, and Rwanda is doing the same in its effort to become a techno-led economic powerhouse in Africa. According to a new survey by MarketsandMarkets, the overall smart cities market, valued at $526.3 billion in 2011, is forecast to double to $1,023.4 billion by 2016, at a CAGR of 14.2 per cent for the period 2011 to 2016.[12]

Replicable approaches

Finally, Cyburbia also recognizes the critical roles that cities play in the global economy, and the notion as Jaime Lerner, former Mayor of Curitiba in Brazil, expressed it, that *'cities are the solution not the problem.'* George Gilder, who made a fortune predicting which ICT stocks would do well based on an intimate understanding of the technology, argued that cities were the leftover baggage of the industrial era which ICT would make redundant because it no longer mattered where one lived.[13] Sixteen years later, cities represent the dwelling place for more than half the people on Earth. They are also praised as the environment that creates 'collaborative brilliance', including disproportionate numbers of patents and innovations in clean technology. Cyburbia also provides the testbed, not just to collaborate but to pilot these innovations for broader rollout. One model of the smart city views the urban environment as 'open-air computers' that produce huge quantities of data that can be used to manage the urban environment more effectively.[14] In addition to being able to control home appliances from any location, access to information about road conditions in real-time reduces traffic and improves air quality. In Stockholm the technology has enabled a road-pricing scheme that shortens the waiting time for vehicles crossing the central district by up to 50 per cent and reduces vehicle emissions by up to 15 per cent.[15] That same data-rich open-air computer makes it easier to keep people safe because the police can monitor data flows to predict crimes before they happen.

Questioning Cyburbia: How Smart is Smart?

On closer examination, there is a paradox to Cyburbia in which there is simultaneously progress away from and regression towards the mass era. The superstructure of the smart city smacks of improvement, but the foundations are the same revolutionary general purpose technology (GPT) whose potential was blocked and then subverted to continue business as usual. The smart city model has many theoretical benefits; but at the same time it could evolve to present social and environmental challenges that threaten its ultimate resilience.

Social exclusion

The first issue is one of inclusivity. New Songdo City will contain just 80000 apartments giving it a population smaller than that of Newcastle upon Tyne

(UK) or Graz (Austria). Five hundred such cities would be the equivalent of ten megacities, but building them is proving expensive. The cost of building Masdar, a smart eco-city in UAE, is estimated to be US$16 billion for a population of just 40000 people, and several green innovations have had to be abandoned to keep the budget under control.[16]

What often emerges from descriptions of the smart city is the impression of an archipelago of islands, linked by the internet but in important ways self-contained and isolated. The blueprint city, as it is currently being developed, is exclusive, welcoming those who have the money, the skills, and the values that it treasures. Good citizens are rewarded with a pleasant lifestyle, but what about those (the vast majority) who are turned away? In Masdar, an army of service workers will descend each day to keep the eco-city groomed, just as similar cohorts tend to the gated communities of Petropolis described in Chapter 4. However, failing an implausible boom in the creation of such cities, most people will be outside the gates and more likely will never see them. These are the people who are central to the demographic change crisis, and for the new city to be a feasible alternative it must acknowledge their situation.

Even with a huge increase in the number of smart green cities, there is little evidence it will be anything other than an exclusive approach. One problem is inequality, and the capital invested in state of the art infrastructure for the few at the expense of the needs of the many. The other is the risk to society of a gated city. As climate change and perhaps social disruption have an impact, these islands may want to protect themselves, investing more of their wealth in resilience and less in stimulating the wider society. If smart cities are successful at fending off natural disasters and social unrest, they will be replicated, perhaps in a bastardized form in which the emphasis is placed on digital protection rather than digital ease. As they grow, they will become more important to the overall economy as a consumer of goods and services, as an investor, and as a protector. The parts of the world reliant on Cyburbia may not have the same knowledge and infrastructure to compete, and will rely more and more on the production and supply of basic commodities that will not generate the wealth needed to reap the demographic dividend or even combat natural disasters and ecosystem degradation. The communities outside of Cyburbia may no longer have the assets needed to trade with smart citizens on equal terms.

A broader social issue becomes apparent when one looks in detail at how ICT might be deployed in the smart city. The risk stems from Cyburbia's top down design, created by experts from their blueprint vision of the city. These cities have many business benefits: the potential for mass production, each one acting as a template for the next, enabling them to be built ever more quickly and cheaply. They consume mass produced goods just as twentieth-century cities did, and because they are often described as innovation hubs serving the needs of the world at large, they are ultimately reliant on mass markets. From inside the bubble they may seem revolutionary, but looked at as part of the entire industrial ecosystem, they are no different in functional terms from the model towns of the Victorian era. They are solidly rooted in the complex interlocking high capex systems of the mass era, and the inequalities as well as the ecosystem degradation they produce.

Environmental disconnection

There is nothing about their relationship to the natural environment that contradicts this conclusion. A lot of attention is paid to the cities' place in nature, but the environment is treated as something to be preserved rather than something to be stewarded. For all of the talk of sustainability, there is no mention of sustenance, and ultimately the smart city depends on what the world beyond its gates can provide. Its model is product-in, trash-out. There is a theme running through descriptions of the cities that nature has been conquered (e.g. by reclaiming land from the sea) and a man-made version of nature is being constructed around and inside the communities, not just with trees, lakes, and parks, but through eco-friendly buildings conforming to architectural standards of what sustainability means.

Civic disengagement

This treatment of nature as something to be dominated but at the same time kept at a distance is evident as well in the society Cyburbia seems to encourage and applaud. There is an environmental disconnect from nature, and a social disconnect from the world beyond the city gates. For all the emphasis put on connectivity, there is an undercurrent of civic disengagement. Is Cyburbia a place one belongs to or escapes from, either by means of the transport systems and nearby international airports, or by losing oneself in work and the array of entertainment available from one's home? Many such cities were built to be detached from a wider sense of citizenship, designed as free trade zones that reject conventional ways of ensuring the welfare of the local community. They are also built from scratch so that every inhabitant is an immigrant who may have more affinity with online communities, work colleagues, and geographically dispersed family and friends, than with his or her neighbours. They are citizens without a common culture, traditions, and way of life.

Even if this was not the case, the way the GPT is used in the smart city can be a barrier to community and gives the sense of inhabiting 'the geography of nowhere'. You may want to help your neighbour whose lights have gone, but there are limited opportunities to do this when whole electrical units have to be replaced rather than simply a fuse. The chances are that public space is

137

privately owned and monitored by security guards to keep citizens safe. Auto-mation of services makes it impossible even for willing citizens to carry out the acts that build community, and in the process this increases the hazards of inactivity such as ill-health.[17] Once the technology of the city is able to open and close, turn on and shut off everything from a toaster to Telepresence, the opportunities to be active members of society are diminished, entrenching the move towards frictionless consumption as opposed to engagement.

Digital control

Sassen calls this the 'sensored city' because every action is monitored by sensors and given a meaning.[18] One fear is that networked data make 'our steps through the cityscape increasingly predictable and, eventually, also controllable'.[19] Turkle talks of society experiencing a 'robotic moment' when it can imagine handing its welfare over to machines in ways envisioned by techno-optimists and pessimists of the past such as Verne, Shelley, Welles, and Orwell.[20] Its citizens live in a place whose functions they cannot compre-hend or control, monitored and spied upon by processes they do not know. In the Panopticon, Jeremy Bentham's model for Victorian prisons, a single person could observe everything that was happening. Writers such as Andrew Keen in *Digital Vertigo* describe Cyburbia as a kind of prison in which there is no privacy.[21] As Foucault pointed out, the power of the Panopticon is not that everything is seen, but that people behave as if that is the case and hence discipline their own actions accordingly.[22]

The non-resilient city

In terms of resilience, the prosperity of Cyburbia is not guaranteed, not least because it is so closely linked to the enfeebled mass era that is struggling to succeed even in its own terms, never mind in terms of external congruence. It does not offer any new ways of increasing productivity and generating wealth. One can argue that those who accept Cyburbia have ceded their independence, for the sake of ease, to incumbent industries from the mass era—a conflux of big oil and big auto, big finance, and big data—that are seeking the latest pocket of superior rents to exploit. But there are other risks as well. More than any other type of settlement, Cyburbia is built on the prospect of continual growth in order that it can constantly upgrade itself. An out of date smart city is a contradiction in terms because once the technol-ogy is redundant, the city itself faces decline. In traditional cities, the landscape is remade in people's image: what has been termed a type of 'open-source urbanism' in which cities are remade through a myriad of interventions and little changes from the ground up.[23] Smart cities by contrast are planned and their technology is hidden from and incomprehensible to most of their inhabitants. Not only does this profoundly affect the relationship between citizen and city, it makes Cyburbia a closed system at risk of obsolescence, and lacking in resilience in the face of climate change or social upheaval. The occupants of the smart city also lack resilience because they are dependent on others to make the system work. Perhaps experts at their particular jobs, they are also at risk of obsolescence themselves if they become so deskilled and dependent that they cannot adapt to the consequences of the crises quadrilemma. In fact, Cyburbia can be accused of producing the very opposite type of city and citizen that our quadrilemma of crises demand. Cyburbia is the mass-produced, high capex, non-resilient city. The risk is that even its putative green credentials prove false when the city itself becomes redundant. Cyburbia risks elevating the unit of disposal in consumer capitalism to a new level, the level of the city.

Cyburbia: built in obsolescence?

The problem with Cyburbia as a solution to society's current incongruence is twofold. First, it is not using the latest GPT to break away from the malfunctioning mass era; on the contrary, it does not offer a substantial alternative to that era at all. Second, it is producing a type of city and citizen that is ill-equipped to utilize the quadrilemma of crises to increase prosperity, or even to survive them. The model Cyburbia citizen is passive, narrowly focused, an expert, whereas the crises require imagination, creativity, flexibility, and a grasp of many disciplines. The smart city, meanwhile, values order, reliability, and predictability; it is exclusive and designed to protect itself from the unknown; it is also high maintenance, prone to obsolescence, and lacks the tools of resilience associated with more conventional communities. By contrast, the uncertainties related to climate change and the often unpredictable consequences of demographic change seem to require that the urban environment be lithe rather than rigid, with the capacity to adapt to the unforeseen, and a surplus of physical assets and human knowledge to develop imperfect but practicable solutions.

All told, the proposed city of the future has the DNA of the past: it has a light green varnish but underneath it is constructed on mass. Cyburbia does little to ignite a new techno-economic paradigm: instead, it is a place where technology is used less to enable real productivity and the flourishing of citizens than the closing of a construction contract. The attitude to humanity embodied in Cyburbia was summed up by T.S. Eliot:

> They constantly try to escape
> From the darkness outside and within
> By dreaming of systems so perfect that no one will need to be good.[24]

139

We may be ambivalent about the type of life one could enjoy in Cyburbia, but the more important issue is whether these cities help address society's and business's turnaround challenge. They do not seem to provide an escape from the mass era, but maybe this would matter less if they could deliver the kind of productivity gains some of our Oracles claimed would allow society to grow its way out of the crises. There is no evidence of this, and the application of ICT innovation to make sushi slicing robots, car elevators, and popcorn ejected automatically into our mouths, as we have seen, suggests that technology does not automatically raise productivity. In Japan, a group of grandmothers rose up in protest against nano-bots that had been programmed to care for them and monitor and report back on their progress. However, perhaps similar technology could be put to different and more productive uses. 1.8 million years ago, human ancestors in the Olduvai Gorge were using hand axes: they controlled the tool; the technology did not control them. In Cyburbia, technology is leading the way, and defining the kind of life people want to lead. Is there a third city where the next GPT is deployed to help society flourish?

This is the option that we explore in the next chapter.

Notes

1. Songdo publicity material citd in http://www.independent.co.uk/news/world/asia/new-songdo-city-atlantis-of-the-far-east-1712252.html, accessed 24 October 2012
2. http://www.independent.co.uk/news/world/asia/new-songdo-city-atlantis-of-the-far-east-1712252.html, accessed 24 October 2012
3. http://newsroom.cisco.com/feature-content?type=webcontent&articleId=633196, accessed 24 December 2012
4. http://archrecord.construction.com/news/daily/archives/090204korea.asp, accessed 24 December 2012
5. http://newsroom.cisco.com/feature-content?type=webcontent&articleId=630153, accessed 24 December 2012
6. Conference overview 'Sustainable Cities of the Future Conference' (2009). http://www.cisco.com/web/KR/scc/index.html
7. http://www.greenbiz.com/bio/marie-hattar, accessed 24 December 2012
8. http://www.puglieseco.com/page/destiny-florida.html, accessed 14 November 2012
9. http://avp4.info/destiny/assets/the-new-American-dream.pdf, accessed 14 November 2012
10. (Lindsay 2010)
11. (Glaeser 2011)
12. (http://www.marketsandmarkets.com/Market-Reports/smart-cities-market-542.html)

13. (Cohen 2000)
14. (*The Economist* 2012); (Ratti, Townsend 2011)
15. (Ratti, Townsend 2011)
16. http://www.thenational.ae/business/energy/masdar-city-clips-another-2-5bn-from-price-tag, accessed 1 November 2012
17. (Pratt et al. 2012)
18. (Sassen 2012)
19. (Pietsch et al. 2012)
20. (Turkle 2011)
21. (Keen 2012)
22. (Foucault 1979)
23. (Sassen 2012)
24. (Eliot 1934)

7

The Return of the Optimist

IN THIS CHAPTER

Explanation of a third option for business and society. Examples of new business models from around the world. How alternative approaches to business generate profit and growth. Why the distinctive features of the new models create the possibility of a new type of capitalism. How the third option tackles the quad-rilemma of crises and builds congruence.

> *'We're bringing the factory back to the individual.'*
>
> Bre Pettis

Beyond Petropolis and Cyburbia

For a long time, the mass era was an outstanding success. Although not everyone enjoyed its benefits, it improved the quality and length of life of unprecedented numbers and became the aspiration for many more. It created the Petropolis in which fossil fuel-powered energy altered the face of production, consumption, and leisure. It made it possible to think of trade as a cause of peace rather than war, and in many countries it broke down hierarchies and increased social mobility.

Nowadays society is witnessing the limits of the mass era, and the Petropolis mirrors its pathologies rather than its aspirations. The fact that emerging economies are enjoying economic growth and new levels of prosperity does not alter that situation. The mass era does not become viable again simply because it is replicated in new locations. In countries that benefited from a thriving Petropolis in the past, the troubles today (e.g. falling incomes, social insecurity, the wealth divide) are different from those in emerging economies (e.g. reaping the demographic dividend, managing wealth), but ultimately the underlying situation is the same.

The mass era is externally incongruent because of climate change and demographic change. In the past, that could be dismissed as a problem to be tackled in the future: now the future has arrived. But external incongruence is not the only difficulty: the mass era is riddled with internal incongruence as well. For all of the effort put into boosting productivity, the return on assets is in long-term decline, and this is worsening because of increasingly lower levels of energy return on energy invested as we showed in Chapter 4. The justification for capitalism is in jeopardy, and in Chapter 5 we showed how the prolonged war between the financial and real economies has worsened economic disparity and social dysfunction. The opportunity to rectify that situation was squandered when the general purpose technology associated with ICT was coopted to perpetuate the mass era, rather than establish a new era of congruence. Thus, for all of the emphasis placed on greening the mass era as the only feasible option, to do so only exacerbates external incongruence. In looking for alternatives to reclaim our rights to optimism, we must therefore leave Cyburbia and the Petropolis and their progeny and look elsewhere.

Techno-Optimism Revisited

In Chapter 3, we were sceptical about what we called techno-optimism in the form of geo-engineering because it relied on lobbing the unavailable and untried into the unknown at an uncertain moment in the future. There are other strands of techno-optimism emerging, however.

The era of abundance

If the first school, the geo-engineering school, focuses its attention on transforming the Earth's biosphere. A second focuses with laser clarity on the human being. For techno-optimists like Diamandis and Kotler, what we are about to enjoy is a new era of abundance. They believe that radical progress will be made in overcoming scarcity by the transformative application of ICT to the world's hardest problems. What lies ahead is digital abundance. Improvements in health care, for example, will radically extend life spans, with the possibility of halting the process of the ageing of cells. 'Deathists,' a new class of cyber-pessmisist, are those who don't believe in the merits or possibilities of eternal life or wish to set boundaries to the scientific advances that would create it. The mathematician, John von Neumann, spoke in the 1950s of 'ever accelerating progress of technology and changes in the mode of human life, which gives the appearance of approaching some essential singularity in the history of the race beyond which human affairs, as we know them, could not continue.' The Singularity, the moment when the collected computing intelligence exceeds and converges with human intelligence, will be accelerated by the internet of things, and its distribution of brain to computer interfaces, providing a non-linear advance in our capacity to solve problems. This moment is predicted by Ray Kurzweil of Singularity University to occur around 2045. Vernon Vinge more optimistically for adherents of this vision predicts some time before 2030.

Backing up the biosphere

Should these technological advances fail to provide the solutions we are looking for, Elon Musk, founder of PayPal, Tesla, and now SpaceX, has a complementary vision: to use space travel as a means to get us to Mars—a project as he puts it to 'back-up the biosphere' in case we run into some limits on Earth.

This second strand of techno-optimists has undoubted merits in its potential to drive forward the boundaries of science. Two core issues emerge, though. The first is social. While these advances may bring, for example, medical benefits, how widely distributed will these be? Are we at risk of creating a medical plutonomy with eternal life offered to the few while health budgets continue to be unable to meet the needs of the many? More broadly, as Jaron Lanier asks in *You Are Not A Gadget*, how desirable for society is the type of vision embedded in the Singularity? The model of the human brain, connected to a series of adjacent brains and hard drives as part of one collective intelligence, is a digital recreation of the assembly line, reducing the human being to a neural factor of production. It is a model that increases our technological capabilities but reduces our autonomy.

On the environmental side, there is a further issue. If Cyburbia escalated the unit of disposal to the city level, the vision of the radical techno-optimists raises it to the level of the planet. Trash the Earth, move to Mars. Mars is though, in real estate terms, what Elon Musk calls a 'fixer-upper' of a planet.

Optimism about people

We have shown two strands of techno-optimism. The first, geo-engineering, offers nothing that is both safe and scalable. It risks moral hazard also, offering the carbon equivalent of a slim-fast diet pill that allows society to maintain the carbon binge confident of the pill's future efficacy. The second was the more radical engineering around the interface of brain and computers, with the potential creation of trans-humans, eternal life, the Singularity, and a back up biosphere.

Neither option, in our assessment, meets the tests laid down of adequacy and achievability as solutions to the challenges that confront us. Previous shifts in the techno-economic paradigm have shown that the transition is contingent. Both the speed at which the new technology emerges, and the specific form it takes depend on the responses of dominant institutions. Mass production, as Carlota Perez has noted, took three different forms under the consumer capitalism of the USA, under Nazism, and in the Soviet Union. Could the ICT GPT have a third form that is capable of meeting the challenges we face? Can ICT address these real questions? Is there a form of optimism that is not Cyburbian optimism about technology but about people, with technology playing a supporting role?

In search of productivity

To answer this question we need to get back to the root of the function of the GPT. Crisis is the essence of capitalism, according to Schumpeter: it is the fuel for the waves of creative destruction that keep capitalism alive. As academics such as Abramovitz and Solow have shown, conventional measures of capital and labour inputs cannot account for 90 per cent of economic growth in advanced industrialized countries. Technological change is what is key.

During what Perez calls phases of gestation and irruption, new general purposes technologies appear and spread due to four main characteristics:

- A wide scope for improvement and elaboration
- Applicability across a wide variety of uses
- Potential to be used in various products and processes
- Strong complementarities with existing or potential new technologies.

Stephenson, Carnegie, and Ford were part of the GPT revolutions of their day. Ford's achievement was to take a technology that had been the toy of the rich for many years, and focus it on customer needs. The Model T was not about speed or leather upholstery: it was about increasing trade, mobility, and empowerment. It brought new power to new people to achieve new things, and all the time the cost of production tumbled to make it affordable to an ever greater number of customers.

The core function of a new GPT, then, is to increase productivity, lower costs and increase capabilities. But as Solow points out, when it comes to ICT, reports of improved productivity show up everywhere except in the statistics. In other words, ICT did everything to create the appearance of prosperity (not least through financial engineering), but nothing to strengthen the real economy as the data on the constant fall in return on assets showed in Figure 2.3.

Getting to the heart of the crisis

The root cause, according to Joseph Stiglitz,[1] of the current 'great stagnation' cannot be resolved by fixing the financial sector: it can only be done by addressing the real economy. Finance, he argues, is a distraction in the search for real solutions, ones that reconsider the kinds of jobs people have, the kind they need, and the kind that are being lost. The mass era took care of those problems for a long time. When it went global, it spread the same justification of capitalism to a wider audience, but it threw the real economy in many OECD countries into what Stiglitz calls a dislocation that has never been squarely faced. Furthermore, the quadrilemma of crises mean that similar issues will spread more rapidly than anticipated to emerging economies as well. For Stiglitz, the current situation is a crisis of production: who is making what.

This is nothing new. During the Great Depression of the 1930s, workers moved from agriculture to mass manufacturing, and a similar phenomenon has been seen in emerging economies since the 1980s. However, the emergence of the ICT general purpose technology—which should have had the same effect on productivity as Arkwright's mill or Ford's assembly lines—has yet to deliver a phase change with a similar impact on productivity, jobs, and economic growth. A central question then is this: can ICT rebuild the real economy?

ICT and the distributed economy

To frame the challenge concretely, let us think once again of the people by the roadside in the post-Katrina photo early on in this book (Figure 2.1). How will the type of capitalism embodied in this new economic model benefit hurricane victims on the roadside, or for that matter ones in Burma, the Philippines, and Bangladesh? The people in that picture have plenty of unmet basic needs: no adequate water, housing, sanitation, health care, power source, or a long-term food source. Their productivity is threatened because they have no long-term income prospects, no prospect of accessing insurance, and limited opportunities to improve their skills. They are disempowered, lacking a voice to engage with government, their communities are damaged, and their opportunities to capture value from their work are limited. Can ICT usher in a new economic model, one that doesn't just bring real sector growth, but also addresses pressing social and environmental constraints?

We believe that this option exists. Moreover, it is not only possible, it is more plausible than the other two options we have discussed. The Petropolis exists only by exacerbating the existential threat of climate change. Examples of thriving Cyburbia are more likely to be found on planners' computers than on the ground. But there are innumerable instances of the third option already independently springing up. We call this third option the distributed economy for reasons that will become clear. It is not exclusive in the way Cyburbia is, nor is it centralized like the Petropolis.

The distributed economy produces cities that more closely resemble a 'polis' in the ancient Greek sense of interdependent urban and rural communities, although we are talking about society as a whole, not simply its towns and cities. It is most definitely a capitalist society because, as we have argued throughout this book, there is no plausible alternative to capitalism within the timeframe available to address the crises. However, it is not a capitalist society like today's model. It contains some of the more useful elements of that model, but mixes them with others that currently are either overlooked or regarded as impossible.

Drivers of new opportunity

Can the GPT of ICT, currently deployed towards Cyburbia, support instead this third city? To answer this, we need to look at what drives a GPT's uptake. Productivity is the acid test. Does the GPT allow new people to do new things? Three factors drive this uptake: (a) the GPT is pervasive in that it spreads to many sectors; (b) it is improved and refined over time and, hence, should keep lowering its users' costs; (c) it makes it easier to invent and produce new products or processes.

Henry Ford's Model T laid down the framework for mass production, and the key principle that products need to be affordable for the common person to buy them. Ford took the car, which JP Morgan had called 'the plaything' of the rich, and made it into a transformational tool for the masses. As we have seen, a series of repercussions followed from his technological and organizational innovations. Figure 7.1 shows the logic of mass production.

- *High product sales*: To achieve market penetration required a low cost product.
- *Low product cost*: This required mass production with increases in productivity over traditional techniques.
- *Low cost assembly line labour*: High plant productivity required improved efficiency of labour with organizational redesign into assembly line processes.
- *High capex plant*: Low labour costs required high levels of automation and high capital intensity plant.
- *Long runs*: High capex plant required long production runs to amortize costs.
- *High investor risk*: Long payback periods before breakeven meant higher risk to investors, and risk-adjusted return to investors.
- *Investor returns*: This demanded intellectual property and brand protection.
- *Brand and IP protection*: Enhanced sales and marketing effectiveness against competitive threats/substitutes, driving increased product sales.

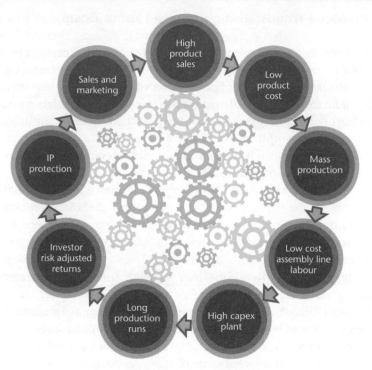

Figure 7.1: The logic of mass production

Challenges to the dominance of mass

As we have shown in our description of the Petropolis, these principles remain intact even though the industries of the real economy have been reshaped by finance. China exemplifies the current model; it is a manufacturing hub designed to allow companies to drive their costs down so that they can compete. Put crudely, one part of the world's task is to produce; the other's is to consume. However two new phenomena are shifting this. The well-documented issues at Foxconn show some of the emerging trends. After a sudden increase of jumping suicides in 2010, Foxconn installed 'suicide cameras' trained on the suicide nets installed at its plants. A full scale riot at the plant in September 2012 added to customer concern, with Apple's chief executive, Tim Cook, ordering an investigation into labour practices. In October 2012 Foxconn revealed that 'interns', some aged 14, had been working at its plants. In December Tim Cook announced that Apple would bring some production of Mac computers back from China to the USA.

Colliding Mega-trends: Rising Chinese Labour Costs . . .

There are two trends emerging behind the Foxconn example. The first is increasing Chinese labour costs. In China, and some other emerging economies, there is increasing upward pressure on wages. In China this stems from a number of factors; from the rising middle class to increasing labour unrest to national-level commitments to reduce inequality in order to stimulate long-term domestic consumption. As Wang Xiaolu, deputy director of China's National Economic Research Foundation, commented, 'If you reduce income inequality you can improve domestic consumption.'[2]

As a result of these factors, the Ministry of Commerce estimates that wages have risen by 33 per cent in the past three years. The 18th National Party Congress furthermore said it wanted wages for lowly paid workers to double over the next seven years, in line with the nation's economic growth and rapid urbanization.

The second trend is there are other signs of social and environmental externalities that have yet to be internalized into these labour costs. In an article for the *Economic Observer*, Sun Liping, a professor at Tsinghua University, referred to research estimating that there were 180 000 protests, riots, and other mass incidents in China in 2010. As the January 2013 Beijing smog highlighted, the environmental costs of mass production are having an economic impact. A recent (2011) World Bank study estimated the economic cost to the environment (2011) of China's development model to be 8.9 per cent of Gross National Income, at US$650 billion.

In 'consumer' countries such as the USA, meanwhile, foreign labour and shipping costs, together with a variety of risks associated with overseas production are starting to resurrect the case for domestic production. GE, which under Jack Welch had pioneered offshoring, setting up one of the very first offshore service centres in Gurgaon in 1997, has moved the production of appliances from Mexico and China to Kentucky. The GeoSpring water heater, as Charles Fishman recounts in the *Atlantic Monthly*, shows the benefits of the model.[3]

The GeoSpring water heater

When GE started manufacturing the GeoSpring water heater in Louisville rather than China, they made two discoveries. First, no products had been manufactured in Building 2 at Appliance Park since 1998. Old oven doors, partially finished, were hanging from the overhead assembly lines. Their engineers had meanwhile forgotten how to do some complex tasks, like correctly soldering the joints on the complex copper tubing. The second was when they did figure it out, they could make it cheaper. To simplify its

HIDDEN COSTS OF MASS

- Equipment and inventory insurance
- Capital tied up in pre-payments
- Shipping costs
- Currency risks
- Loss of contracts from delays in filling order
- Delivery risks (customs etc.)
- Quality control risks
- Stockout and resupply
- Supplier issues (labour strikes, shut down etc.)

Figure 7.2: Hidden costs of outsourced mass production

manufacture, they eliminated 20 per cent of parts, shaving 25 per cent off the cost of the materials and cutting assembly time from ten hours to two. The China-made GeoSpring retailed for US$1 599. The Louisville-made version hit the shops at US$1 299, 20 per cent cheaper.

As a glance at Figure 7.2 will show, there are a number of hidden costs to outsourced mass production that increase the volatility and uncertainty surrounding the current model.

The hidden costs of mass

To these can be added factors such as resource nationalism, carbon costs, protectionism, and supply chain vulnerability associated with our four crises. While China itself may be outsourcing, this may not provide a solution. Other countries, including Vietnam, Indonesia, and the Philippines, may offer low wages, but they fail to provide China's efficiency, volume, and supply chain infrastructure. The result, as Peter Marsh of the *Financial Times* highlights in *The New Industrial Revolution: Consumers, Globalization and the End of Mass Production*, is the beginnings of a movement towards re-shoring. It may be more of a trickle than a flood, and some highly labour intensive industries such as textiles look set to remain localized where wages are cheapest, but long-term business planning now appears to be revisiting the offshoring model.

Yesterday's model?

Caterpillar, the *Economist* explains in a special report entitled *Coming Home*, is building a new factory in Georgia.[4] Otis Elevator is moving a factory from Mexico to South Carolina, Ford is moving manufacture of medium duty trucks from Mexico to Ohio. Chesapeake Bay Candle is moving from China back to

Maryland. Cleantech companies are also coming home. Seesmart, for example, is a small lighting company in the USA that has decided it makes more sense to manufacture in California than pay the cost of air freight, and deal with the logistical issues faced in China.[5] Seesmart estimates that shifting production from China to the USA has cut logistics costs by about 30 per cent, and, despite higher wages, production in the USA is cheaper than overseas.[6] The same trend is found in other industries: electric motors for windscreen wipers, for example, were 45 per cent cheaper to make in China than in the USA in 2005; now the gap is down to 18 per cent and according to an Alix Partners analysis could fall to 9 per cent in 2015.[7] It is also a phenomenon that goes beyond the USA. In the UK, as James Shotter highlights in the *Financial Times*, Lancashire's Paper Cup Company is following the same logic of re-shoring. After seven years of production in China, a quarter of its production will be moved to a factory in its home town of Clitheroe, with the UK base allowing them to reach customers within three to five days of their ordering.[8]

GE was one of the pioneers of offshoring with its Gurgaon centre outside Delhi in 1997. Jeff Immelt, successor to Welch at GE, is now recruiting several hundred IT specialists at a new centre in Michigan's Van Buren Township and calls outsourcing 'yesterday's model.'

... and Decreasing Costs of Local Manufacturing

A survey by the Hackett Group consultancy found that 46 per cent of executives at European and North American manufacturing companies were considering re-shoring some production to the USA from China. Twenty-seven per cent said they were actively planning for or were in the middle of the process.[9]

Is this optimism about a manufacturing renaissance well-grounded? Is this just temporary labour 'arbitrage,' with companies analysing that the combination of stagnant American and European manufacturing pay and rising Chinese and Indian, may make re-shoring the smart medium-term option? Or could other advances in manufacturing accelerate the speed, volume, and durability of the move towards re-shoring?

The Airbus 380 seat buckle

The seat buckle on the Airbus A380 may give a clue. A standard airplane buckle is made of steel and can weigh as much as 155g. Commercial airplanes can have anything up to 850 of them. Working with the MERLIN consortium of aero engine manufacturers, Rolls Royce coordinated a team to redesign the belt to lower the weight using 3D printing. Making the part with 3D printing (or additive manufacturing) meant it was possible to build a lighter buckle that combined previously welded parts into one, reducing post production finishing as well as weight. When made in Titanium with additive manufacturing, the weight is reduced to 68g without compromising strength. This is a maximum potential weight saving of 87g. This saving, according to Helm and Lambrecht, leads to a 3 300 000 litres fuel saving over the life of the plane and 0.74 Mtonne less CO_2 emissions.[10]

Advances in additive manufacturing

In a first for medicine, a team of medical researchers from Belgium and the Netherlands has replaced the jaw of an 83-year old woman with a 3D printed model. Infection and the patient's age had prevented the doctors from carrying out traditional reconstructive surgery. The researchers, working in conjunction with implant company Xilloc, replaced the entire lower mandible with a 3D printed one.

Back in the aviation sector, Airbus has announced their intention to build entire fuselages with giant 3D printers by 2050. GE, the leading manufacturer of jet engines, made claims that they will manufacture approximately 50 per cent of the jet engine parts with 3D printers by 2016. Figure 7.3 illustrates the potential impact of additive manufacturing on efficiency across traditional value chains.

As Will Sillar, partner at the Legerwood management consultancy which advises companies on 3D printing, comments, 'Up to 50 per cent of the working capital of a business is currently tied up in stock and working capital...

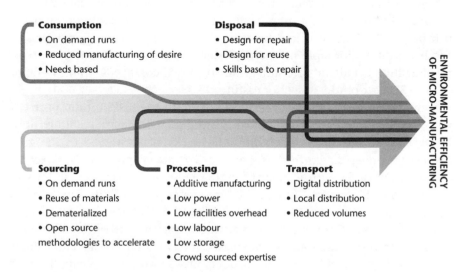

Figure 7.3: The logic of additive manufacturing across the value chain

Eliminate that, and the finance director is going to be the happiest man in the world.'

With all the current excitement around additive manufacturing, it is tempting to pronounce eulogies over the corpse of mass-production based subtractive manufacturing. The reality is additive manufacturing is only just beginning to emerge from its niche as an R & D technology into something that has potential for manufacturing. It has nevertheless started to make progress in grappling with the core challenges it faces, around speed, range of materials, cost, and quality.

Towards the democratization of making

In terms of ease of use, Google Sketchup gives easy design in three dimensions. FARO Technologies produces a handheld laser that you can point at an object. The laser will create a CAD/CAM file of what you're pointing at in real time. If you see a vase, you point your laser and click and get a 3D replica waiting on your desk. Pirate Bay, the prime source of illegal downloads, now offers downloadable physical object models, called Physibles, that could make 3D files widely available. Society is a long way off that, but if the evolution of hardware continues to parallel the digitization of print and media, the next step is the arrival of a 3D equivalent to iTunes. This potential 3D iTunes, formalizing 3D downloads as iTunes formalized music downloads, would have a transformational impact on retail production and distribution.

The quality of materials also is evolving rapidly. 3D Systems raised the bar when they came up with Nano composites, different blends of plastics, and different blends of powdered metals. These improvements in materials from waxy plastic to steel substitutes have driven 3D from printing prototypes to printing parts. Stratasys now has three main technologies: Fused Deposit Modeling (FDM) for rapid prototype design, PolyJet for high-end prototypes needing high detail and fine surface finish, and Solidscape Drop-on-Demand ('DoD') 3D wax printers used for casting.

Some 120 types of material are now used across the 3D printing spectrum, with combinations of colours, and companies such as Organovo bio-printing living tissues. Bond's Aston Martin DB5 in Skyfall, destroyed to the great dismay of global car enthusisasts, was a 3D model, printed by Voxeljet's massive 3D printer with a capacity of 283 cubic feet. Each car, at 1:3 size, was assembled from 18 individual components with real-life functionality including opening doors, trunks, and hoods but not an ejector seat.

The challenge of raw materials remains. While most 3D printers use oil-based resins or plastics, some are bio plastic such as polylactic acid that allows you to grow your own 3D supply. Filabot is already working to create a system that will grind up waste plastics and turn them into 3D printing filament.

Transport Intelligence estimates that by 2016, 50 per cent of products will involve some form of additive as opposed to subtractive manufacturing, and by 2020 potentially up to 80 per cent.[11] As Bre Pettis, CEO of MakerBot Industries, comments, '[W]e're bringing the factory back to the individual.'

Finally, in terms of cost, while the costs of basic desktop 3D printers have dropped to around US$600, the Rep Rap3D printer is open source and comes with instructions on how to print other 3D printers. It is, in other words a freely downloadable and self-replicating printer.

Structural or Surface Change?

Wikispeed: disruptive change in action

But, for all the buzz around 3D production, is there in all of this, 100 years after Henry Ford, the potential to undo the logic of Fordism? To get a feel for what this could look like, let us examine another car, constructed around principles as foreign to mainstream manufacturing as the Model T was to artisanal craftsmen in 1908.

Joe Justice and the Wikispeed team set themselves a target: to build a car that can do 100 mph, plus meet all road-legal safety requirements, plus one extra dimension, that none of the big auto companies have mastered. Do 100 miles to the gallon, slashing carbon emissions. Plus be switchable to electricity for areas where there's charging. And have a chassis that you could switch from sports car to SUV.

Justice had no cash, no equipment, no factory, no auto experience (his background was software) but he knew how to blog, and he liked the sound of winning the Progressive Insurance X Prize—the US$10 million prize for a working prototype for a 100 mpg car that had got him thinking about it, and beyond, in the first place. Three months later, he had a team of 44 members in four countries and a functioning prototype. Within six months they had produced the C3, Comfortable Commuter Car (C3). Top speed 149 mph, 100 mpg, switchable from gas to electric, fully compliant with the USA Department of Transport road-legal safety specifications. Price range US $18000 for an on-the-road vehicle, and US$10000 for a kit you can assemble yourself.

In its present form, it looks as primitive as the Apple II or the Acorn computers once did, but to that extent it may bear the hallmark of disruptive innovations. As Christensen pointed out in the *Innovator's Dilemma*, such innovations look so basic the competition does not register them as threats; but they can improve fast, and gain market share to the point where the incumbents cannot catch up.

BARRIER TO ENTRY	TECHNOLOGIES AVAILABLE AND WIKISPEED RESULT
Team recruitment	Open source/crowd-source inputs (Community noticeboards, social media) • 100+ volunteers, in 8 countries, high levels of intrinsic motivation
Design	Open source software (rapid prototyping, visualization tools) and Open source hardware (e.g. Raspberry Pi computer built for hackability) • Speed of design: 3 weeks for design from new, contrasted to auto-industry multi-year cycle • Cost of design: Iterated a process that brought the cost/time of a full structural carbon fibre car body down to $800/3 days • Car built for further re-design: 8 core modules, with protocols on docking/interoperability. Every system in the car can be as modified rapidly as a tire change
Seed finance	**Crowd-financing** • Indiegogo financing of prototype underway
Access to finance	**Working protoype** • Working prototypes used as model to attract potential investors, reducing investor risk
Printing and production	**Additive printing** • 3D printing techniques available for rapid prototyping and low cost additive printing approach • Reduced all costs in tooling, machinery, and complexity to eliminate sunk costs and allow immediate redesign • The parts for the frame of the car can be built with stock 4" aluminum tube, an US$80 band saw, and a used-kit-built CNC milling machine

Figure 7.4: Technology and the shrinking barriers to entry to manufacturing

Part of the story is technology. Figure 7.4 shows the impact of new technology is reducing barriers to entry, and not just 3D printing but a stew of less publicized machinery. They may not yet be, as Chris Anderson, in *Makers*, describes them, 'ankle high.' But they have started to drop.

As important as the innovation in technology, though, is the innovation in process. The approaches of Wikispeed reverse the efficiency-focused principles of production and operations management that have come to be known as Taylorism.

- *Collaboration, not silos*: The C3 was built using distributed, collaborative teams with access to free online tools. They worked in pairs because putting a newcomer with an experienced person reduces training time. 'Equipotentiality' replaces hierarchy with all valued for their potential and leadership is context specific, based on the ability to contribute to the task at hand.

- *Last minute decisions*: Decisions are made at the last responsible moment because this is when there is the most knowledge available to find the best solution. The typical approach is to start with the minimum useful solution and then take that through an iterative process to improve visible value and come up with an efficient solution.

- *Open source IP*: The Wikispeed project uses open source IP with creative commons legal licences, reducing legal fees, contracting and process. Contracts focus on what matters to quality, including issues like the docking of component parts that are essential to the modular approach.

- *Design for testing at subcomponent levels*: Rather than testing the final product, Wikispeed carries out immediate testing of all designs e.g. passing the 100 mpg criterion.

- *Intrinsic motivation*: Test passes are celebrated. Where tests fail, teams 'swarm' the problem with fresh perspectives, not anchored in previous approaches, to identify rapid solutions.

Ford versus Wikispeed

As the eminent economist John Kenneth Galbraith said of Henry Ford, 'If there is any certainty as to what a businessman is, he is assuredly the things Ford was not.' A century later, the same could be said of the Wikispeed team. A comparison of the model above with aspects of the value chain of industry leader, Apple, reveals the extent to which Wikispeed is defying mainstream business practice.

There are not many people in modern corporations who are yet to be told the importance of team-work, trust, efficiency, and so on, but there are genuine differences between Wikispeed and the car industry of the Ford era. The C3 is easy to maintain, for instance, (just like the Model T) and that reduces the temptation to dispose of it at regular intervals. It has been funded partly through crowd-sourcing which enables lots of people to put small amounts of money quickly into projects they like. Profits are distributed amongst contributors to the project in a way that Justice claims generates the same amount of profit, but in a way that is more equitable. There is also the possibility that in such a system labour stops being seen as a cost in accounting terms, and is recognized as an asset: if not, the dispersed nature of the contributor/labour

SOURCING	PRODUCTION	DISTRIBUTION	CONSUMPTION	DISPOSAL
• Scarce metals • Petroleum based • Water intensive	• Outsourcing • Labour issues in supply chain • Iconic design Designer as hero	• Plane cargo • Legal copyright • Closed system (iTunes)	• Design-based obsolescence ('This changes everything') • Product incompatibility • Managed timeline of introductions	• Unfixable • Designed for replacement

Figure 7.5: Apple value chain: the logic of late stage mass production

force means they can up and leave, taking their skills and experience to the next collaborative project. This is in keeping with the newest of capitalism's orders of worth, the networked world touched upon in Chapter 5; a world of heightened employment insecurity in the Petropolis or Cyburbia, but one that lends itself to a new type of inclusivity and engagement in the distributed economy.

One of the biggest differences between Wikispeed and Henry Ford is that the former lends itself to low capex, micro-production that allows the C3 to be built almost anywhere, and is not dependent on high capex factories and distribution networks. Wikispeed is not unique. The Open Source Ecology network has identified and designed 50 technologies that it considers essential for a sustainable, comfortable life, ranging from cars to wind turbines to 3D printers. These comprise the Global Village Construction Set and are intended to be built almost anywhere: for instance in FabLabs, small-scale workshops that offer the facilities to fabricate almost any digital device normally associated with mass production.[12]

The contributors to Wikispeed, and the creators of the Global Village Construction Set may all look back to the Apple II as the model of inspired imperfection that they are emulating, but the modern Apple Mac exemplifies how different their approaches to manufacturing are (Figure 7.5). Whether one is looking at labour, intellectual property, R&D, human resources, customers, shareholder value, the legal basis, or the manufacturing process, the different underlying philosophies of mass manufacturing and manufacturing in the distributed economy are clear. Central to the difference is the role of the worker. Where Fordism and Taylorism aimed to reduce labour as a cost, the distributed economy uses technology to unleash it as the central unit of value added.

Relaxing control of the means of production

In other words it is a shift in the control of the means of production, with new tools and processes that democratize production and put it back in the hands of the small business and maker. Technologically, these advances are exciting because they put a factory in a metaphorical suitcase. However, in terms of society they promise a shift from a system in which valuable machines were run by cheap people, to one where valuable people run cheap machines.

The model of the distributed economy, then, uses advances in nanotechnology and 3D printing to lower barriers to entry and put manufacturing back within the hands of small business. But just as important, as the example of Wikispeed shows, is the open process that reverses conventional assumptions around labour. Instead of squeezing commodity labour costs to boost productivity, it aims to mobilize the range of unused assets that the community can bring. The classic example of the value of the crowd is the apocryphal tale of an audience guessing the weight of the prize pig at the market. This is the mass production view of the crowd, a view that reduces it to a data point on a spreadsheet. A broader range of forms of productive crowd collaboration is beginning to emerge.

- *Asset matching*: The average car sits idle for twenty-two out of 24 hours. Building on the successful models of ZipCar and AirBnB, Wikit uses a GPS device to connect up available cars and drivers, with software to match location and willingness to pay. 'The future of transportation will be a blend of things like ZipCar, public transportation, and private car ownership,' says Bill Ford, Executive Chairman of Ford.

- *Capital*: Crowd financing sites such as Indiegogo, MyC4, Kiva, and Kickstarter tap into crowd willingness to invest, often for 'blended returns' that combine the economic with the social or environmental.

- *Network*: social media sites and online fora from Tumblr to Twitter generate crowd technical input and momentum. For Wikispeed it made the difference between one man in a garage and a network of 100 + volunteers.

- *Specialist knowledge*: Wikipedia is the result of some 120 million hours devoted voluntarily to the project of universal free access to knowledge. The Wikipedia project to build an online encyclopaedia currently has an estimated 67 000 active contributors working on over 4.6 million articles in more than 100 languages.

Unlocking the genius of the crowd

The open approach also brings in the possibility of unlocking the genius of the crowd. Major Peter Flynn of the British Army was stationed outside Kabul and discovered that his satellite communications system was not working. A local teenager came up and asked if they needed a satellite. Within three hours the boy had turned a bag of Lilt and Coke cans into a satellite dish that could

159

receive 360 channels, including Al Jazeera broadcasts that were used to brief Flynn's brigadier.

Another Afghan, Massoud Hassani more recently has built Mine Kafon, a US $53 mine clearer. According to one report, about 1 million Afghans live within 500 metres of areas expected to contain landmines. The device, inspired by childhood toys he would play with in Afghanistan, rolls across the fields with the wind. This 'Mine Kafon' is a spherical mobile made out of biodegradable plastic and bamboo, light enough to roll but heavy enough to set off land-mines as it rolls over them. With each detonation the Mine Kafon loses just one or two legs so it could potentially destroy three or four landmines in one journey.

It is a phenomenon that taps into the skills of generations brought up with manufacturing. The USA's Air Force Research Laboratory put out a call for innovations to help disable fleeing get away vehicles safely without high speed chases that threatened other motorists. A sixty-six year old retired mech-anical engineer from Lima, Peru, won the challenge with a simple idea. A remote controlled miniature vehicle, armed with an air bag, would accelerate under the car. The air bag would then inflate, leaving the vehicle immobilized.

Meanwhile GE has launched a US$100 000 prize for a model that could help civil pilots improve their decision-making process with 'real time business intelligence.' A 2008 analysis by the Joint Economic Committee of the US Congress suggested that domestic air traffic delays in 2007 alone cost the economy as much as US$41 billion, including US$19 billion in increased operational costs for the airlines and US$12 billion worth of lost time for passengers. The GE model would allow them to make adjustments to their flight patterns.[13]

Madness

The crowd can also outfox even the British Geological Survey. On the evening of the 8th of August 1992, the police station at Finsbury Park, London started getting calls. Apparently there was an earthquake in London. Tower blocks were shaking, concrete cracking, residents fleeing their blocks. With quaking estimated at 5.0 on the Richter scale, the police ordered the evacuation of the building and contacted the British Geological Survey for emergency advice. Evacuate, came the response. As residents assembled on the streets, a local, Alice Walker, called the police and told them she thought the rumbling could be a Madness concert at Finsbury Park. In the words of lead singer Suggs, 'It was the first time we'd opened a gig with "One Step Beyond", and it's a fairly up-tempo song, so there were about 45 000 medium to large middle-aged men all jumping up and down at the same time.' Result: one 'earthquake'.

The combination of nanotechnology, 3D printing, and the Open Source Movement present shifts in manufacturing. The first is new tools; a range of manufacturing tools turn processes into low cost tasks for startups, that used to take a factory. These include precision milling and lathing tools, and rapid prototyping and 3D printing. The second is new processes; new processes and protocols around Agile Manufacturing and Open Sourcing allow small business to reduce the costs of production.

But how big a deal is this? Is this fringe? Or are these cost lowering shifts that have the potential, like Ford's Model T one hundred years ago, to transform markets? Should it make us more optimistic about the quadrilemma of crises?

Drogba and D.Light

In 2010, the British Museum and the BBC listed the 100 objects that explained the history of the world. They included the Olduvai hand axe we mentioned in the last chapter, and went through the steam engine and semi-conductor on to the present day. The choice of the final two objects lay between Didier Drogba's football shirt, and a solar-powered portable light called D.Light. In what could have been an allegory for the struggle between the Petropolis and the distributed economy, the shirt of an Ivorian striker playing in London wearing clothes designed in Europe and made in Asia, lost out to a small light-cum-phone charger powered by a solar cell, designed to meet the needs of people without access to the electricity grid.[14]

There is no getting away from the problem of access to power as we discussed earlier. For the world's 1.6 billion without power, there are three difficulties. First, there are the economic costs, estimated at 25–40 per cent of the incomes of the poorest of the poor. Second, there are the health impacts (two million air quality deaths a year according to WHO estimates). The third difficulty is loss of productivity: the main alternative fuel, paraffin, is a scarce and expensive resource. The D.Light, and products like it (e.g. Nokero; 8.19), address all three of these problems. They get rid of the paraffin costs, reduce the health impacts, and lower carbon emissions (estimated at 150 million tonnes a year globally from paraffin for lighting). A study in Karnataka (India) showed D.Light increased study time and raised exam pass rates from 67 per cent to 82 per cent.[15]

But what is interesting about D.Light in terms of scaling up to the 1.6 billion off-grid people it is aimed at, may be not the light itself but a combination of the light and two other inventions that were not on the British Museum list.

Mama Felix and the Pink Lady Salon

Mama Felix runs the Pink Lady Hair Salon in the Mathare slum in Nairobi (Kenya). When mobile phone services launched in sub-Saharan Africa, she was clear how she could benefit. For the first time she could have a phone, and it was cheaper than a landline, and enabled her to make calls to whoever she wanted, whenever she wanted, in or out of the house. As the technology spread, the power of the tool in her hand increased. The more people calling, the more she could call.

Mobile telephony-laying the rails for development

The story of the growth of mobile telephones in Africa is one of rapid and unexpected change in communications technology. Sixty per cent of Africans now have mobile phone coverage compared to almost none in the 1990s and there are now over ten times as many mobile as landline phones in use.[16] Initially this was nothing technologically extraordinary; the early phones could not be used to access the internet, which in any case was read-only. However, in several cases mobile phones could be shown to improve people's welfare. A study on grain traders in Niger, for instance, found phones allowed traders to obtain better information about grain prices across the country without incurring the high cost of having to travel to different markets.[17] Phone-owning traders had 29 per cent higher profits than their competitors. Other studies have suggested that increased mobile ownership is linked to higher economic growth, especially where the starting point of infrastructure is so much lower in terms of landlines and broadband access.[18] A 2012 World Bank study showed mobile phones had a positive impact on eight aspects of the Millennium Development Goals including education, poverty, and health. Mobile technology has lower investment costs than traditional infrastructure, and other benefits include increased telecom-based tax revenues, greater employment opportunities, and overall increased productivity, not to mention a thriving telecom industry that attracts foreign direct investment.

Nonetheless, mobile services for poor people are still expensive, amounting to nearly 16 per cent of monthly average income in developing countries compared to about 5 per cent in more developed ones. Coverage in remote areas is often lacking, and at least 40 per cent of people in the least developed countries are not covered by a mobile network.[19]

Mobiles and the challenge of access to finance

Mobile phones, like D.Light, have been advances in their own right, but their real value is revealed when they are linked to other innovations. As Sam

Goldman, CEO of D.Light, commented, 'The technology is necessary, but insufficient.' The first problem is access to finance. Roughly one billion people with a mobile phone have no bank account. The absence of such basic financial services slows economic growth, and worsens inequality.[20] *The Economist* picked up on a breakthrough in this area in Kenya; its headline, 'Dial M for money: Beating banks at their own game.'[21] The story concerned M-PESA, a mobile-payment scheme run by Vodafone and Safaricom, a Kenyan telecoms operator, with the backing of the British government's Department for International Development. M-PESA is an alternative to banks, and most of its customers have no bank account. Instead, they withdraw cash, make payments, and transfer money using their mobile phones.

The M-PESA story has been told a number of times in business books.[22] What it helped to deliver for people like Mama Felix was another key capacity, the power to transfer money. It uses simple SMS technology, but it enhanced productivity, reducing the time, cost, and risk of money transfer. When riots broke out in Nairobi after contested elections, mobile phone users, able to transfer and receive funds, buffered themselves against the costs of disruption. In Kenya in general, households with access to mobile money are better able than those without to manage negative shocks (e.g. job loss, death of live-stock, problems with harvests), and in such circumstances households without M-PESA saw consumption fall by 6–10 per cent, while M-PESA users were often able to fully absorb the shocks due to receiving more remittances and losing less to transaction costs.[23]

In 2008, Vodafone partnered with Roshan, Afghanistan's primary mobile operator, to provide 'M-Paisa,' a new brand of M-PESA. It was initially used to pay police salaries, and soon after it was launched the Afghan National Police found that under the previous cash model, 10 per cent of their workforce did not exist; their salaries had been taken by others. The funds recovered were then used to increase police wages. However, the police are not the only financial beneficiaries. M-PESA quickly captured a significant market share for cash transfers, and grew quickly, capturing 17 million subscribers by December 2011 in Kenya alone. The same explosive growth was also reflected in the increase in M-PESA agents which grew to over 18 000 service locations by April 2010, from a base of approximately 450 in mid-2007. This compares to just 491 bank branches throughout Kenya, 500 postal-bank branches, and 352 ATMs.[24] Three and a half years after its launch, over 70 per cent of Kenya's households and more significantly over 50 per cent of poor, unbanked rural populations are M-PESA users.[25] According to the Communications Commission of Kenya (CCK), between September 2010 and 2011 69.5 per cent of mobile subscribers—18.4 million people—use M-PESA. Safaricom, the mobile operator offering M-PESA, reported mobile money revenues for the first half of 2011 equivalent to

US$90 million. In addition, cash agents also gain commercial benefit from the fees they receive.

Mobiles and the challenge of access to energy

Despite the mobile phones and M-PESA, Mama Felix still faced a problem: the robust solar systems of the type that she could use to light the salon after dusk were too expensive. This is where M-KOPA, the second brainchild of Nick Hughes one of the initiators of M-PESA, comes in. M-KOPA Solar set out to remove barriers to market uptake by making solar home systems affordable and accessible to low income consumers. In October 2012, M-KOPA partnered with Safaricom to launch the first ever GSM (Global System for Mobile Communications) enabled pay-as-you-go solar solution that customers could pay for using mobile money. This credit-sale model is targeted at low income households in rural areas currently dependent on paraffin for lighting and local mobile service locations for phone charging. This market includes about three million homes that spend a significant portion of their daily income on paraffin and charging.

M-KOPA Solar allows customers the use of a D.Light solar home system that has a Safaricom enabled SIM card in it. Using M-PESA, they pay installments of Kshs 40 a day for 12 months, about Kshs 30 less than the cost of paraffin and charging. They also have to pay an initial deposit of US$30. In return, they get the M-KOPA system comprising a base-station with a solar panel, three lamps and a charging kit for phones. This is equivalent to an entire electrical system for a small house which would normally cost around US$200. Customers in Kenya pay US$30 up front and then pay off the balance in small installments using their mobile phones until they eventually own it outright.

Payment is flexible because by using M-PESA, relatives working in the cities can contribute back home, and farmers can vary the size of payments depending on their cash flow. It also provides a mechanism for the government to provide welfare payments to households with infants, or children studying for exams. The base-station is also able to provide a payment record which could be used by banks as a credit history when offering loans or mortgages.[26]

It is a model being adapted elsewhere by initiatives such as Eight19. People new to the concept often dismiss it as non-commercial, government-subsidized aid.[27] However, M-KOPA is a commercial proposition that has had two stages of seed funding. First, in 2010, Signal Point Partners Ltd secured convertible equity and R&D grant funding from the Shell Foundation (UK), DOEN Foundation (Netherlands), and d.o.b foundation (Netherlands). The following year, M-KOPA concluded a Series A investment round of equity and debt financing from investors including Gray Ghost Ventures (USA) and the Acumen Fund (USA). It is now considering offering other 'pay-as-you-go' products to markets in developing countries including irrigation systems, refrigerators for shop-owners to cool drinks and snacks, as well as sewing machines.

Mobiles and the challenge of access to insurance

The convergence of the mobile phone, finance, and energy sectors has been good news for Mama Felix and her fellow businesswomen who can call each other with the mobile service, transfer money via M-PESA, get access to power at prices they can afford, and buy the D.Light system with M-KOPA. However, none of this necessarily results in making money. According to the UN Food and Agricultural Organization, up to 70 per cent of smallholder farmers are women. In Kenya, only half of these invest in improved seeds and nutrition for their crops, often because they fear poor conditions such as drought will make their investment worthless, depriving them of both crops and savings.[28] Insurance is difficult to obtain, expensive, and time consuming with long delays before the eventual payout.

A possible alternative is the Kilimo Salama programme which uses the M-PESA payment system as the basis for micro-insurance for farmers included in every bag of fertilizer they buy. According to the programme's managers, agro-dealers registered and trained by Kilimo Salama have a camera phone which they use to scan a special bar code at the time of purchase. The policy is instantly registered with UAP Insurance via the mobile data network, and this is confirmed by a text message sent to the farmer's mobile phone. Weather stations in the targeted regions broadcast regular updates on rainfall and other weather conditions. When data from a particular station indicates that drought or other extreme conditions (including excessive rains) are likely to affect harvests, all farmers registered with that station automatically receive payouts directly via M-PESA's mobile money transfer service. With access to finance via M-PESA, power via M-KOPA, and insurance via Kilimo Salama, smallholder farmers can mitigate risk allowing them to invest in the land to increase their productivity.

Mobiles and the challenges of clean water

Another way to increase productivity is to keep people healthy. One in eight people in the world lack access to clean, safe drinking water, and this, plus lack of basic sanitation, accounts for 80 per cent of all sickness and disease. According to Water.org, it is a bigger killer than all forms of violence, including war, causing 3.5 million deaths each year. Slingshot is a water purification system that runs on low levels of electricity. The Slingshot unit can be plugged into the local grid or powered by other locally available and renewable power sources such as solar cells and batteries. The system boils and evaporates any dirty water source, including river water, ocean water, and even raw sewage. It then allows the pure water to condense and be collected. According to its advertising, a Slingshot unit can purify up to 300 000 litres of water each year, enough daily drinking water for roughly 300 people. It can also produce ten gallons of clean water an hour while consuming less than a kilowatt of electricity.[29] It was invented by Dean Kamen, better known for the Segway, a technology more associated with Cyburbia and plutonomy than the distributed economy. However, in partnership with the Coca-Cola Company which aims to replenish 100 per cent of the water it uses in its beverages by 2020, the Inter-American Development Bank Group, and Africare, the aim is to bring Slingshot technology to communities where potable water access is limited. To date, it has only been tested at five schools near Accra, Ghana, but during that time it provided 140 000 litres of clean drinking water to 1 500 school children over a six-month period.

Mobiles and the challenge of irrigation

Another water-related way to increase productivity is irrigation. The FAO says that only 4 per cent of cropland in sub-Saharan Africa is irrigated, despite there being large untapped reserves of groundwater, and large potential to harvest water runoff. KickStart, founded in Nairobi, has developed what it calls a 'mobile layaway' plan enabling farmers to pay for hand-operated micro-irrigation pumps by phone. The MoneyMaker Hip Pump, for example, costs US$34 but aims to give a return on investment after three months, potentially making smallholder farming more profitable than working in a city, and encouraging farmers not just to stay in rural production, but to bring more land under cultivation.

Each pump, KickStart claims, can increase farm income by up to ten times by enabling three or four crops of vegetables and fruit to be grown. That extra income can be invested in additional labour as well as the farmer's subsistence. Once basic needs are met, farmers are able to make other productivity boosting investments, including cows, chickens, cell phones, solar lighting, and smart irrigation systems.[30] Because of the large number of women amongst smallholder farmers, KickStart can lift women out of poverty. What makes it accessible to such women is that they can pay for the pump with mobile money, using KickStart's Mobile Layaway to save for a pump by sending micro-payments through their mobile phone. Pilot test results show that with this system, the time to save for a system has fallen from ten months to ten weeks. Unlike M-PESA, there has not yet been much independent research into KickStart's impact, but the non-profit organization claims it has sold 63 000 pumps in Kenya, Tanzania, and Mali, and estimates that

US$45 million in profits and wages have been generated by 'kick-started' businesses.

From the intensive to the extensive economy

These models mark the beginnings of a shift between two types of economy. The first is intensive, catering to the fixed market of the urban and suburban wealthy, and maximizing volume by the manufacturing of desire. The second is the extensive, distributed economy, addressing the underserved with products and services that enhance welfare. Figure 7.6 illustrates clearly the difference between them in terms of market, marketing, and method of finance.

The examples we have provided, however early they may be in terms of their rollout as business models, are all working businesses that are exploiting a dynamic essential to the Schumpeterian process of creative destruction.

CHARACTERISTICS	INTENSIVE ECONOMY	EXTENSIVE ECONOMY
Market	Urban and suburban billion	Global population including the underserved
Marketing	Manufacturing of desire/wants based	Needs based as well as wants based Crisis of humanity
Method of finance	Credit fuelled debt	Productivity enhancements from product purchase

Figure 7.6: The intensive and extensive economy

They follow Christensen's logic of capitalism in which the incumbent focuses on its existing customers at the costs of service, decreasing margins, decreasing profitability, and erosion of capital, outlined in Figure 7.7, while in the meantime unknowingly opening a space for the innovator.

FORCES OF CREATIVE DESTRUCTION

- Competition from mature markets
- Decreased price/Increased specification to differentiate
- Increased costs of development
- Increased marketing
- Decreased margins
- Reduced capital for R&D
- Reduced long-term returns
- Increased pressure for short-term results from investors
- Reduced capacity to invest in strategic realignment

Figure 7.7: Creative destruction at the maturity phase

Lessons for Business: Innovation Aligned with the Market

There are five big implications for business from this set of linked examples.

Technological advances, lowering costs, can crack open unaddressed markets

The first lesson concerns new markets. Our examples illustrate the role of technology in opening up previously unaddressable markets. At the heart of the subprime crisis was a technological innovation, the capacity to use advanced mathematics to slice and dice packages of mortgages, turning them into collateralized debt obligations that were sold off in risk-sorted tranches to global investors. But the ICT revolution has also created the capacity to open up new markets whose economic characteristics are the opposite of the subprime market.

The market is big

The second lesson is that Prahalad and Hart were right when they highlighted the market potential of the bottom of the pyramid. The products we have described address the needs of huge markets: 1.6 billion without power, 1.4 billion without clean water and basic sanitation, and one billion mobile users without bank accounts. As Prahalad observed in *The Fortune at the Bottom of the Pyramid,* for basic needs such as credit, potable water, diarrhoea medication, and rice, the poor pay from 1.2 times to as high as 53 times more in the shanty town than in wealthy parts of Mumbai. J.P. Morgan, in conjunction with the Rockefeller Foundation and the Global Impact Investors Network (GIIN), examined the potential for investment into the delivery of affordable services that address basic needs for the poor, as well as the potential profit opportunities for businesses involved. These are set out in Figure 7.8.

The study focuses only on the BoP segment of the customer base for impact investments and analyses only five subsectors: urban housing, water for rural communities, maternal healthcare, primary education, and microfinance. In housing alone they identified capital requirements ranging from US$214–US$786bn and potential profits of US$177–US$648bn.

Moreover, as the demographic change crisis shows, these markets are growing as we saw in Chapter 3, as well as the technological barriers to serving them dropping.

The market is willing and able to pay

The third lesson is that it is a market with the capacity to pay. The poorest of the poor already spend an estimated US$36 billion globally on paraffin and

SECTOR	POTENTIAL INVESTED CAPITAL (US$BN)	POTENTIAL PROFIT OPPORTUNITY (US$BN)
Housing: Affordable urban housing	$214–$786	$177–$648
Water: Clean water for rural communities	$5.4–$13	$2.9–$7
Health: Maternal health	$0.4–$2	$0.1–$1
Education: Primary Education	$4.8–$10	$2.6–$11
Financial Services: Microfinance	$176	Not measured

Figure 7.8: Potential invested capital to fund selected BoP businesses over the next 10 years in US$ bn

Source: J. P. Morgan *Impact Investments: An emerging asset class*, November 2010

firewood, US$10 billion in sub-Saharan Africa alone. The poorest of the poor currently are forced to pay the highest rates for the essential goods and services they access, and the poor in Dhaka (Bangladesh) are said to pay 1000 per cent more than their rich countrymen do, while a slum inhabitant of Barranquilla (Colombia) pays ten times more than someone in New York.

The more you serve it the more it grows

A fourth lesson is that these investments have a positive impact on productivity. It is a business model that is the opposite of subprime. If someone gets a predatory loan, with a hidden ballooning interest rate payment at the end of a short grace period, what has been created is an unsustainable market where value is eventually going to get destroyed. If someone gets micro-irrigation, and their incomes increase, that investment is productive not predatory: for each dollar put in, more than a dollar comes out, and the more that happens the more one creates the conditions for growth.

Solutions to scarcities can multiply

A fifth and final effect is that solutions to various scarcities can then multiply: access to power can reduce paraffin and health expenses, freeing up income to invest in agricultural productivity, including insurance and irrigation hand pumps which in turn drive up returns. Figure 7.9 makes it plain that those who have access to the power of D.Light and some of the other innovations we have covered are on the pathway to greater wealth and income; those who do

169

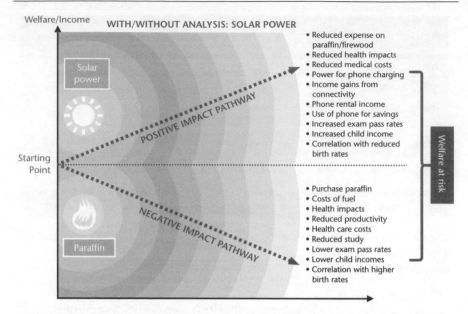

Figure 7.9: The impact of intervention—with/without analysis for solar power

not are increasingly exposed to risk, and this is a situation that over time will be exacerbated by facets of climate change and population growth.

Moreover, the productivity impact is felt at the regional as well as the individual level. Figure 7.10 shows a generic 'impact pathway' from the input of an irrigation pump, through to the output of access to water year round, including short-term outcomes such as increased productivity and the capacity to invest, and long-term outcomes such as enhanced food security and decreased urbanization.

Innovators and Incumbents

A feature of this emerging new market, as Christensen has illustrated, is that industry incumbents will not respond to it. They are too focused on beating the competition by adding new features or slashing prices to maintain market share to notice a disruptive, lower cost, lower performance technology that suddenly brings a whole new raft of customers into play.[31]

While they may be at early stages of growth, this disruption, as we have shown, is what M-PESA is doing to finance; what D.Light and M-KOPA are doing to traditional power supply; and what Kilimo Salama is doing to insurance. The evidence of this linked set of examples suggests though that this shift will not be reversed. Once a foundation technology is in place, it lays the

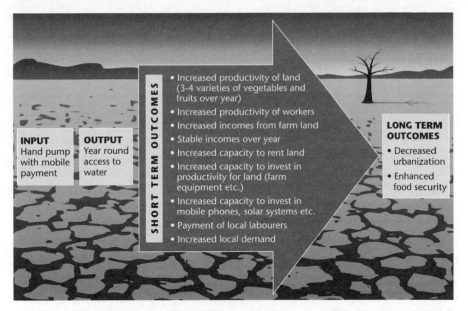

INPUT
Hand pump with mobile payment

OUTPUT
Year round access to water

SHORT TERM OUTCOMES

- Increased productivity of land (3-4 varieties of vegetables and fruits over year)
- Increased productivity of workers
- Increased incomes from farm land
- Stable incomes over year
- Increased capacity to rent land
- Increased capacity to invest in productivity for land (farm equipment etc.)
- Increased capacity to invest in mobile phones, solar systems etc.
- Payment of local labourers
- Increased local demand

LONG TERM OUTCOMES

- Decreased urbanization
- Enhanced food security

Figure 7.10: Rural productivity—countering urbanization

rails for complementary technologies to advance. Mobile phones lay the rails for mobile money transfers, and then mobile payment for solar lights, insurance, and desalination. The innovators can leverage the installed base of other innovators to accelerate penetration of the market.

Do the changes in manufacturing that we outlined above have the potential to create market disruption? While a review of the strategic implications for different sectors is beyond the scope of this book, there are already examples in play of potential disruptors emerging. Just as Ford's assembly line drove down prices to the extent that he democratized car ownership, these shifts in technology have the potential to undercut the costs of mass assembly, removing not just material but plant and process. The result, as with Ford, is they acquire the potential to accelerate into previously unserved markets. What follows is a snap-shot of the phase that Carlotta Perez describes as the transition period, where technologies have irrupted and are beginning the journey towards synergy.

Scanning for the Disruptors

Automotive sector

Alongside Wikispeed as innovators in the *automotive* sector, Teijin and Stratasys have a quick press manufacturing model for vehicles. The Urbee, its shell

3D printed, uses electric motors, backed up by a small ethanol-powered engine. It is capable of 70mph and does 200mpg. It is built to last 30 years and could be mass produced at a price tag of US$10000.

Healthcare

In the field of *healthcare*, the potential is for companies like Organovo to harvest a grown adult's stem cells by drawing blood, use a specialized 3D printer to build an organic, polymeric scaffold in the shape of the organ or tissue that needs to be replicated, then grow a kidney, heart, or lungs, within a period of days or weeks without risk of rejection. While the US military explores AugCon (augmented cognition) for complex environments, Berlin's Campus Party plays host to Neill Harbisson, founder of the Cyborg Foundation, and the first passport-accredited cyborg. Born colour blind, Harbisson states that he became a cyborg when the union between his organism and cybernetics created new neuronal tissue in his brain that allowed him to perceive colour through a new sense. Harbisson, who composes and performs chromatic scale music, is exploring how to partner with the medical community to make the approach more broadly available.

DIY healthcare

Tim Cannon, co-founder of DIY body-hacking group Grindhouse Wetware, sees the coming convergence of 3D printing with body-hacking.[32] Short-term projects include subdermal navigation systems, wireless file storage, and brain-only thermostat control for the house. Five to ten year projects include heart replacement and sensors on remaining major organs and brain-to-brain wireless interface.

More immediately, the cost of a high quality artificial limb replacement is estimated to be in the six figure range. Bespoke Innovations, based in San Francisco, has been creating some of the functional prototypes for artificial limbs with moving parts using 3D printers, at a cost of between US$5000 to 10000.

Construction

In terms of *construction*, a Dutch architectural firm is now printing out a 3D house. The wiki-house project runs a global programme for local low-cost housing. As well as the US$35 hackable Raspberry Pi computer, the Digits to All project in Bangladesh is an example of how underserved markets can access ICT. It distributed custom developed US$100 Amadeyr (and later Amadeyr II) tablet computers to over 100 households in a rural village to test their feasibility. The tablets used software specifically designed and customized for use by semiliterate, illiterate, and bottom-of-the-pyramid users, and a touchscreen operated by seeing pictures and hearing instructions in Bengali. Villagers who had never used computers or the internet were able to use the tablets within a few days, suggesting that the barrier to crossing the digital divide in rural communities is not lack of skills but the lack of communication technologies tailored to meet local needs.

Retail finance

In *retail finance*, among a range of crowd-funding initiatives, Kiva, for instance, is a charitable organization providing loans from individual donors to developing countries. Started in 2005, it has made over US$380 million in loans with a repayment rate of 99 per cent. The same kind of approach has been employed commercially in advanced economies where the likes of Kickstarter and Zopa have helped small borrowers avoid the credit drought in banks while offering lenders a better market return than most retail offerings.

Bond rating

For *bond ratings*, meanwhile, Wikirating and Public Sector Credit Solutions (PSCS) employ crowdsourcing techniques to improve credit ratings, with a 'radically reduced' cost of entry. While Wikirating gathers and aggregates information and views about credit quality for different types of bond, PSCS has released an open source software tool that calculates default probabilities for government bonds, along with fully transparent sample models and data sets. PSCS recently estimated that Italy's ten year default stood at 2.59 per cent, and concluded that investors in Italian sovereign bonds were being well compensated.[33]

Defence and space

In July 2012, the US Military rolled out 3D printers to the Afghan frontline in shipping containers that act as mobile production labs. The US$2.8m labs house 3D printers and CNC machines to make parts from aluminium, plastic, and steel. The labs also have the potential to fabricate spare parts to repair them, according to Pete Newell, head of the US army's Rapid Equipping Force. NASA and the Singularity University are reportedly planning to use 3D printers for future *space missions*, dealing with the Achilles Heel of space travel, resupply. Supplies of silicon dioxide, which is commonly found near the Earth's surface, could be combined with a binding agent to form a raw material source.

Agriculture

In *agriculture*, 3D printing of chicken is already on the menu, with benefits in terms of both carbon and food security. At the other end of the spectrum, the arrival of the smart phone has started to improve existing agricultural practices. In Senegal, mobile phones linked to the Manobi market information service connect farmers to European and US importers. Trade at Hand in Mali, Wougnet in Uganda, and Tradenet in Ghana offer similar services, all designed to be accessible to and usable by often illiterate farmers. In Kenya, iCow, an SMS and voice-based application for small-scale dairy farmers, helps farmers trace the oestrogen cycles of their cows, and also gives technical advice on issues such as animal nutrition, milk production and gestation. Users of the application have reportedly seen their incomes increase by 42 per cent, with milk retention increased by 56 per cent.[34]

M-Farm, a Kenyan agribusiness company, has partnered with Samsung to launch a new SMS tool which allows subscribing farmers to obtain real time price information, buy farm inputs, and find buyers for their produce. The M-Farm SMS tool was founded by three Kenyan women who met through the iHub in Nairobi. Their idea, facilitated by a group called Akirachix, a community of over 200 tech women, was developed at the m:lab incubator at Nairobi's iHub and launched after they won a 48-hour boot camp event and €10 000 of investment.

Education

Education is critical to productivity, and internet access opens up new possibilities for education. Udacity, Coursera, P2PU, and University of the People are pioneering online further education using MOOCs (massive open online courses). MobilEd has piloted an audio wikipedia to allow children to access audio encyclopaedic articles via SMS. MPowering is already at work in Orissa, India, using a payment by results model to incentivize increased attendance at school among communities living on US$2 a day. Participating families receive mobile phones. A child going to school, for example, logs in to the 'school' option on the mPowering mobile app and scans the barcode to check in with a picture-based app, so users don't have to be literate. At the end of each month, the families pool together their points to score medicine, food, and clothing from the nonprofit partners.

In the *gastronomy* business, finally, Ferran Adrià, who was Head Chef of El Bulli in Spain, is creating La Bullipedia. La Bullipedia aims to reverse the hierarchical model of cuisine, allowing users to tap into a crowd-sourced curated database that captures every possible combination of foods and methods of cooking that have been applied. It is a project to link cooks with ideas they would never have had access to, right down to white chocolate with sardines, and to allow them to adapt and modify what they discover.[35]

Business Implications: Resolving the Crises of the Quadrilemma

What do these examples mean for business? How do they help address the Turnaround Challenge? It is important not to exaggerate the strategic impact or productivity boosts of some of these initiatives. Cutting out the middle man in agriculture for example, can be a mixed blessing because research over the years has shown the importance of these traders, not least when small-holders are under stress. Fairtrade, an approach to engineering the market in favour of small producers, has not always benefitted farmers and farm communities,[36] and the highly praised micro-finance model to empower the poor through small loans has been persistently criticized for not living up to its promises.[37] Initiatives associated with bottom billion capitalism and social entrepreneurship have often struggled to get beyond the stage of a handful of pilot projects, and lack a sustainable financial basis.[38]

Four parallel shifts in the model of growth

But a pattern emerges. In Chapter 2, we framed the Turnaround Challenge around four decision points for business, representing the environmental, social, economic, and governance crises confronting us. The examples we have reviewed suggest the emergence of a new set of innovators in line with the logic of capitalism but breaking away from business as usual.

1. *Fossil fuel to renewable*: The first, to deal with the carbon constraint, is the transition from fossil fuel to the renewable production of energy (see D.Light).

2. *Mass to micro*: The second, addressing the social constraint, is the move from mass production to micro production driven by new advances in nanotech, picotech, and additive manufacturing (see 3D printed spares and the Rolls Royce Buckle).

3. *Intensive to extensive*: The third is the transition from the intensive economy, serving the wants of already saturated wealthier markets, to the extensive economy addressing the needs of the many (see M-PESA).

4. *Closed to open*: The fourth is the move from the closed economy, with guarded IP, and labour minimized as cost, to the open economy capturing the value of the team and its resources (see Wikiratings, and GE air traffic guidance for pilots).

Responding to the shifts

These shifts are unresolved. Today's business operates at the point of transition between them. As a complex and unresolved set of crises hitting business at a time of economic vulnerability, they represent something of a perfect strategic storm. One risk is what is termed the threat rigidity thesis—precisely when business needs to be agile, the complexity of the threat leaves it paralysed. Hallmarks of threat rigidity vary across business. For a finance function it may be exploring new financial engineering that is not part of the core business. For sales it might be the mis-selling of products such as insurance. For marketing it might be surface green differentiation or 'tooferization,' or the development of other campaigns based on the over-delivery of performance to saturated markets to maintain or claw back market share at the cost of margin.

Is there a win-win?

But the strategic response of business is critical, not just for shareholder value, but for the successful emergence of a new wave of growth that brings productivity to the economy. Put simply, without big business today's incumbents, the new wave of growth will not happen. Is there a form of synergy that helps innovators and incumbents? In Chapter 5, referring to Figure 5.5, we explained the evolutionary pathway of techno-economic paradigms. Let's revisit Perez's model to see what it tells us about the transition process and the role of business.

Irruption of new sustainability innovators

As we saw, the installation of the new GPT involves two phases. In Phase One, after a gestation period during the maturity of the old paradigm, new technologies 'irrupt.' They are featured in Wired. They get invited to do TEDx talks. They are often loss-making. They are short of finance, and they require risk-taking capital and the skills and resources of groups like the Skoll Foundation, and Ashoka, as well as the seed capital of smart impact investors like IFC, the Shell Foundation, and Acumen. DFID, remember, offered a critical early stage £1 million to Nick Hughes to get M-PESA off the ground.

Frenzy of new social enterprises

In the second period, there is a frenzy of investment as the innovators demonstrate their potential to boost productivity. With a lot of pent up capital from the previous GPT, and a limited supply of innovators, the frenzy sparks a rise in asset prices. The rise, based on companies that disrupt the incumbents and therefore have few channels into mainstream markets, ultimately becomes a bubble. Returns from the innovators eventually no longer support company valuations, and the bubble bursts.

Turning Point: collapse of the bubble

At this stage there is a turning point or transition phase 3, a period of economic stagnation after the bursting of the bubble. A new phase of growth begins when one critical thing happens. This is when 'productive capital,' business in other words, stops putting money into speculative projects to try to find returns, and starts to invest it in the new productivity boosting GPT.

Synergy of innovators and incumbents

This is the fourth phase, synergy. The GPT is then rolled out across the economy, deployed in waves across sectors of the economy until it reaches the fifth and final phase of maturity.

Maturity

As it deploys, it brings increased productivity, long-term growth at the national level and superior returns to the industries that have gained first mover advantage by understanding and aligning with the dynamics of the new technology.

The critical role of incumbents in transition

So the strategic response of incumbent business is critical, not just at the level of the firm, but at the level of the economy. We have seen the options in terms of potential directions for the ICT deployment, from the blueprint eco-cities of Cyburbia, to large scale geo-engineering to trans-humanism and the Singularity. Our assessment of each of them has been that they fail to meet the test of providing a scalable solution to the challenges that confront us. If Perez's model of transition is correct, managing the transition (see Figure 7.11) depends on a group of existing business leaders avoiding the innovator's dilemma and finding ways to gain from the deployment of the new technology. The speed and direction of the new GPT depends on this synergy; on productive capital having the incentives to scale up the potential winners that speculative capital has installed, and then deploy them across the economic base towards their most productive use There will be a short-term bust if the shift from financial to industrial capital is successful; but if that shift does not

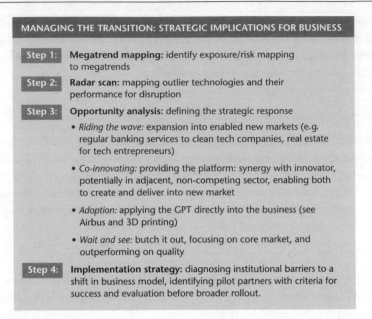

Figure 7.11: Managing the transition: strategic implications for business

happen, there is likely to be a prolonged recession if productive capital fails to deploy into the new paradigm or subverts it towards long-term unproductive uses.

The strategic response for business

Perez's model has four strategic implications for incumbent business.

Megatrend mapping

The first is *megatrend mapping*, identifying external megatrends that show the current GPT is no longer externally congruent. Our analysis in Chapter 2 identified four separate challenges or megatrends, economic, social, environmental, and governance. Each of them, as we have discussed, presents a decision point and potential shift for business and society that would bring it into congruence with the external environmental.

Scanning the business horizon

The second step is to *scan the business horizon* for specific companies, even small cap, whose business model fits the GPT and could disrupt your business.

Critical to this phase is to understand the specific benefits that the new technology brings and the new dimensions on which disruptors may undercut your business. Examples of the disruptive benefits of the cluster of technologies underpinning the ICT revolution (nano, additive, and open) might include speed of prototyping, and localization.

Speed of prototyping: For companies where the product is based on qualitative judgement (the customer can't judge it till they see it) such as fashion, design, and the automotive sector, the disruption may be the capacity of a competitor to undercut you with a model of rapid prototyping that means the customer can have the product and the customer's own iteration of it printed out live in front of them to approve.

Localization/omnipresence: The already low cost of 3D printing and its potential to be a freely downloadable machine that can print other printers (super-exponentially) suggest more 3D printers around. With growable feedstock, 3D printing becomes available even in zones where supply has been impossible (from space to the Antarctic). Competitors will also be disruptive if they provide the technology in high urgency markets where supply is slow from the customer point of view. These include medical applications (replacement jaws), breakdowns and repairs (indicator lights) and ICT and military (equipment replacement).

Triggers for disruption

A broader analysis is beyond the scope of this book, but other factors suggested as triggers for disruption might include the following:

- *Structural integrity* (see Rolls Royce buckle, where additive manufacturing allows single piece components, reducing weight and cost).
- *Lower cost of production* from reductions in materials, plant, and process (Wikispeed, Urbee, GM's water heater) allowing increased market share with existing segments or the spread into new previously unaddressed markets.
- *Advanced data analytics* from crowd information (GE and air traffic patterns).
- *Speed to customer* (Lancashire Paper Cup Company).
- *Costlessness of complexity* (see 3D printed hearts).
- *Environmental return* from low carbon model (see Abyd Kamali of Merrill Lynch and the structuring of a multi-million CER (Certified Emissions Reductions) agreement with Nuru Energy, a social enterprise that seeks to provide an affordable and clean off-grid lighting system).

- *Social returns from inclusive business* (See St Giles's Trust and payment by results for reduced prisoner re-offending and mPowering in Orissa. See also the range of initiatives funded by Kickstarter and impact investors).

This list is not exhaustive, and will evolve as the technologies evolve. The relevance and the potential for disruption will vary. There may also be multiple points of disruption. The strategic challenge is to identify the ones that matter to your current and potential customer.

Opportunity analysis

The third step is *facing the music*, looking for opportunities a) to grow the business by riding the wave, b) co-innovating, c) integrating the GPT into operations, or d) butching it out with a wait and see strategy because you believe that this isn't going to happen at the scale or speed to be a strategic threat.

Riding the wave: This strategy involves anticipating market growth, then delivering core products and services into the market that innovators have helped to create. The 'with/without analysis' around power and the generic impact pathway for rural irrigation in Figure 7.9 showed how single interventions can create a series of effects that raise incomes and enable markets. The spread of the mobile phone for example, triggers indirect market opportunities in fertilizer sales because the new mobile weather insurance offered via Kilimo Salama makes it worth taking the risk.

Co-innovating: Co-innovation is an essential mechanism for synergy in the transition process. The innovator and incumbent combine to roll out propositions into the market. The approach allows innovators to tap into the platform of the incumbents, giving them the access to markets, distribution, contacts, and resources of the larger firm. For incumbents, the partnership with the innovator provides the means to address the innovator's dilemma, harnessing market insight that their customer focus will have blinded them to and a pilot test to explore the pitfalls and potential of the new GPT for their business. Examples highlighted include Merrill Lynch's Nuru Energy project and Coca-Cola's partnership with Slingshot to deliver distributed water. An emerging example involving multi-partner synergy is Unilever's partnership with Wassup and Diageo to deliver sanitation to the poor, using human waste as low carbon feedstock for a local brewery, and using the revenues to help support the costs of rolling out sanitation in slums. Successful co-innovation may often occur in adjacent, non-competitive sectors. The GSMA has played a critical role in convening potential collaborators and in helping to identify, amid the hype of the mobile revolution, the uses of mobile technology that are linked to development impact. Emerging combinations where mobile phones provide the mechanism for synergy between non-competitors include telecoms and finance (M-PESA), power (M-KOPA), health (eHealth-Point), education (mPowering), insurance (Kilimo Salama), and agriculture (Kickstart).

Adoption: The adoption strategy involves the 'productive capital' of capital of business going directly into the new GPT. Examples highlighted include the Rolls Royce buckle and Airbus's commitments to 3D printing.

Implementation Strategy

The fourth strategic step is to map barriers, an essential step if the institution is going to align and deploy its capital successfully into the new GPT, gaining productivity and providing a demonstration effect to other companies. This process will reveal (illustrated by Figure 7.12) that the transition from the principles of the mass era to the principles of the distributed economy run counter to the assumptions built across business functions.

The downside is that this is complex and high risk. But as the ICT related collapse in January 2013 of three high street stores in the space of a week suggests (Jessops the camera retailer, HMV the music store, and Blockbuster the movie rentals business), the impacts of disruption can arrive fast for weakened businesses. The upside, as Geoff Moore, author of *Crossing the Chasm*, suggests, is that associating with innovators in developing new

ROLE	MASS	◀ VS ▶ DISTRIBUTED ECONOMY
HR	We need to reduce labour costs. But we need to pay top dollar to get the best people, especially management. Extensive training will induct people into the business.	Labour is the chief source of competitive advantage. Motivation is intrinsic. Our HR policy assumes all people have capability (equipotentiality). Fresh ideas are needed to solve entrenched problems. Barriers to contribution are low, training on the job, with reward for results
Legal	We need to control IP like you wouldn't believe	We need to open up our IP, and focus on contracting around shareability
R & D	We need our own R&D teams	We can tap into the crowd and harness new resources
Customers	We need to deliver more value to our customers	We need to focus on customers with unsolved problems
Manufacturing process	Quality comes from high capex mass production	Quality comes from high precision low capex tools
Shareholders	We are under pressure to generate superior returns by whatever means we can. We need to focus on shareholder value	What matters is a long-term strategy for growth that is fit for purpose. We need to focus on delivering social outcomes, shareholder valuing will follow

Figure 7.12: Principles of mass versus distributed economy

markets might help incumbent companies return to their roots and act like entrepreneurs once more.

Two sets of colliding megatrends

We began this chapter looking for a new GPT that might have the potential to usher in a new wave of growth. Two trends, as Figure 7.13 shows, are colliding. The first is the rise in Chinese and other emerging market labour costs. The second, driven in large part by new types of ICT, is the declining costs of local production.

But the balance looks finely tipped, with the move to date more of a trickle than a stampede. While the trends may be real, survey the landscape as a CEO and CFO and it's not clear what the time horizon is for these changes.

One of the defining features of general purpose technologies, as Solow has indicated, is their capacity to evolve, rolling out in waves across the economy. The first wave of the ICT revolution, Internet 1.0, covered the period from irruption up to the feature phone and the read-only internet. During this period ICT had limited productivity effects. It was used instead to prop up a mass production paradigm that had reached maturity, and that tried to maintain its competitiveness by offshoring to emerging markets. The second phase of the ICT revolution, Internet 2.0, brought revolutions in technology that

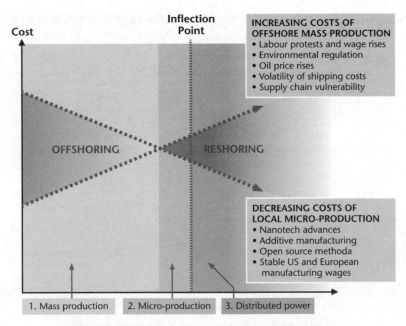

Figure 7.13: Shifting economics of local production

have the potential to transform manufacturing and markets. This transformation, combined with rising costs of offshore manufacturing, presents the possibility for a continued shift towards re-shoring. This is a big stride forward. Not just jobs, but jobs with the potential to be small business jobs. ICT is beginning to gain some credibility as a candidate for the role of GPT. But is this as good as it gets? Or are there tipping points that might bring us closer still to the city we want to live in? This is the question we will explore in Chapter 8.

Notes

1. (Stiglitz 2012)
2. http://online.wsj.com/article/SB10001424127887324640104578161493858722884. html, accessed 5 December 2012
3. http://www.theatlantic.com/magazine/archive/2012/12/the-insourcing-boom/309166/
4. http://www.economist.com/news/special-report/21569570-growing-number-american-companies-are-moving-their-manufacturing-back-united
5. Since writing this chapter, Seesmart has been acquired by Revolution Lighting
6. (Anonymous 2012)
7. http://www.alixpartners.com/en/WhatWeThink/Automotive/IsChinaStilltheLCCD efaultOption.aspx, accessed 6 December 2012
8. http://www.ft.com/cms/s/0/633ed984-71b0-11e1-b853-00144feab49a.html#axzz 2Izd0QdxF
9. http://www.thehackettgroup.com/research/2012/reshoring-global-manufacturing/
10. http://lib.bioinfo.pl/projects/view/22292
11. http://www.transportintelligence.com/forms/get_whitepaper.php?wpID=76
12. http://opensourceecology.org/gvcs.php, accessed 12 October 2012
13. http://www.gequest.com/c/flight
14. By way of consolation to the shirt manufacturer, the Museum also acquired as a 'companion object' to the shirt, a fake bought in a market in Peru. http://www.bbc. co.uk/blogs/ahistoryoftheworld/2010/10/100th-object-contenders-1.shtml
15. http://www.socialedge.org/blogs/let-there-d-light/?b_start:int=20&-C =, accessed 5 December 2012
16. (Aker, Mbiti 2010)
17. (Aker, Ksoll)
18. For instance http://www.icrier.org/pdf/public_policy19jan09.pdf
19. (World Bank 2012; Blackman, Srivastava 2011)
20. (Beck, Demirgüç-Kunt, & Levine 2009)
21. *The Economist*, June 28, 2007
22. For instance, (Blowfield 2012)
23. (Jack, Suri 2011)

24. Mas and Ng'weno, 2009, cited in http://www.econ.brown.edu/faculty/David_Weil/Mbitiper cent20Weilper cent20NBERper cent20workingper cent20paperper cent2017129.pdf, accessed 5 December 2012

25. http://www.cgap.org/blog/10-things-you-thought-you-knew-about-m-pesa, accessed 5 December 2012

26. http://www.economist.com/node/21560983

27. This has been our experience teaching business school students, for example

28. Mobilemoneyafrica.com, accessed 5 December 2012

29. http://edition.cnn.com/2009/TECH/09/11/kamen.water.slingshot/index.html, accessed 6 December 2012

30. www.atatwork.org, accessed 6 December 2012

31. (Christensen 1997)

32. http://www.wired.co.uk/news/archive/2012-09/04/diy-biohacking

33. http://prnewswire.netpr.pl/en/pr/228418/crowdsourcedcredit-rating-providers-join-forces

34. http://www.ventures-africa.com/2012/07/kenyas-konza-tech-city-a-step-too-far/

35. ttp://www.wired.co.uk/magazine/archive/2012/10/features/staying-creative-ferran-adriper centC3per centA0?page=all, accessed 10 December 2012

36. (Blowfield, Dolan 2010; Dolan 2008)

37. (Rogaly 1996; Roy 2010)

38. Blowfield & Dolan forthcoming

8

The City of the Future: A Place for People

IN THIS CHAPTER

What distinguishes the distributed economy from Cyburbia and the Petropolis. A new approach to energy. The third wave of ICT and the rollout of a new general purpose technology. Technology as amplifier of intent. Testing it against three stubborn challenges of mobility, political engagement, and work.

> '(W)e slipped into a fiction which was that it is actually possible to make a blueprint of a piece of the environment or the completed environment, and have it work.'[1]
>
> Christopher Alexander, 2004 Schumacher lecture

Internet Eyes, a company based in Cornwall, pays Australian citizens to monitor UK CCTV footage remotely. The company allows its 8 000 subscribers, who pay £1.99 a month, to scrutinize 10 minutes of footage at a time and to make five alerts a month reporting suspicious activity. Prizes of up to £250 a month are given to viewers who detect shoplifting or other crimes in action.[2]

Camover, meanwhile, is a German game where civil rights activists in Berlin team up to destroy public surveillance cameras as part of an 'anti-oppression Olympics,' then post a YouTube video to win points for innovation in cam-removal technique from viewers and other players. The site has been shut down several times by its internet server hosts.

Saskia Sassen, as we have seen, talked of the potential of the smart city, for all its virtues, to become not just sensored but censored. As sites like *bigbrotherwatch* and the writings of Henry Porter in the *Observer* newspaper have suggested and as the 2013 revelations about foreign intelligence gathering made clear, this potential appears to be already emerging, with the smart city revealing aspects of the model, described by Andrew Keen in *Digital Vertigo*, of Jeremy Bentham's Panopticon. We have shown the growing limits of both Petropolis and Cyburbia as places for human beings to flourish. Furthermore, the quadrilemma of crises mean they are not cities in which business can flourish in any real sense. But are the contours of another city emerging?

From Smart Cities to Smart Citizens

The hypothesis of this chapter is that a new city model is already emerging from the bottom up, that its critical factor is people, and that ICT technology, with the right intent, can play a positive role. As Jane Jacobs put it, 'Cities have the capability of providing something for everybody, only because, and only when, they are created by everybody.' What is needed in other words is not the blueprint smart city but smart citizens.

What are the critical factors in the development of this city? What is the role of business? In the previous chapter we showed the emergence of new forms of manufacturing with the potential to transform markets. We saw how rising Chinese manufacturing costs and lowering costs of domestic manufacturing are helping to reverse the quarter-century-long trend of offshoring. Optimists though we are, we don't see this as an immediate game-changer. Could this not be just another round in the game of labour arbitrage? What is the long-term driver, beyond short-term cheaper production costs, that could bring enduring manufacturing and prosperity back to the city?

The Great Texas Blackout

Let's start with a power cut. On 2 February 2011, Texas was hit by a series of rolling blackouts. An estimated 50 out of the State's 550 power plants went down, knocking off 8000 mw, or about 12 per cent of demand. The alleged cause? Two new coal-fired plants owned by Luminant (a subsidiary of the former TXU) had had pipe issues in the cold. Another 12 000 megawatts worth of plants were already offline for maintenance. Natural gas plants were turned on to make up for the coal-plant failures, but power cuts affecting stations compressing natural gas sent them offline too. The next morning, 3 000 mw of plants were reportedly still offline because of the cold. Prices surged to the cap of US$3000 per megawatt hour.

The challenges of the grid are not going away. Electricity is the fastest growing form of end-use energy. In the USA, according to the Energy Information Administration, power generation will increase by 77 per cent between 2006 and 2030. But the average USA substation transformer is 42 years old—two years past the 40 year life expectancy. It has been claimed that energy already costs 21 per cent of total income for about half of households, up from 12 per cent 11 years ago.[3] With blackouts affecting a daily average of 500 000 people, an estimated US$1.5 trillion would need to be spent to upgrade the electric grid over the next 25 years.

With only one new coal-fired power plant on the books, state regulators, to attract new investment, proposed tripling the maximum price Texas generators can charge during periods of heaviest demand from US$3000 a megawatt-hour to US$9000 a megawatt hour by 2015. The dilemma for Texan business is either to pay higher rates to encourage investment in the grid, or face escalating levels of blackout.[4]

This is not just a Texan problem. In 2003, this time in the sweltering heat of an Ohio summer, a sagging high-voltage power line in Northern Ohio brushed against some overgrown trees and shorted. The alarm system at the local utility company failed and the cascading blackout that followed caused the shutdown of over 100 power plants. It was the largest blackout in North American history with 50 million people losing power. The event contributed to 11 deaths and cost the economy an estimated US$6 billion during the four days before full power was restored. Just under ten years later, though, the July 2012 India blackout made Ohio and Texas look like a dress rehearsal. The Indian blackout, the largest power outage in history, affected about 9 per cent of the world's population (620 million people), spread across 22 states in Northern, Eastern, and Northeast India.

Austin, Texas: rethinking the grid

The issue here is long-term resilience. Changing weather patterns can disrupt energy capacity, but what all of the cases reveal and is spelled out in full in Figure 8.1 are structural challenges with centralized power grids.

For the city of Austin, Texas, this dilemma of more blackouts or higher bills hit home hard. 'From 2000 to 2010,' says Jose Beceiro of Austin's Chamber of Commerce, 'the city lost roughly 30,000 high-tech jobs.' This formed part of a broader total estimated by US Department of Labor to be some 81 600 manufacturing jobs lost in Austin during the recession. Every US state lost manufacturing jobs from May 2007 to May 2012, according to an *On Numbers* analysis, but Texas had the eighth largest decline, with 8.72 per cent of manufacturing jobs lost (down from 935 600 in May 2007 to 854 000 in May 2012).

Local business, in other words, could neither afford the higher bills nor the blackouts.

Pecan Street: Producing local power

Three miles from the Texas capitol building, at the disused airstrip that is the home of Austin's Mueller community, there is a locally-grown response to the twin challenges of energy and economic downturn. The project is for a different type of grid, not centralized and fossil fuel driven, but decentralized and green—the smart micro grid. Pecan Street is the location for a five-year demonstration project to deploy smart grid technology—home energy

GRID CHALLENGES	CONSEQUENCE
1. Centralization	• Centralized structure results in high levels of loss in transmission and distribution as well as unserved populations (Global 1.6bn without access to power) • India's aggregate technical and commercial losses are thought to be about 25-30%, but could be higher given the substantial fraction of the population that is not metered and the lack of transparency
2. Peak load capacity needed	• The centralized grid has no local storage capacity, so has to have idle excess capacity to make sure it can cover peak load. • With growing populations and consumption levels, peak demand, continues to outpace India's power supply. Official estimates of India's demand shortfall are 16% for peak demand, with over 34% of the country off grid
3. Energy price rises	• The grid relies on fossil fuels and is vulnerable to rising fuel costs
4. Operating costs increasing	• As the grid ages, its complex physical chain requires higher operating and maintenance costs
5. Lack of resilience	• The grid's centralized structure makes it vulnerable to domino effect blackouts, where failures cascade down the system
6. Lack of data on supply side	• The grid gives no real time information for the power providers to monitor demand and adjust supply to match
7. Lack of data on customer side	• The grid gives no real time information for customers to monitor energy prices and consumption levels and adjust demand
8. Vicious circle	• With decreasing profits, and decreasing capital to invest, the centralized grid has decreasing capital to improve efficiency and levels of service. The result is a service with decreasing quality and increasing cost for consumers

Figure 8.1: Structural challenges with the power grid

management systems, solar panels, electric vehicles, new pricing models, and more—in about 1000 homes in and around Mueller. To date a third of the homes have solar panels, and a hundred have Chevrolet's battery electric Volt. The aim is to connect an entire neighbourhood with solar panels, electric vehicles, utility smart meters, and household batteries in what some have called '*a giant green power blender.*'

Rooftop solar panels will calculate how much energy they'll produce that day based on the morning weather forecast then set up a schedule for using the energy or selling it back to the grid at peak demand. The solar panels will help charge electric vehicles. But it's not just 'plug the car into the house'. The collective battery network of electric vehicles can serve as reserve storage capacity for a micro-grid to help balance an unanticipated outage or shortfall in supply. In other words, the house gets plugged into the car. The Electric Power Research Institute estimates that the same vehicles could reduce fuel consumption by about 60 per cent compared with non-hybrid vehicles.

The target is to reduce carbon emissions by 64 per cent compared to an average Austin neighbourhood, and for solar panel fitted homes to produce zero net carbon emissions. More significantly, though, is Mueller's role as a living laboratory to test ideas and technologies that will make the USA's US$1.3 trillion electricity market one in which energy is cheap, abundant, and clean. This expertise will provide Austin not just with the increased margins and resilience of a smart grid, but expertise in a critical growth sector for the future.

Co-designing the New Energy Economy

The new, US$1.5 million Pike Powers Laboratory, located right next to Mueller, will research how a new generation of appliances, electric vehicles, air conditioners, and solar panels can be developed to fit the needs and use patterns of the community. As a lab, Pecan Street aims to be where the New Energy Economy is designed, and verified before it goes to market, and a base for both innovators and incumbents.

Partners involved in Pecan Street include General Motors, Sony, Intel, SunEdison, Whirlpool, and Toshiba, together with the Environmental Defense Fund and the University of Texas. In the words of Brewster McCracken, Pecan Street's executive director: 'We are going to revolutionize how energy is produced, transported and consumed in America.'

The principles of distributed renewable power for resilience are not new. Guessing, on the Austria-Hungary border, with a population of 3 811 (2011) used energy independence as its central turnaround strategy. In 1988, the Guessing region, briefly part of the Soviet Union, was one of the poorest in terms of per-capita income in Austria, with high unemployment, collapsed infrastructure, post-Soviet failures of energy efficiency, weak transportation links to major cities like Vienna and a high rate of emigration to other regions in Austria. A strategy of energy efficiency and biomass district heating systems now enables it to produce more heat, fuel, and electric power from renewable sources than it uses, with annual added value of €13 million (calculation based on 2005 figures) per year. Fifty new enterprises with more than 1 000 direct and indirect jobs were created in the renewable energy sector for the region. Guessing has now developed into a hub in the fields of wood products, hardwood drying, and environmental technologies, attracting investment in 1996 in the form of the European Centre for Renewable Energy, whose focus is regional and community-based concepts for energy conservation and generation.

The emergence of the smart micro-grid

Over 400 smart micro grids, deploying the sensing technologies of the 'energy internet,' are now in operation globally. These range from TERI and the Indian Government's trial at Gurgaon, where GE launched its first fully controlled offshoring centre and where Google now has its India operations, to the PowerMatching City in the Groningen district of Hoogkerk and the Cloud Power trial on the Dutch island of Texel, to the Jeju Island smart grid pilot in South Korea. The US$58 million Jeju Island project is the Korean government initiative to build and demonstrate the world's largest Smart Grid in action as part of a twenty year vision to see its US$58.3 billion electricity market connected in a smart grid that overlays a series of smart micro grids, and to win 30 per cent of the global smart grid market (estimated between US$20 billion to US$160 billion) for its home industries. According to the Korea Smart Grid Institute, the smart grid will save the country about US$10 billion a year in energy import costs and reduce the country's CO_2 level by 30 per cent. By 2030, the South Korean government plans to engage 30 per cent of all citizens in a real-time power trading market, allowing them to produce and sell renewable energy back to the grid.[5]

Prospects for the future

Consistent with the Korean government's view, Southern California Edison (SCE) sees rapidly growing market potential for the smart grid. Between 2009 and 2012, SCE plans to replace more than five million traditional electric meters with next-generation smart devices, making possible money-saving, time-differentiated rates, and demand response options as well as home area connectivity with appliances of the future. The new meter system will allow customers to set smart, inter-connected thermostats and appliances to respond automatically to periods of peak pricing and grid emergencies, potentially reducing overall peak demand on SCE's grid by as much as 1 000 MW—the output of a major power plant. In a historic twist, the company also has a joint programme with the Ford Motor Company to explore plug-in hybrid vehicles and vehicle-to-grid technology. Ford, the company that helped inaugurate the mass era, may also play a role in stabilizing the game-changing technology for the distributed era, the smart micro grid. SCE estimates that plug-in electric vehicles in SCE's service area will exceed one million before 2025.

They argue that the decade will see the mass introduction of zero net energy residential and commercial buildings in California that may incorporate onsite renewable supply, energy storage, high efficiency envelopes, energy smart appliances/devices, and autonomous control systems interfaced to grid and wholesale market operations. SCE sees as a result, 'an integrated network with the potential of 20 million agents (people & devices) on SCE's system.' It further believes that 'vehicle-to-grid, micro grids and dynamic scheduling . . . using distributed resources will become operationally and economically feasible options.'

The implications for competitiveness are clear. This third wave of the internet (see Figure 8.2), applied to the energy grid, has the capacity to lower the costs of production for business. It has the potential to take energy, an increasingly expensive factor of production, and either reduce it substantially or in some cases turn it into a revenue stream. Figure 8.2 shows its potential role in helping to accelerate a third wave of manufacturing. Wave 1 presents the decline in OECD manufacturing associated with the full deployment of mass. Wave 2 presents the rising costs of offshore manufacturing. Wave 3 presents the falling costs of micro-manufacturing and smart-grid energy as drivers of localized production with the potential to stimulate investment and jobs. Austin based Incenergy is a start-up that exemplifies this trend. Founded in 2009, it designed the energy monitoring devices in the Pecan Street smart grid, allowing remote control of electricity use. The company is growing rapidly. CEO Barry McConachie comments 'Energy is a US$1.3 trillion industry in the U.S. alone.' Prof. Michael Webber at the University of Texas adds 'I see smart grids as a huge economic growth engine, just as when we built the grid 100 years ago.'

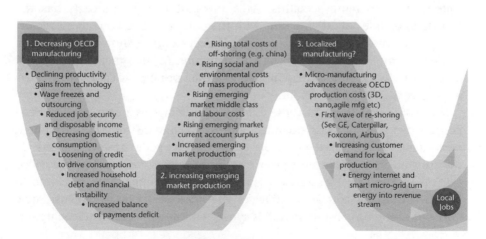

Figure 8.2: Waves of production

Accelerating Transition

The emergence of the energy internet marks a significant potential milestone in terms of transition. Over the last 150–200 years, as Carlota Perez identifies, there have been five great surges of development from water power and the weaving looms and canals, to coal and the steam engine, to electricity and the transmission lines, to oil and the combustion engine; each of these great surges coinciding with a new energy source, getting distribution, allowing large groups of people to improve their productive capacity. The energy internet has the fundamental implication of ushering in a new source of energy and a mechanism for distributing it. In terms of productivity gains, it is an energy source that has the potential to be both globally available and free, with a transformational impact on the energy return on energy invested once installed.

According to the criteria identified by Lipsey, Bekar, and Carlaw,[6] GPTs share four primary characteristics:

(1) wide scope for improvement and elaboration;
(2) applicability across a broad range of uses;
(3) potential for use in a wide variety of products and processes;
(4) strong complementarities with existing or potential new technologies.

Energy alone, no matter how smart, is only part of the prosperous future city. Genuine growth in a real economy as opposed to a financial one builds on the transformational benefits of a new general purpose technology. The technology is at the pilot stage, with wide scope for elaboration, but its applicability is already being broadened, for example, to the water internet and waste, with smart technologies in South Korea monitoring household waste volumes and immediately charging accounts. As a low-cost energy source it has the broadest possible potential for use, with the potential to roll out across sectors and geographies. Moreover, as the Pecan Street example shows, it is a system that can complement the existing grid structure. As the synergy of Ford and SCE shows, finally, it has the potential to attract productive capital to accelerate rather than delay its rollout.

Successful transition, as these examples illustrate, is not a head-to-head contest between the mass era and the new. Wikipedia, the bastion of openness, depends on closed protocols protecting its code. The Wikispeed C3 depends on mass produced rubber tires and a highway infrastructure rolled out under Fordism. Kickstart's hand pumps are manufactured in China to keep them as low-cost as possible for the poor. What accelerates the new GPT out of the turnaround period is synergy between the old and the new.

From Laboratory to City

Pecan Street is a small scale laboratory for an alternative grid. The FabCity project in Barcelona (Spain) is a laboratory for an alternative city. The city's chief architect, Vincente Guallart, and deputy mayor, Antoni Vives, aim to build Barcelona 5.0, a FabCity built on an interconnected community of neighbourhood fabrication laboratories (FabLabs) like the one in Texas. They want to encourage entrepreneurship and innovation, bringing factories back to the city in ways that enable a new industrial revolution built on new production methods and social bonds. At its heart is a focus on what the local community needs. 'There is no blueprint,' Vives comments, 'there is no template that you can build the productive city on. The vision has to respond to what they term the "City Anatomy," the unique configuration of needs and capabilities across the city.'[7]

The FabLab in action

Each FabLab is driven by a mission for the district, defined in collaboration between the local communities and city council. As with the Pecan Street project, they want to create a foundation funded by the public and private sectors. Each FabLab would produce devices and products for the local community, and these would eventually be managed by the neighbourhood's residents. All FabLabs will be connected by telepresence, and will share a repository of designs and educational material. The FabCity will support them with training concerning digital fabrication, ICT, and innovation at different levels (e.g. FabLab Kids, Fab Academy, advanced vocational training, programmes for senior citizens), and will itself collaborate on research projects with universities and other centres. The aim is not just to increase skills, but to build a FabCity productive model that accelerates business incubation, prototyping of ideas and products, development of new online sales platforms, development of new products and services associated with digital fabrication (remote 3D printing, 3D modelling, and consultancy for electronics projects and business programming, etc.). According to Vives, 'We are convinced the challenge [for cities] isn't just being more efficient or sustainable, but changing the model and turning sustainability into a productive model as well ... The internet has changed our lives, but not our cities—yet.'[8]

The FabCity model shows some of the potential of localized, interlinked production we discussed in Chapter 7. It encourages business incubation, the prototyping of ideas and products, the development of new online sales platforms, and the creation of new products and services associated with digital fabrication. For Barcelona as a whole this enables the creation of a range of clusters, addressing local needs and opportunities for growth. In the Les Corts district, for example, the FabLab being developed is dedicated to medical applications such as prostheses, mobility devices, and implants. It partners with the city's technical college, an employment centre for people with cerebral palsy, and the Wikispeed car initiative. The city is often the contracting agent for services and an important source of demand. Other FabLabs focus on textiles and fashion, industrial design, mobility, water, and energy.

The replicators

If you doubt the capacity of such ideas to spread, you only need to consider the way innovations now taken for granted have grown using the same infrastructure. In March 2003, there were just 100 000 blogs; today there are more than 100 million worldwide, with 15 more added in the time it takes to read this sentence.[9]

Part of it is demonstrating the possible. Ten years after an Afghan youth built the British Army a satellite from soda cans, as described in Chapter 7, Afghans who had attended the local Jalalabad FabLab team built a 'FabFi' (cf. Wi-Fi) network that uses the water tower at a local hospital to transmit Wi-Fi signals. The physical and metaphorical visibility of the tower encourages people to point downlink antennae at the FabFi. The FabLab team then offers people the chance to make an antenna for about US$70 in materials, and community interest puts pressure on the hospital to keep the resource working and serviced.

Beyond demonstration effects like these, and the self-replicating and open source tools, highlighted in Box 8.1, the FabLab project has two replication devices of its own.

Box 8.1 KEY SUCCESS FACTORS FOR BARCELONA'S FABCITY

- Defining goals, setting strategic direction based on community identified needs

- Training for lab leaders, with business model to spread based on replication model of Benedictine monks who moved from Mother monastery to set up new ones

- Government as broker of strategic partnerships, identifying companies focused on delivering services, consulting advice on how to make the market work as opposed to selling into the market

- Government contribution in kind, including e.g. unused spaces/buildings and staff input

- City contracts for goods and services from the labs (efficiency in procurement process as well as economic and social effects)

The first is rotation. FabLab leaders rotate through multiple labs, their role modelled on the Benedictine monks who would leave the mother monastery to serve in the surrounding areas. The second is the City Protocol (CP). CP facilitates a *peer-to-peer network* that aims to make it possible for cities to find other cities to collaborate with to tackle common problems using small, delivery-focused task-and-finish teams. Critical to the success of the project is the ecosystem approach with a trusted cross-sector partnership of the local community, academia, business, and the city council. In July 2012 over 200 participants, representing 33 cities, 20 major businesses, 14 universities, and 20 other organizations, convened in Barcelona to initiate the City Protocol Society and establish an Interim Steering Committee (ISC).

Virtuous circle

As with many other examples from energy to civic engagement to local manufacturing, once the interest to participate is in place, other technologies can amplify it and help citizens to create what has been described as the bottom up city.

In this way, represented by Figure 8.3, business is part of a virtuous circle in such cities.

A critical mass of makers is formed with the capacity to share resources, skills, and goals. This critical mass helps to implement energy self-sufficiency projects, reducing energy costs and strengthening the culture of autonomous production. The companies that prosper in this ecosystem have the advantage of low-cost energy, skilled and motivated labour, access to markets, and enhanced manufacturing capacity. That competitive edge increases the demand for labour and strengthens local markets that appeal to new artisanal trades. The Barcelona, Wikispeed, and Austin examples suggest that visible projects also attract participants, raising the level of engagement and reshaping the sense of what is possible. Technology enables new forms of collective engagement that increase the appetite for more involvement in local decision-making. This combination in turn enhances the desirability of the location, attracting more entrepreneurs, investors, active citizens, and civic funding.

Ecosystems of actors

This virtuous circle highlights the importance of multiple actors forming part of an ecosystem approach able to serve the specific needs and resources of each city, and thereby accelerate its transformation. It is not wholly top-down nor bottom-up. We have mentioned the role of the city council as a democratic convenor, able to help identify community needs and then bring together the business, NGO, academic, and other relevant resources. It can also provide

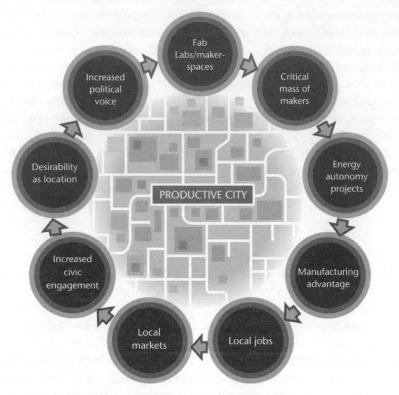

Figure 8.3: The virtuous circle of productive cities

funding, in cash or in kind in the form of seconded staff, or access to unused buildings. It can also stimulate the market by becoming a customer and opening up its own procurement contracts to the new producers.

The community sets the broad direction of demand and forms the testing ground for products and services. Business drives the innovation, addressing local community needs and opportunities for national and international growth, drawing on micro-fabrication technologies and other processes to gain competitive advantage. As we have demonstrated, these range from open-sourced methodologies to low-cost additive printing to crowd sourcing; from highly motivated labour to customer demand for locally-sourced products.

Democratizing power

One of the challenges for business in building the productive city is that each location has its own issues and complex network of stakeholders. What works in Barcelona may not work in Berlin. At present, major companies tend to parachute-in models, backed by statistics, indicating how many jobs a retail outlet of a certain size will generate, the tax revenues that can be anticipated, and the number of consumers who will be served. This top-down approach in general has been successful but in places, such as, Totnes, Devon (UK) and Sharon, Massachusetts (USA), has met with local resistance. It is, moreover, not well-suited to the distributed economy. Instead of master plans, the emphasis is on process and how different sectors get the basics right in each locality. As Hamdi describes it, it depends on trickle up rather than trickle down: 'a city plan made of small, networked interventions.'[10]

As David Roberts comments in 'Local Power: Tapping Distributed Energy in 21st-Century Cities,' democratizing power, just like democratizing computers, may result in a new wave of innovation and experimentation.[11] 'Spurred by the dispersion of energy technology,' Roberts comments, 'they will leave behind brittle 20th-century energy systems to create new models of resilient, self-reliant and sustainable prosperity.'

From Consumer to Producer

We have followed the drivers of increased local small business production; the rise in the costs of energy and of overseas production. We have also seen the trends of lowering solar costs and the advance of the energy internet as drivers for the switch to distributed energy. This switch in turn improves margins and attracts local economic growth. It also has a more subtle effect on agency. In co-producing power and an economic model for the new energy future, the Pecan Street residents shifted in identity from consumers to producers. This energy localism then has an indirect but observed impact on engagement. They went from managing power consumption to sorting rubbish. 'You build it through city pride,' says one Pecan Street leader, 'It's a visible thing people feel proud about. Then they're more amenable to doing other things.'

What has shifted here is not just identity, from the consumer to the producer, from the disconnected to the connected, but intent. The act of co-producing energy opens up the possibilities and rewards of civic engagement. Technology, as Kentaro Toyama argued, is not the answer. It is the amplifier of an existing intent. This intent can then be coupled with and amplified by well-chosen ICT to help create a flourishing city. Let's look at a couple of examples of this intent in action against three of the most intractable challenges confronting the city, mobility, political engagement, and good jobs.

Challenge 1: The Car-shaped City

Martin Melosi, in *The Automobile Shapes The City*, refers to the four phases in the evolution of the city, from walking city to streetcar city to automobile city to freeway city, and the extent to which the automobile has in some ways separated us from each other and reduced our capacity for this intent. Donald Appleyard's Project for Public Spaces, replicated in the UK in 2008 by Joshua Hart, demonstrated the social impact of the car, with residents of the San Francisco street with low car traffic volume having three times more friends than those living on the street with high car traffic.[12]

The turnaround of Curitiba

Curitiba (Brazil) gives some idea of the impact of intent in action. Back in 1970, crime in the overcrowded city of Curitiba was rampant, traffic blocking the streets. Each of the city's inhabitants had less than 1 m^2 of green area. Mayor Jaime Lerner had a people-centred approach to the turnaround of Curitiba. He put in place a Bus Rapid Transit programme that now carries two million passengers a day. The bus fare is the same wherever you go. People live within 400 metres of a bus stop. Most importantly, the bus gets priority on the roads, with sensors on the buses synchronizing with the traffic lights to allow them to cut through traffic. The system has proved good enough over 30 years to have caused a 30 per cent decrease in car use even as the population tripled; the reduced use of cars has also had a number of indirect benefits. Curitiba has the world's largest pedestrian shopping area. In addition, with a network of almost 30 parks and urban forested areas, Curitiba now has 52 m^2 green area per inhabitant. This in turn aids flood control. Instead of concrete canals, it controls floods through its park system, including the use of sheep as the preferred method for lawn cutting. Curitiba reports high levels of citizen satisfaction (70 per cent of residents in Sao Paolo want to live in Curitiba), and average income since the 1970s has gone from less than to 66 per cent greater than the national average. The city is Brazil's fourth richest and has a GDP in excess of US$17 billion, according to IBGE (Instituto Brasileiro de Geografia e Estatística: http://www.ibge.gov.br/home/).

Bogota's Ciclovia

Ciclovía, as another example, is a weekly, city-wide, car-free day in Bogotá that puts 76 miles of roads, including La Septima, the city's main commercial centre, off-limits to cars. It's been running since 1974, with more than 2 million people coming out every week to cycle and above all hang out on the street. Inspired by Bogota's 'ciclovia,' Los Angeles has started its own 'cicLAvia'. The event, covering over ten miles of Los Angeles downtown, opens the city up to bicycles and pedestrians. The lesson is summed up by Jaime Lerner. Curitiba is 'a city for people,' a place for coexistence, and the ability to be with each other is one of its core attractions. As James Button says in *Liberating the Heart of the City*, 'People are drawn to crowded, bustling spaces, where those unpredictable, surprising actors, other human beings are on centre stage. People make detours on their walking journeys to pass through busy streets. Pensioners take long bus journeys just to pass a morning.'[13]

The value of liveable cities

The return of manufacturing to the local community can therefore help create a virtuous circle where it reduces the need for the commuter car, frees up public space for parks and markets, and creates the space for engagement. Cortright's study of housing value in the USA found that houses with higher levels of 'walkability' (i.e. the mix of common daily shopping and social destinations within a short distance of the home) were worth US$4 000–34 000 more than those with average levels.[14]

ICT can then play a direct role again in helping to create some of the engagement on the streets. Local loyalty schemes such as MyCard and WiganPlus help ensure that more wealth stays inside a community, and initiatives such as Totally Locally demonstrate the large amount of money that can go into a local economy as the result of relatively small—£5—extra expenditure in local shops and businesses. Local online enterprises such as OurGoods, Freecycle, and Neighbourhood Goods also illustrate people's willingness to trade with others in their area. Incredible Edible Todmorden demonstrates how unlikely approaches such as growing vegetables in public spaces can change the look, feel, and reputation of cities, attracting people into the centres and boosting the trade of independent retailers and chain store managers alike.

Challenge 2: Political Engagement and Results from Government

The second challenge is political, creating local engagement in the political process and ensuring the crisis of governance has a positive impact on our crises quadrilemma.

Improving government is one of the ways these citizen networks can improve cities. Uchaguzi, for example, is an IT platform, used in Kenya's March 2013 elections, that allows citizens, NGOs, election observers, police, and humanitarian agencies to monitor the election process and immediately report incidents. MobileActive and Tactical Tech are international groups supporting people to use mobile phones for advocacy and campaigning work. One of the first uses of text messaging for social change was in the Philippines in 2001 when political activists sent SMS text messages urging Filipinos to assemble at Epifanio de los Santos Avenue (EDSA) in Manila to demonstrate for the impeachment of then-president Joseph Estrada. The message was short—'Go 2 EDSA. Wear blk.'—but over the next few days more than a million people arrived and seven million texts were sent. Within a month, Estrada had resigned.[15] Similar incidents have been reported in Moldova (the 2009 Twitter Revolution), and Côte d'Ivoire (Wonzomai 2010). In India, ipaidabribe is used to combat pervasive corruption by allowing users to report the dates, times, amounts, departments, and cases when bribes were paid. It has spread to Kenya, Greece, and Pakistan, and Russian users of the Bribr.ru app can also submit information on the locations and the amounts of the bribes they pay.

Ushahidi and the crowd-sourcing of solutions

Civil governance is just one of the ways a redirecting of ICT as general purpose technology can bring about better cities that foster external congruence. The technical possibilities offered by the second generation of the internet to create two-way communication, as well as the increase of information available, provide the right circumstances for hands-on involvement of articulate citizens and companies in formulating local policies. Urban citizens can also create new structures themselves—by calling on the government to take responsibility, by focusing attention on tangible problems, and by searching for solutions. Ushahidi was used during the 2010 Haiti earthquake to text help messages, but it has also been employed to monitor elections and helped people trapped in blizzards.

SeeClickFix is part of a movement to initiate community reporting of quality-of-life issues such as potholes, graffiti, rubbish, or broken street lights. It is software that allows users to show on a map where incidents occur, and forward that information to local government. As well as informing officials, it lets users see all of the complaints made about a particular problem and to add their voice to existing ones, thereby pushing the incident up the priority list. As well as letting government know that people are concerned, it has also prompted actions by companies, NGOs, and individual citizens, including a carpenter who fixed park benches SeeClickFix identified as broken. In a separate initiative in Paris, 200 citizens were given devices to sense ozone and noise levels as they went about their daily lives, and that information was shared via the Citypulse mapping engine.

Participatory budgeting

Porto Alegre (Brazil) has pioneered the use of participatory budgeting which has been praised for increasing the amount of public housing, bringing sanitation and water connections to 98 per cent of households, and quadrupling the number of schools over twenty years.[16] Since 1997, Ipatinga (Brazil) has provided online geo-referenced information about budgetary allocation and the status of public works projects. In the South-Kivu region of the Democratic Republic of Congo, mobile phones have been used to mobilize citizens to attend participatory budgeting meetings, to vote on budgetary priorities and to update citizens on the status of public works selected. In La Plata (Argentina), a combination of offline, online, and mobile channels is used to promote the engagement of citizens in the direct allocation of the investment budget of the city.[17]

Participatory budgeting is also found in Germany and the USA. In Hamburg, citizens have an opportunity to have their say on the medium-term city budget until 2016 using an online budget calculator and online forum. 50000 people are believed to have participated online, with over 2 000 budgets submitted.[18] In 2012, during its first year in New York City, participatory budgeting engaged 8 850 people, including neighbourhood assembly participants, budget delegates, and above all, voters. Residents submitted nearly 2 000 project ideas, and 44 per cent of the voters involved said they had never been involved in community problem-solving previously. Participation was especially strong amongst those the government recognizes as marginalized; and racial minorities and low-income people participated at higher rates than in traditional electoral politics.[19] The head of the project, Josh Lerner, concluded, 'New York has joined over 3 000 cities around the world that give residents real power over real money.'[20]

Enabling localism

This is not just about government action, but about enabling and facilitating localism. Citizens, instead of waiting for often unresponsive central government, are helped by it to discuss and decide what to do in their local patch. They are given back control, creating the urban environment that works for them, attracts other people, stimulates a vibrant marketplace, intensifies innovation and drives up the value of the area, with economic following social capital. The city shapes us, but its survival depends on us shaping it too. These principles apply from the macro level of town planning decisions to the micro of vegetable planting, where citizens worldwide share their knowledge and experience of innovative techniques to grow vegetables indoors, using hydroculture techniques (see www.rndiy.org; www.windowfarms.org). As Ratti and

Townsend comment, 'Rather than focusing on the installation and control of network hardware, city governments, technology companies and their urban-planning advisers can exploit a more ground-up approach to creating even smarter cities in which people become the agents of change.'[21] This is the distinction between the top-down blue-printed vision of Cyburbia and the bottom up vision of the distributed economy. Technology's intent is not to create cyber-space but to shape a new form of civic activism. Antonio Vives in Barcelona says that it is not government's role to lay down what a project should look like, or come up with a blueprint; one of the main contributions governments can make is ensuring that what happens is designed by people, for people. It is this public involvement, rather than categorical definitions, that creates what the New Economics Foundation calls the 'home town' as opposed to the architectural equivalent of the Invasion of the Body Snatchers that defines the 'clone town'.

Challenge 3: Good Jobs

A problem with the mass era today is work. One of the early justifications of capitalism was that it inspired creativity and enabled artisans to flourish. That 'inspired order of worth', the first justification of capitalism of Figure 5.2, was displaced in the lives of most people by other ones, but work, employment, and jobs have remained central to the expectations people have of business. Even when, in some parts of the world, the market order of worth predominates, manifesting itself in consumption, purchasing power, and the manufacture of desire, work itself is essential to participating in the capitalist system. Beruf, to borrow Weber's term, is still what makes us legitimate citizens. However, as we have shown, employment is problematic. In OECD countries, employment is as important as ever as a membership card to society, but part-time work, underemployment, youth unemployment, stagnant incomes, and job insecurity are undermining this relationship. Business is a victim of this in that it is inheriting the wrong kind of workforce for its needs and is suffering from the impossibility of the mass era reverting from a financial to an industrial economy but it will always be considered a cause of it as well if it continues to rely on financial engineering, and now intellectual property wars, for company growth, and persists in using redundancies, low wages, and underemployment as the primary way to boost productivity.

Emerging economies too are not immune from employment problems. We do not want to read too much into the slowing growth in some countries, and do not want to give too much weight to economists' predictions about stalled development, wage inflation, and possible trade and currency wars. Whatever the short- and medium-term trends may be, the quadrilemma of crises means that the model of economic development those countries relied on cannot continue without reaching dangerous levels of external incongruence that bring with them existential risk. As we have discussed, demographic change in such countries makes economic growth essential, but climate change puts those same people at enormous risk.

A major claim of green business as usual (GBAU) is that green growth creates green jobs. Stern called GBAU the most promising growth strategy for the future, and political leaders such as Obama and Merkel have stressed the employment benefits of shifting to clean energy. There is not yet much hard evidence for these claims. Creating a low carbon energy system replicating the mass era's high capex, centralized model would create jobs, but perhaps only enough to replace the jobs lost in fossil-based facilities. Building the generation and distribution system offers a Keynesian way of addressing recession by stimulating demand and increasing short-term job opportunities, but OECD countries are hesitant about this kind of economic stimulus because it implies taking on yet more debt. Even if that were not the case, it is unclear why applying green technology to sustain the mass era would have a positive impact on employment.

The Cyburbia alternative emphasizes the potential to change the way people work and to improve their quality of life, but the benefits only apply to those who live on the islands of green prosperity. In the worst case scenarios, work for the majority of people could be a terrible experience if, for example, a supplicant-tribute system emerges. The truth is that the impact of Cyburbia on work has not been properly thought through. Techno-optimists are the inheritors of an Edwardian dream that technological advances will allow people to lead better lives and work less, but that is an assumption with conflicting theoretical and empirical backing, and at the very least would need rigorous examination if Cyburbia were to be taken seriously.

Jobs and the distributed economy

The relationship between the distributed economy and work is still emerging and there is much more still to be found out about it. The FabCity model shows some of the potential of localized, interlinked production. It encourages business incubation, the prototyping of ideas and products, the development of new online sales platforms, and the creation of new products and services associated with digital fabrication. For Barcelona as a whole, this enables the creation of a range of clusters, addressing local needs and opportunities for growth. The advantages of cities with FabLabs compared to those without can be seen in Figure 8.4, which shows the pattern of value distribution this cluster of technological advance allows. Level 1 represents the mode of the bottom of the pyramid with ICT applications helping to deliver unmet

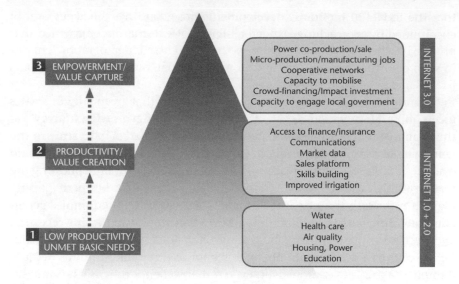

Figure 8.4: ICT and empowerment

basic needs such as power and clean water. At level 2, ICT applications enable employment, productivity, and the creation of value by the worker. At Level 3, ICT has the potential to support not just the creation but the capture of value, empowering the citizen.

This is also the context into which the value of clean tech jobs needs to be put. According to research in 2011, the USA has nearly 2.7 million clean tech jobs, equivalent to 60 per cent of the size of the IT sector (4.8 million jobs), and larger than its fossil fuel industry (2.4 million jobs). However, not all of these jobs have the same significance. Some are to do with renewable energy and resource efficiency which will aid emissions reduction but tied into the mass era will not result in absolute decoupling or climate stabilization. Some jobs are in environmental management, reuse, and recycling which are areas of important innovation, although whether they offer better employment prospects than other industries is not known. Other jobs are in agriculture and natural resources conservation, education, and compliance. However, the emerging growth opportunities appear to lie with new clean tech industries across multiple segments including wind power, battery technologies, bio-fuels, and smart-grid technology. These segments grew at about 8 per cent a year between 2003 and 2010, twice as fast as the rest of the USA's economy. They are productive, with export potential, accounting for almost US$54 billion of exports in 2009, twice as export-intensive as the national economy with over US$20 000 worth of goods and services sold for every job compared to just US$10 400 in the economy as a whole. These are the types of job, exemplified by Incenergy, that the Pecan Street project is creating in Texas.

Innovation, manufacturing, and exports

In contrast with much of contemporary industry, clean tech industries appear to support an innovation-driven productive economy. The same study of the situation in the USA shows that 10 per cent of clean economy jobs are in the fields of science and engineering (twice the figure for the USA economy overall), and 26 per cent of them involve manufacturing, compared to 9 per cent of jobs in the economy as a whole. The figure in some sectors is even higher: two-thirds of jobs in solar and wind energy, for example, are in manufacturing, and in segments such as appliances, water-efficient products, and electric vehicle technologies the figure is over 90 per cent. The potential is for the return of not just jobs but skills focused on innovation.

Clusters of innovation

However, this is not simply a story of manufacturing or entrepreneurship. It is the story of a new living environment. Although we described the distributed economy as inclusive, clean tech innovation to date highlights the importance of cities and metropolitan areas for agglomeration, networks, and clusters. FabCity is an urban initiative, and in the USA the clean tech experience reinforces Porter's thesis that clusters aid competitiveness, rewarding metropolitan areas that facilitate them with better growth performance. Urban regions are estimated to have produced ten times more renewable technologies patents than rural ones. According to the London School of Economics, there are numerous examples of clean clusters throughout the USA, including professional environmental services in Houston, solar photovoltaic in Los Angeles, fuel cells in Boston, wind in Chicago, water industries in Milwaukee, and energy efficiency in Philadelphia.

The example we gave in Chapter 7 of the interconnection of solar lighting, money transfer, and farm insurance shows how a cluster of ideas can evolve in a developing country setting. A thick web of specialized services increases the competitiveness of a locality, and fostering this sort of creative-productive-consumption can increase the value of human capital, suggesting that young people that participate in such activities today will be tomorrow's innovative entrepreneurs.

This is in keeping with Jacobs's notion of cities from the 1960s. In 1962, she argued that cities were the primary drivers of economic development, and that explosive economic growth came about from replacing urban imports, as happened for example when bicycle factories replaced bicycle importers in nineteenth-century Tokyo. Anticipating what is happening with FabLabs and projects such as Pecan Street, she believed that import replacement built up local infrastructure, skills, and production.

An emerging new 'order of worth'?

The work situation we have described conforms to the new network order of worth identified by Boltanski and Chiapello. It is a justification of capitalism built around networked groupings that value entrepreneurship, creativity, and relationships, and is in marked contrast to the idea of the 'company man' or 'salaryman' that lingers as an ideal but is increasingly difficult to find in reality. The stresses of modern work life have been touched on at different points in this book: labour exploitation in emerging country factories, job insecurity and underemployment in OECD countries, and the erosion of social welfare safety nets worldwide are some of the ones we have mentioned. There are plenty of people who say that this is the price people must pay for the benefits of capitalism; but as we have argued, this type of capitalism will not deliver sustainable prosperity for society, and will not even benefit business. More importantly, many people already accept the network order of worth, and do not trust governments or companies to honour the social contracts of the past. Therefore, the kind of work and manufacturing associated with the distributed economy does not require a leap of faith, it complements a transition that is already well-advanced.

After Ford, and after homo economicus

The motivations for participating in a FabLab or a project of civic engagement or a wikispeed agile manufacturing experiment will vary, revealing a wider set of desires to engage more consistent with Amos Etzioni's *I-We* paradigm than the neo-liberal assumption that humans are *homo economicus*.[22] Motivations are affected by blends of financial, social, and environmental outcomes, and also include ones purely anchored around the process of producing. There is a distinction within Platonic thought between two types of desire: productive desire (the active desire to make things), and desire from lack (the passive desire for things one does not have). Productive desire is the driver of *homo faber*, humans as the maker of things. This is not an urge that the mass era has favoured; the mass production process turned the craftsman in to the labourer and the creator into a factor of production. Their role became fragmentary, static, not allowing people's skills to grow, and without a clear result in terms of impact to give it meaning. This is reflected in the changing justifications of capitalism we visited in Chapter 5, and in particular the diminution of the artisanal order of worth.

Man as maker

What micro-production responds to is productive desire, giving people the chance, at varying levels of engagement, to make productive contributions. It is the opposite of the desire from lack. This passive desire for things not possessed is already dominant, and looks set to grow as the world's population heads towards the nine billion mark. The mass production, intensive economy has focused, quite rationally, on serving the customers who could pay, and its core target has been the urban and suburban consumers with disposable incomes. As Prahalad, Hart, and others recognized, the model leaves unaddressed the basic needs of the billions at the bottom of the pyramid.

At the heart of the new model is a productive economy that addresses these failures by linking the two desires together. The active desire to create is satisfied in the production of goods and services that address the needs (the passive desires from lack) of the broader community. In the mass production model a limited number of experts design and create content. Product is then mass produced, with labour receiving enough wages to enable it to participate in the market as mass consumers. A portion of the profits from sales are returned to investors. In the collaborative/creative economy model, design is crowd-sourced, drawing on the needs and expertise of a broad range of contributors using open sourced materials. Production is then done at the micro level using micro-production technologies.

Portrait of the possible

Some of what we are describing echoes theories found in other schools of thought from social entrepreneurship to libertarianism. As we said earlier on, the nature of the quadrilemma of crises means they cannot be addressed by resorting to outdated ideas or rejecting the new. The bottom-up city is more complex than making shops more attractive or greening public transport. It is also not about expecting everyone to be entrepreneurs. Nonetheless, there are non-philosophical reasons to be enthused by the prospects of productive cities.

In the short term, people in OECD countries are living in an austerity economy but do not want austerity experiences; the cities associated with the distributed economy not only lay the foundations for future prosperity, they can also provide good experiences and a sense of belonging now.

As with all of the ideas we have set out, what unfolds will depend on human decisions and actions. One might believe that once social capital is created in the heart of communities, the economic capital will follow, but what will it take to make this happen more broadly? Can cities, large and small, be engines of a new productive economy, or is it that the small town will remain somewhere to escape from? Will investment in cities result in localized innovation and manufacturing, or will the attraction of retail-led generation continue to dominate because people want to buy, to shop, to park their car, and to parade their brands. In Oxford (UK), where we are writing, planning permission for a FabLab was rejected, despite this being a renowned hub of scientific, humanities, and social innovation, despite the need for better jobs, and despite the weekly closure of retail outlets large and small. The sparks of what is possible from KickStart to WiganPlus, FabCity to Pecan Street do not mean that the transition to the distributed economy will happen inevitably. As Jamie Lerner, ex-mayor of Curitiba says, 'The soul of the city—the strength which makes it breathe, exist and progress—resides in each one of its citizens.' That strength may reside in citizens, but unleashing it to create the productive city is a task that requires both business and government. It is this process that we turn to in the final chapter.

Notes

1. (Alexander 2004)
2. http://www.bigbrotherwatch.org.uk/
3. http://www.businessweek.com/news/2012-02-09/energy-takes-twice-as-much-income-for-half-of-u-s-households.html, accessed 13 December 2012
4. http://www.businessweek.com/news/2012-06-01/texas-may-triple-power-prices-to-avert-summer-blackouts
5. (Korea Smart Grid Institute: http://www.smartgrid.or.kr/10eng3-1.php
6. In Helpman 1998, pp. 38–43
7. Antoni Vives speaking at the Global Clean Energy Forum, Barcelona, 3 October 2012
8. Antoni Vives speaking at the Global Clean Energy Forum, Barcelona, 3 October 2012
9. (Lessig 2008)
10. (Hamdi 2010)
11. http://www.scientificamerican.com/article.cfm?id=distributed-energy-urban
12. http://www.pps.org/reference/dappleyard/
13. (*The Age*, 6 September 2002)
14. (Cortright 2009)
15. (Shirky 2010)
16. (Wampler 2007)
17. http://www.presupuestoparticipativo.laplata.gov.ar, accessed 29 December 2012
18. http://www.hamburg-haushalt.de, accessed 29 December 2012
19. https://s3.amazonaws.com/attachments.readmedia.com/files/39068/original/PBNYC_Data_Summary_4_3_12_Final.pdf?1333509153, accessed 29 December 2012
20. http://www.nynp.biz/index.php/breaking-news/9842-communities-and-cbos-benefit-from-participatory-budgeting-project, accessed 29 December 2012
21. http://www.scientificamerican.com/article.cfm?id=the-social-nexus
22. (Etzioni 1989)

9

Transition: The Turnaround

IN THIS CHAPTER

The ecosystem of innovation. The unique role of the entrepreneurial state. Redefining the new order of worth. The elements of producer capitalism.

> *'If something cannot go on forever, it will stop.'*
>
> Herb Stein

Innovation and the Entrepreneurial State

When Louis Blériot climbed triumphantly out of the wreckage of his plane in a Dover field on the morning of Sunday 25 July 1909, the first thing he reached for was the pair of crutches he had strapped to the fuselage. Financially broke, crippled from previous crashes, Blériot had just won the Daily Mail's £1 000 challenge to cross the channel by plane. He was taken to Dover for an English breakfast to celebrate, but there he was accosted by three UK customs officials who checked him for contraband and infectious diseases.

There is a ready conclusion to draw from this story—private sector innovation versus the dead hand of the state. The reality however is more nuanced. Guiding Blériot's path was *Escopette*, the French destroyer laid on by the French Government to help Blériot compete against Britain's Hubert Latham. *Escopett*e, complete with Mme Blériot on board, was Blériot's signpost for the way to Dover (he had no compass or watch). Having rapidly passed *Escopette*, he circled back to give the vessel and his wife a chance to catch up but lost them again, and decided to press on. While the private sector was the driver, an ecosystem was at work. Among others, the state, with the destroyer *Escopette* in the background and rapidly overtaken, had played a guiding role.

This book has focused on business and its role in society. We have said little about the role of government. An often polarized debate pitches austerity against stimulus. One side asks how can economic cuts ever be the route to growth? The other dismisses stimulus packages as little better than Maynard Keynes's proposal to boost the economy by burying money in disused mines. Is this is a false dichotomy? Can the state, at the point of transition in the technological cycle, make targeted investments that can help generate large scale and superior returns for the economy? Is there, in other words, a role for what the think tank Demos calls the 'entrepreneurial state'?

The case against government involvement in innovation has a long history. Herb Stein's dictum that what cannot go on forever will stop, acquired canonical status as Stein's Law. And this advice from Stein, former Chairman of the USA's Council of Economic Advisers under Richard Nixon, sums up one of the guiding principles of non-interventionism; things self-correct. It is not just that there is no need for intervention. Stein would argue that to do so introduces distortion. In ancient Sparta, the Greek historian Plutarch (48–122 AD) tells us, the elders would order parents to leave children overnight on Mount Taygetus to be sure that only the strong would survive.[1] This, echoing the laissez-faire-ism of Stein's Law, is the theoretical essence of the Schumpeterian model of creative destruction. A vibrant economy depends on strong companies surviving and weak ones going down, devoting resources not to the 'hopelessly unadapted', as Schumpeter put it, but to the potential winners. In this model, the market, not government, needs to be the mechanism.

Waves of growth

In the Schumpeterian-based model, GPT's bring waves of growth, but only insofar as they are fit for purpose, adapted to the needs of the external

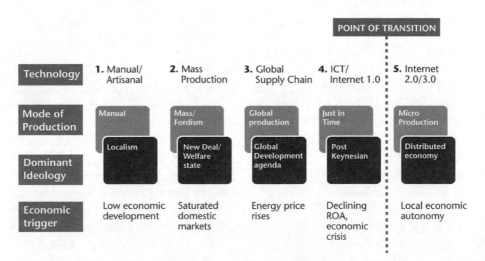

Figure 9.1: Technological waves

environment. As Figure 9.1 shows, each wave raises welfare but as it reaches maturity succumbs to, and in some cases contributes to, an economic 'trigger' environment or new set of needs that helps precipitate the technological breakthrough and accompanying mode of capitalism of the wave that follows. The new technology gains traction in part because of its fit with the new needs of society, i.e. its congruence with the external environment. The low levels of economic development of the artisanal era, for example Stage 1 in Figure 9.1, acted as one of the triggers for the steam age technologies introduced by Stephenson and Ford's mass production. This new mode of production accompanied by New Deal policies that spread wealth, culminated in saturated markets. The saturated domestic markets of mass production in OECD countries are driving the logic for, and help trigger the globalization of, mass production and consumption across a new wave of markets. Rising fuel prices and the mounting complexity of logistics support the introduction of ICT into the supply chain.

Capitalism that fits the world around it

In our hypothesis, finally, at the most simplified level of analysis, declining economy-wide gains in productivity, consistent with a mature set of mass technologies, are now linked to economic crisis. This economic crisis, coupled with environmental and social crises now paves the way for the emergence of a new dominant technology and accompanying mode of capitalism to replace a current model both delegitimized and weakened. 'Capitalism', as Klaus Schwab stated at the 2013 gathering of the World Economic Forum in Davos, 'does not fit the world around it.' The pattern of Schumpeterian waves of development suggests that what will emerge are both a new technological paradigm and a model of capitalism with a better fit to the world around it.

For Herb Stein, what is central is the pattern. Without intervention, the technological waves roll in; the invisible hand of the market passes the metaphorical lime of a new General Purpose Technology for the barman to squeeze until it's dry. This is the genius of capitalism, and for Stein, as for many others, it is the reason why government is superfluous. The reality, however, as Veblen and congruence theory identify (Chapter 5), is that social and economic institutions coalesce around a technological paradigm and can have the capacity to lock it in, with institutions, including regulators themselves, captured by the very markets they are supposed to regulate. As we showed earlier in Chapter 2, the failure to achieve binding legislation on climate change to avoid more than 2°C of warming remains a paramount example of this lock-in in action. As Simon Johnson, former Chief Economist of the IMF, comments in *The Quiet Coup*, Wall Street's political power is a function not just of the surface capture of regulation through lobbying and the dense interchange of personnel, but also of the deep capture embodied by the belief that what was good for Wall Street was by definition good for the country.[2]

The Economist's review of state support for entrepreneurs[3] critiqued government's inability to pick winners, favouring horizontal strategies to support innovation broadly over vertical strategies that targeted specific companies or sectors. China's 13th Five Year Development Plan appears though to blur that distinction, providing not just horizontal support such as tax breaks for R & D, but vertical support in the form of US$1.7 trillion committed to seven strategic sub-sectors including Clean Tech, Biotech, and Nanotechnology. The reality is that in successful economies, not least in emerging countries, government is playing a role that goes beyond developing infrastructure and setting the rules, and instead delivers active support for high growth sectors. The impact of this support has proven, historically, to be critical. From space exploration to the US Defence Department's support for ARPANET, a precursor of the internet, to the grant-funded algorithm that was the foundation for Google's search engine, to the UK's Medical Research Council support for research into molecular antibodies and DFID's grant to M-PESA, state funding has played a catalytic role. Block and Keller found that between 1971 and 2006, 77 out of the most important 88 innovations rated by *R&D Magazine*'s annual awards were found to have been fully dependent on federal support.[4] Successful transitions, as Perez suggests, are accelerated by governments, as part of an innovation ecosystem, coming up with the right interventions at the right time to identify, support, and direct breakthrough technologies. What do those interventions look like?

Three Cities of the Future

This book has mapped the contours of three 'cities' or models of the economy of the future, cities we have labelled for shorthand as Petropolis, Cyburbia and the distributed economy. As society moves, by necessity, beyond Petropolis, only two options are left that appear to offer external congruence: Cyburbia and the distributed economy. These two models represent two different deployments of the new ICT paradigm. Where we differ from the laissez-faire approach of Stein, and follow Perez, is that the form of deployment remains open rather than determined. Just as with mass production, the technology can take different forms and the role of the state can be critical in directing and accelerating the transition. Modern Nairobi offers an illustration.

Nairobi

Figure 9.2 shows a group of people standing against a fence in the savannah outside Nairobi. Some gaze at the camera. Some gaze at the land that is going

Figure 9.2: Konza Technopolis: Source Erik Hersman

to be transformed. The billboard above the fence is for Konza Technopolis, the US$14.5bn blueprint of the Konza Technopolis Development Authority (KOTDA), now under construction 60 kilometres from Nairobi. Konza City will have state-of-the-art information technology, onsite healthcare and education facilities, monitored air quality, purified water from the specially constructed Thwake dam, and high speed rail links to Jomo Kenyatta International Airport. The city to some extent complements Nairobi, and its appeal betrays some of the challenges the ageing Kenyan capital confronts. In many ways it is Nairobi's mirror image.

A third city, though, is also represented in the photo, an addition to the dyad of old Nairobi and its glimmering Konza cyburb. The group standing in front of the perimeter gate are members of Nairobi's iHub, part of a network of sixteen innovation spaces across the city that have earned Nairobi the nickname 'Silicon Savannah'. It was the iHub that incubated M-Farm and played host to Akirachix, Kenya's network of 200 female technology entrepreneurs. All three cities of the future are present in the photo. The iHub team, representatives of the distributed economy, standing in front of the fence are on a day trip to visit the site of Konza Technopolis, the design antithesis of old Nairobi.

These three potential pathways or cities illustrate a decision point—a crisis—for Kenya about its model of future growth. In this case it is Kenya's crisis, but it is also a global one. Urbanization and population growth are expected to bring

3.2 billion new people to the world's cities by 2050. Thirty-five megacities with over 10 million people will emerge by 2030, with twenty-two of them in Asia. A hundred and thirty-six new cities, according to McKinsey & Co., will enter the world's top 600 by 2025, all of them from the developing world.[5]

The three cities represent separate development approaches. First, to shore up existing infrastructure enabling the city to continue to absorb refugees from the countryside into its slums (the model of Petropolis); second, to invest from scratch in the greenfield smart city (the model of Cyburbia); or, third, to use technology to adapt the city from within to address the emerging needs and opportunities facing its people, both inside and outside the city (the model of the distributed economy).

The challenges for Petropolis

The fossil fuel driven mass production and consumption model of the Petropolis, as we have shown at the start of the book, is running up against structural limits. Over time, as the *Shift Index* revealed, productivity gains and return on assets decrease. Wages stagnate, manufacturing gets exported overseas, consumer spending decreases, debt-fuelled consumption increases, and household debt and national balance of payments deficits increase. In the case of fossil fuel driven mass production and consumption, climate change, and social issues create separate and mounting sources of instability. Capital constraints then prevent the Petropolis from investing in major overhaul. The Petropolis loses its ability to recruit and retain the best businesses and talent. The construction of a new model of the city gains competitive logic.

The challenges for Cyburbia

What form, though, does that new model take? The image on the boundary of Konza shows two distinct options, both ICT driven, but confronting very different challenges and presenting very different approaches to the potential of local people. The first is the blueprint smart city. Such cities offer the chance for infrastructure investment, and can form knowledge centres that accelerate innovation and spearhead new clean growth in the economy, a growing focus, for example, for the knowledge cities in the Pearl River Delta in China. They also run the risk, if not designed from the bottom up, of losing the qualities that attract the smartest and most creative citizens. China's Dong Tan eco-city, and Malaysia's BioValley (later nicknamed 'BioValley of the Ghosts') showed that where the smart city is built from the top down the Cyburbia model, not anchored in the needs of the local market, creates real estate projects that are harder to fill with people than to plan.

The challenges for the distributed economy

The other alternative to Petropolis is the city of the distributed economy. The model has compelling up-front logic; the rise in offshore manufacturing costs, combined with low capex micro-manufacturing techniques provides the economic trigger for a return to local manufacturing. The potential emergence of the plug and play smart micro grid transforms the costs of production, turning energy for local producers into an income stream not an expense. A new culture emerges based around producer capitalism and connectedness that drives local competition around fabrication. It is a bottom-up, demand-led initiative but, as the group standing beneath the billboard for Konza show us, this city's growth is not certain. The bottom-up city has no government requisitioned land, no capital, and no convening power. In order for the ventures the iHub is incubating to reach profitability, a lot of things have to go right. Above all, as the examples of their fellow innovators in the cluster that produced M-PESA, M-KOPA, and Kilimo Salama illustrate, the pathway to scale often depends on getting access to the platform resource and markets of an incumbent business.

Synergy and the Role of the Entrepreneurial State

We have outlined two opposing visions, neither on its own seemingly capable of delivering society's needs at scale. The reality though is more nuanced, and the plans for Nairobi involve something closer to the synergy Perez says is crucial to transition. There are two forms that cities like Konza can take, competitive or collaborative. The first is the blueprint city, built to meet the market opportunity defined by the mass paradigm, with state of the art facilities for multinationals and jobs focused on business process outsourcing. In this model the city could in some cases undercut the community of the iHub. The iHub members could be left standing at the perimeter fence of a new smart city with the potential to make life more precarious for them in a number of ways:

People: Rather than accelerate an indigenous innovation economy, will the smart city harness the talent of the iHub and deploy it to attract ever cheaper outsourcing?

Space: Konza, as the iHub trip members were quick to blog, could house 100 iHubs. Will Konza city, with potentially unfilled tech real estate if it is not built around the preferences of local people, make it harder to argue for space and government support to expand in Nairobi?

Access to local users and business collaborators: Market innovations depend on knowing the customer's unmet needs. M-PESA's access to local markets,

215

for example, was critical in getting the message from consumers that they wanted money transfers not banking. Likewise the build-out from M-PESA to M-KOPA and Kilimo Salama depended on close contacts between innovators, incumbents, and end-users on how systems could inter-operate. If the smart city breaks up the density of exchange, it breaks up the innovation ecosystem, reducing the potential for the synergies between innovators and incumbents that drive transition.

The second form is a collaborative one, where Konza accelerates synergy between the iHub's start-ups and the multinationals and larger players of Konza. Dr Bitange Ndemo, Permanent Secretary at Kenya's Ministry of Information, is explicit that the model is one of collaboration. 'We have this huge number of youth-run businesses that, if we don't nurture; if we don't help in the growth stages, will die. A lot of small enterprises collapse because they do not have an incubation centre. So what we want to do is create a large incubation centre, not just in IT, but also other peripherals like animation. We will have a studio centre, an IT centre, a research centre, and a technology and science centre. For this, we have brought universities, the private sector and the government together, creating a triple-helix congruence.'[6]

The smart city, in other words, if done smartly, could be a critical part of an innovation ecosystem that will help companies grow. The government can shape and accelerate the direction of growth, playing a critical role in designing the new city to create synergies between the tech city and distributed economy that enhance both. It is government that may be vital in helping the bottom-up city to flourish. The point is not to substitute for the market. What the collaborative model depends on is what Anne-Marie Slaughter describes as 'government as platform'. Slaughter, a former US government senior policy advisor, argues that the most important role of government is not displacing business or the community, but providing the space in which they can operate most productively.[7] This synergy, or interplay between members of the ecosystem, is at the heart of successful innovation.

Examples of the entrepreneurial state in action

Government support, then, as the Nairobi case demonstrates has a role, but one thing that is critical is timing. What accelerates growth at one phase of the transition cycle can hamper it at another. Figure 9.3 shows the phases of transition, from irruption through to maturity, and the opportunities for an entrepreneurial state to support innovation at different stages. While the focus of this book is on the broader waves of growth as opposed to specific policy instruments, we will briefly give some illustrations of this macro-economics of innovation in action.

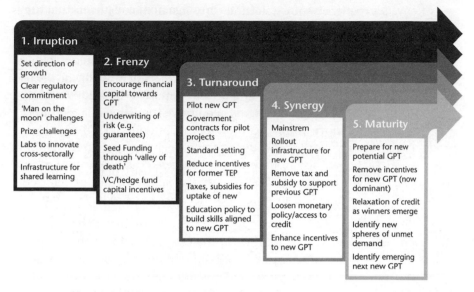

Figure 9.3: Accelerating transition: phases of government support

PHASE 1: IRRUPTION PHASE: ACCELERATING NEW ENTRANTS

At the Irruption phase, while the central role is unquestionably the innovator's, the government can play a strategic role, scanning the horizon during the maturity phase of the prevailing paradigm for disruptive new entrants with the potential to transform markets. This fit between widespread market need and emerging technological capabilities can help set the direction of growth. China's model, as an example, is based around a five year development plan with constituent sub-sectors identified as strategic priorities. This is where the action is going to happen, and the government uses its cross-sectoral role to get a read on it in a way that innovators and incumbents with vested interests cannot.

This strategic task is then supported by a series of interventions to stimulate innovation. The 'Man on the Moon' challenge used by J.F. Kennedy was recently reprised in Al Gore's challenge for zero carbon growth. As Diamandis and Kotler have shown, prize challenges are also powerful signals of intent, and can harness the genius and passion of the crowd, from Blériot, crutch-bound from crashes, to the sixty-six year old retired mechanical engineer from Lima, Peru, with his airbag-powered device to disable getaway vehicles.[8]

As critical, is government's convening power. The example of Pecan Street illustrates the importance of cross-sectoral collaboration. The Pike Powers Lab, sited in the heart of the community piloting the smart grid, gives a chance for entrepreneurs to collaborate with customers, government, and academia, as well as big business partners with the potential to scale up innovations.

As Kenya's experience shows, getting early installation of infrastructure is also critical to accelerating growth. Bitange Ndemo's 2005 appointment as Permanent Secretary to the Ministry of Information and Communications technology played a role in kick-starting government support. Ndemo brought four undersea internet cables to Kenya, causing a bandwidth explosion that has contributed to a trebling of internet users since 2009. Physical infrastructure also counts in the digital economy. The Barcelona 5.0 project, with its vision to move from the product-in-trash-out (PITO) city to the productive and energetically self-sufficient one, is giving up unused buildings to a network of 12 FabLabs around the city. Targeted cash contributions can also have a catalytic impact. What's the cost of a FabLab? At the extreme end, Harmen G. Zijp of the FabLab Amersfoortnetwork has produced a guide to setting up a fully equipped and functioning FabLab in seven days for under €5000. His 'instructable' in the Annex at the end of this chapter lists what that sum gets you.

PHASE 2: FRENZY

At the frenzy stage, the key transition risk is a failure of capital to finance the emerging technologies and a key role is that of risk capital. While popular rhetoric demonizes the financial sector as predatory, looking for nothing but returns, in the Schumpeterian model, in the Frenzy stage you need some smart financiers prepared to take some risk with disruptive companies. In this phase, high risk, high reward capital looks for companies associated with the new GPT and invests in them to get some upside. This high risk equity financing at the installation stage is a different beast to the low risk financing of the deployment phase. Economic theory has applied many terms to this distinction, from the old German distinction between 'schaffendes Kapital' (creative capital) and 'raffendes Kapital' (grabbing capital) to Schumpeter's distinction between the sphere of money (Geldgrössen und monetäre Vorgänge) and the sphere of goods and services (Güterwelt). At its heart, is the difference between Keith Richards and Cliff Richard. Keith is who you turn to for some Rock'n'- Roll, to get the party going. Keith is the economic Start Me Up. Cliff, once the new technology is established and is safe for pensioners to invest in, is closer to Congratulations.

The frenzy stage needs its Keiths. It depends on financial capital taking risk on new ventures, but a key transition risk is the failure of that capital to support the breakthrough technologies that need it. Marianna Mazzucato highlights a critical stage in the development of new enterprises when private sector investment is unavailable and government investment is required.[9] Venture capital, in essence, understands risk but not uncertainty, and therefore works with companies in a sector whose track record allows one to assess risk. Disruptive technologies, by definition, do not have that track record. They fall into the category of Knightian uncertainty where the investor just does not know what will happen because there is no historical record.

Size also presents a challenge. Companies can grow too large to get any more impact and angel investor support, but will still not be strong enough to attract venture capital. This will remain true even with the emergence of crowd-funding and the relatively low capex requirements of the technologies associated with the new economy. Furthermore, fund structure presents a challenge. Venture capital funds typically have a ten-year time horizon, and the need to set up a follow-on fund based on demonstrated returns leads to investment in companies with the fastest pathways to profitability and the easiest exit pathways. It is quite common therefore for start-ups to be ready for sale within five years, with the result that '[v]enture capital funds tend to be concentrated in areas of high potential growth, low technological complexity and low capital investment.'[10]

The state, recognizing the gaps in the market, can not only proactively create strategy around a new high growth area, but can fund the most uncertain phase of the research that the private sector is too risk-averse to engage with, seeking and commissioning further developments, and often even overseeing the commercialization process.

Alongside China and Korea's programmes, the US ARPA-E programme, for example, is having a catalytic effect on clean tech financing in the United States. Guarantee programmes such as OPIC's and the IFC's can also help underwrite risk.

PHASE 3: TURNAROUND

Phase 3 represents the critical stage for government. In the bust that follows the boom, the weak will have perished, and the strong, the companies with the potential for deployment into the mainstream market, will have survived. While a broad new general purpose technology may emerge, there will nevertheless be a range of potential directions it could be deployed in. As we have discussed before, the GPT can emerge in multiple forms. Just as the technologies associated with mass production took different forms in the USA, Russia, and Nazi Germany, ICT is now emerging in a number of linked but distinct models of growth. These forms, rapidly evolving, include:

- *Extending mass production*: ICT as the driver of an extended era of oil and fossil fuel driven mass production (acting as Botox to the mass era's Joan Collins).
- *Geo-engineering*: ICT as a means to maintain man's control over the ecosystem, moving natural resources into the management domain via large-scale actions such as cloud-seeding the stratosphere or changing the

alkalinity of the sea. Trans-humanism applies these principles to the constraints of the body.

- *Cyburbia*: ICT as the nervous system of the blueprint smart cities, deploying large scale capital for the top-down city, presenting the visible and invisible firewall against the mass era's excesses.

- *The distributed economy*: a model of connected and productive communities drawing on micro-production and smart micro-grid technologies.

Critical moves

The role of the government in this phase is not only to help select the direction of the new GPT, choosing the model with the greatest benefit for society; it is to then accelerate its rollout. The private sector will fall into two camps: the incumbent companies with revenues dependent on the current dominant paradigm (TEP), and the innovators that are seeking to disrupt it. Government alone has the independent capacity to objectively evaluate the stage of the technological cycle. Has the dominant general purpose technology and the TEP that supports it reached maturity? Is there a new TEP that is waiting in the wings? The government's job is not just to figure this out, but to help provide the conditions for the new GPT to succeed. Specifically, it has a critical task to address market lock-in and internal incongruence, removing the barriers in terms of tax, regulation, incentives, and skills which prevent markets from supporting the next generation of enterprise and levelling the playing field so that the market can identify and roll out the set of enterprises that will drive the next wave of growth.[11] Figure 9.4 illustrates

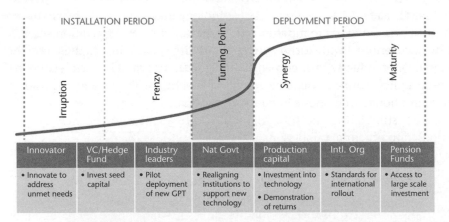

Figure 9.4: Institutional moves across technological cycle

the institutional moves across the technological cycle, showing the pivotal role of government in addressing institutional lock-in and re-aligning institutions around the new GPT and direction of growth that fits the external environment.

While a review of government policy at the transition stage is beyond the scope of this book, critical moves include: closing off the loopholes that might allow production capital to continue to find speculative returns; putting in place market incentives to motivate industry incumbents to explore the market; standard setting, in particular getting industries that need to collaborate across sectors to agree on interoperable standards (see, for instance, the Pecan Street smart grid). Collaboration is key. A perfectly reasonable fear of collusion dating back to Adam Smith and warranted by the behaviour of big business, has resulted in all manner of laws designed to stop companies working together. By contrast, ideas from social entrepreneurship to resilience to corporate sustainability all emphasize the importance of collaboration and partnership. As Awa Coll-Seck, Senegal's Health Minister, has said, talking about the impact internet innovations are having on developing country health care, 'Nobody, working alone, can have results.'[12]

A fourth critical opportunity is for the government to act as pilot customer. In Barcelona, the city council looks to stimulate the market, ensuring through its procurement practices that it buys from FabLabs and other suppliers that meet social and environmental criteria. Using solar energy for schools or electric cars for the postal service (if it is publicly-owned), or other similar decisions can create enough of a local market to foster competition and rapid learning for eventual export. Finally, as examples from Estonia to Colombia show, there needs to be training, ensuring the next generation is capable of not just adopting the technology but accelerating its next wave of growth.

PHASE 4: SYNERGY

As the economy starts to move into the synergy phase, the transition starts to gain momentum, with early movers deploying production capital into the new GPT, productivity increasing and growth returning to the economy. Credit policy can be loosened as it will be fuelling production as opposed to consumption driven boosts in demand. Subsidies for the previous GPT can be reduced, stimulating the flow of production capital into the new GPT as opposed to potential bubbles. As viable substitutes to the dominant technology emerge, it also becomes politically easier to tax it. China's February 2013 introduction of a local carbon tax both depends on and may accelerate the viability of lower carbon alternatives. Finally there is deployment infrastructure. Just as seven successive USA administrations built 47,000 miles of roads over 35 years, and constructed ports and harbours, government may also support the rollout of infrastructure that is critical to deployment but not financeable wholly by the private sector.

PHASE 5: MATURITY

The new technology, as it gets deployed by early adopters across the economy, shows its capacity to address unmet needs and raise productivity. What wins, works. Political, economic, social, and legal institutions, as Veblen identified, then align around it to drive the technology towards full deployment and maximum gain to the economy. It is this impact on productivity, provided lock-in around the previous TEP has been addressed in the synergy phase, which then accelerates alignment and the further uptake of the technology. The level of institutional lock-in and inertia will be an index of national capacity to gain first mover advantage. In the maturity phase, finally, as it moves towards full deployment, the new technology becomes common sense. As Boltanski and Thévenot put it, the new technology redefines capitalism's 'order of worth', depicting a new city on the hill that represents how we can thrive. Just as mass production shaped the suburban American dream, the new technology shapes the model of capitalism and its accompanying vision of the good life, eventually into one that, in Žižekian terms, seems always to have been there.

What does this emerging city on the hill and its accompanying model of capitalism look like? We believe we stand at a point of transition between the mass era and its successor. Neither mass, nor post-mass—but at a stage for which one term might be the 'pre-post mass'. It is a stage, in other words, where precise prediction is impossible. One pattern is clear though, that capitalism, as Klaus Schwab commented, succeeds when it fits its external environmental and that the direction of opportunity, in response to the challenges of the new external environment, is again shifting. Four parallel shifts, reflecting the crises highlighted in Chapter 2, appear to be underway. Together, they may reveal some of the contours of what may emerge as the next model of capitalism, and the opportunity is for business to thrive and government to accelerate their success.

The quadrilemma of crises that we highlighted identified four major decision points for business. Mass or micro production? Fossil fuel or renewable energy sources? Closed or open models of governance? Intensive or inclusive visions of the market? The criteria for an architecture of capitalism that would work were twofold. Were the approaches adequate to the economic, environmental, and social crises that confront us, and were they achievable given the starting point of the system we have, i.e. anchored in the need for growth? Figure 9.5 shows an evolution in capitalism that responds to this dual logic.

TYPE	CRISIS	DECISION POINT	RESOLUTION
Economic	Declining productivity	Consumption or production led growth?	Production led growth
Environmental	Climate change	High carbon or low carbon growth model?	Low carbon growth
Social	Demographic change	Intensive economy or extensive economy (addressing unmet needs)?	Extensive economy
Governance	Path-dependency	Distributed or centralised forms of governance?	Distributed governance

Figure 9.5: Resolving the quadrilemma of crises

The transition towards a form of capitalism that is sustainable is one from mass towards micro production, fossil fuel towards renewable energy, intensive towards inclusive markets, and from closed towards open governance.

Moving to Producer Capitalism

Micro-production, in this model, brings back business and manufacturing to the city. It presents a model of growth that considerably reduces the need for high capex investment and the waste of long-run production lines and subtractive manufacturing. It has the power to help regenerate communities and allow the small businessman and woman to share in the value they produce. The writer, G.K. Chesterton once commented that 'The problem with capitalism is not too many capitalists, but not enough capitalists'. What was needed, in other words, was less of a system that concentrates wealth into the hands of a few, and more sharing of that wealth among its producers. The transition from mass to micro will be a gradual one, and that is important to bear in mind given the time-bound nature of the crises. The micro depends on the mass, but ankle high barriers to production and distribution hold out promise for a move in the direction of the distributed model that Chesterton referred to.

Inclusive markets present the logical next phase of growth. Just as Ford's mass production techniques lowered costs and made goods accessible to the masses, new nanotechnology and open source approaches are making goods and services available to the underserved. These goods and services, anchored in delivering unmet needs, enhance productivity, raise incomes and help stimulate broader demand. Renewable energy, including the smart micro-grid, has, as Jeremy Rifkin explored, the potential to transform energy from an increasing cost to a source of return for communities of producers. Its impact, though, is not just on energy costs.

Civic intent

ICT, up to and including Internet 1.0 (the read only internet), delivered little in terms of empowerment. The governing principle of the era of mass production was to minimize labour as a cost, a principle that remained as the era of mass harnessed ICT to extend its shelf life. The next wave, Internet 2.0, brought progress. Nanotechnology, Open Source software/hardware, and additive manufacturing radically reduced the costs of production and the barriers to entry for local manufacturers. It is in the third wave, Internet 3.0, that the smart micro grid enables people to be independent co-producers of power. The impact is not just on energy costs: they become a group animated by the collective intent to build the city they want to live in. The impact is therefore also on civic intent and empowerment.

It is this civic intent, enabled further by technologies that promote empowerment, from participatory budgeting to monitoring of corruption, that helps accelerate the final shift. This is the shift from a top-down model of governance towards one that is distributed. The city on the hill that is aligned, then, with this new order of worth, the successor to the suburban dream of the mass era, is that of the distributed economy.

The city of the distributed economy goes under a range of names, from the iHub and the FabCity, to the Home Town and the Polis. There is no fixed term because this is a city defined from the bottom-up, not by a master plan. Across this range of names, though, there are a number of unifying elements. One of them is a move towards what Antoni Vives of Barcelona refers to as the productive city, and a form of producer capitalism rooted not in the belief that man is a factor of production, a cost to be minimized, but in a trust in the diverse capacities of people, and in the potential for technology to empower us further.

Donald Appleyard's studies in *Livable Streets* showed, as mentioned earlier, how residents of the street with high car traffic had three times fewer friends than those living on the street with light car traffic.[13] Another unifying element is a move, partly enabled by local manufacturing, away from the car and commuter-shaped city, towards the walking city. Similarly, there is a move away from the product-in-trash-out city; an urban island with its slums as the last refuge for a destitute rural population, towards one where the city depends on and thrives within a productive local region. The ancient Greek word *politeia* denoted both citizenship and the rules of citizenship. It is a move away from our identity as consumers toward a role as citizens where our connection is not to a device but to each other.

Schumacher's cattle

A further element is above all a move away from disconnection. There is a story the Austrian economist E.F. Schumacher tells in *Good Work* of his time as a farm labourer during the Second World War. He was an economist, so he was given a task suited to his skills, counting cattle.

> . . . (M)y task was before breakfast to go to yonder hill and to a field there and count the cattle. I went and I counted the cattle—there were always thirty-two—and then I went back to the bailiff, touched my cap, and said, "Thirty-two, sir," and went and had my breakfast. One day when I arrived at the field an old farmer was standing at the gate, and he said, "Young man, what do you do here every morning?" I said, "Nothing much. I just count the cattle." He shook his head and said, "If you count them every day they won't flourish." . . . One day I went back, I counted and counted again, there were only thirty-one. . . . And we went together and we searched the place and indeed, under a bush, was a dead beast. I thought to myself, "Why have I been counting them all the time? I haven't prevented this beast dying." Perhaps that's what the farmer meant. They won't flourish if you don't look and watch the quality of each individual beast. Look him in the eye. Study the sheen on his coat.

What gets lost in the counting (and accounting) of economic rationality is that people are all, in their way, like Schumacher's cattle. We all need someone close to us to feel the sheen on our coats, to check our tongues and the clarity of our eyes. We are all, as MacIntyre & Carus put it, dependent rational animals, unable to thrive without each other.[14] The Cyburbian city, sensored and censored, has the capacity to count us not as individuals but as part of the herd. We need instead a city, shaped for people, that allows us to connect with each other, to know each other, and to understand each other's needs. We need a market driven not by the manufacturing of desire but by the intrinsic and extrinsic rewards of delivering on those needs. Key to the project of the distributed city, one where we and our neighbour live well, is a form of community that admits and allows our dependence, not just on each other but on the ecosystem of which we are part.

Recapturing the ICT techno-economic paradigm for the purposes of jobs and vibrant, interdependent communities may appear radical. There are many people who, faced with the major crises of the twenty-first century, do not want to treat them as moments for decisive change. They may prefer instead to say there is no alternative to the present situation, or that solutions will arrive of their own accord. We believe that the distributed economy, while not a panacea to all of society's challenges, can combine with the assets built up by the mass era to help create a prosperous future. In terms of adequacy, it presents a model of growth that is both green and inclusive. In terms of achievability, it makes sense according to the underlying logic of capitalism. What is more, the key technological foundations are already laid, and as Kenya's innovation spaces, Barcelona's Fab City, and Austin's Pecan Street, among many others, show, it is already starting to happen on the ground. 'The fields', as Ben Okri said, 'are sprouting strange new mushrooms.' What is sprouting is the distributed city.

Reasons for Optimism

We started this book with an elaboration of the grounds for pessimism. The challenges, climate change among them, remain formidable. We believe, though, there are some long-term reasons for optimism. From the macro perspective, there is specific justification in two colliding trends. First, energy costs for fossil fuel are increasingly volatile and the return on energy invested is declining, while the costs for renewables are going down. The Lawrence Berkeley National Laboratory reported that in the last twelve years, home solar costs have fallen by 43 per cent, with an accelerating trend.[15] Second, the costs for mass production and global distribution are rising, China's labour costs being an example, whereas the costs for micro-manufacturing are going down, and technologies like the RepRap open source 3D printer have the potential to grow exponentially pushing prices down further. These two trends, neither of them going away, give plausibility to the distributed economy scenario of productive communities engaged in clean and local manufacturing. It is a transition that is gradual (although there is potential for acceleration by the entrepreneurial state), but it is one whose basis is the same as that of the previous great surges of development since the Industrial Revolution, i.e. a new technology that brings new people new powers to do new things, transforming productivity, growing markets and bringing widespread gains.

It is a transition, that also, critically, works for many incumbents and has the potential to attract them and the platforms for synergy they can bring. In Austin, where Ford and Southern California Edison collaborate with the Pecan Street Project on plugging houses into the electric car, the very companies that initiated the mass era are collaborating to explore its successor. This synergy is not yet the norm. Society is not at a tipping point in the deployment of production capital into this new model of growth, nor in the recognition of the logic and value of targeted government support to accelerate it. The transition constitutes the Turnaround Challenge for business, from a city it knows but is failing to one that is unknown but promises the potential for greater congruence and prosperity. Against this note of caution about the future, our final reason for optimism is anchored in the past. What the distributed economy represents is less something radically new than a return to two things society knows well: Man as maker, *homo faber*, and Man as a social animal. For all of our pathologies, humans ultimately prosper together, not apart. The distributed economy, or more accurately the distributed society, draws not just on the impulse to create, but on our instinct to be together. As the architect Jan Gehl, points out, the park benches that people most like to sit on are the ones that face the crowd.[16] What it holds out, if we can manage the challenges on the way, is the promise of the community in which we and our neighbours will flourish and prosper rather than merely survive.

ANNEX: The Grassroots FabLab Instructable

HARDWARE

- Mantis Small DIY mill suitable for PCB milling. URLs: makeyourbot.wikidot.com, wiki.protospace.nl
- Calortrans CT-60 Cheap vinyl cutter. URLs: www.signseen.nl, inkcut.sourceforge. net, www.craftrobostore.com
- Morntech Chinese laser cutter. URL: www.morntech-europe.com, wiki.laoslaser. org
- Ultimaker DIY 3D printer developed at ProtoSpace. URL: wiki.protospace.nl
- USBtinyISP USB AVR programmer. Works together with Arduino. URL: www. ladyada.net/make/usbtinyisp
- Acer Aspire One netbook, with a solid state drive and a Linux operating system. URL: www.linux-netbook.com
- Mini ITX, free screens (except flat) URL: www.mini-itx.com

SOFTWARE

- Crunchbang Linux A minimalist Linux distribution with an active community and helpful forum. URL: www. crunchbanglinux.org
- Inkscape Software for 2D vector drawings, with plugins for generating HPGL and gcode. URL: www.inkscape.org
- Blender Software for 3D design (and animation). URL: www.blender.org
- Pycam Toolpath generator for 3-axis CNC machining. URL: pycam.sourceforge.net
- ReplicatorG 3D printing software that connects to most DIY 3D printers. URL: www.replicat.org
- Processing Cross platform rapid prototyping in software. URL: www.processing.org
- Arduino Programming tool for the AVR family of microcontrollers. URL: www.arduino.cc
- Ekiga Voice-over-IP software to connect to the FabLab video channel. URL: www. ekiga.org
- Dosis Configuration script to install all softare on Crunchbang Linux install. URL:
- www. giplt.nl/ dosis
- Linux-cnc Dedicated Linux distribution optimized for milling equipment over a parallel port
- URL: www.linuxcnc.org

WEBSITE

- Hypha Lightweight user-friendly wiki/cms for running a website. Modules for including SVG files and fabmoments/ instructables also under development. URL: www.hypha.net

Notes

1. (Plutarch)
2. {{2643 Johnson, Simon 2009}}
3. 'Picking winners, saving losers' Aug 5th 2010
4. (Block, Keller 2009)
5. http://www.mckinsey.com/insights/mgi/research/urbanization/urban_world
6. http://www.nation.co.ke/Features/DN2/Unveiling-Konza-Africas-first-technopolis-/-/957860/1672974/-/m24xqk/-/index.html, accessed 31 January 2013
7. (Slaughter 2005)
8. (Diamandis, Kotler 2012)
9. (Mazzucato 2011)
10. (Mazzucato 2011)
11. (Ruttan 2004)
12. http://www.guardian.co.uk/sustainable-business/business-women-children-health-development, accessed September 2012
    EF Schumacher, Good Work
13. (Appleyard 1980)
14. (MacIntyre 1999)
15. http://www.nrel.gov/news/press/2012/2038.html, accessed 1 January 2013
16. (Gehl 1987)

References

Abramovitz, M. 1962, "Economic growth in the United States", *The American Economic Review*, pp. 762–82.

Adams, R.B. 2009, *Governance and the financial crisis*, Finance Working Paper N°. 248/2009, European Corporate Governance Institute.

Adams, R.B. 2012, "Governance and the financial crisis," *International Review of Finance*, 12:1 pp.7–38.

Aker, J. & Ksoll, C. 2012, *Information technology and farm households in Niger*, Working Paper 2012-005: February 2012, New York, United Nations Development Programme.

Aker, J. & Mbiti, I. 2010, "Mobile phones and economic development in Africa," *Center for Global Development Working Paper*, no. 211.

Alderson, A.S. & Nielsen, F. (2001) "Globalization and the great U-turn: Income inequality trends in 16 OECD countries," *American Journal of Sociology*, 107:5 pp. 1244–99.

Alexander, C. 2006, *Sustainability and morphogenesis: The birth of a living world*. Center for Environmental Structure. Berkeley. CA.

Allegre, C., Armstrong, J.S., Breslow, J., Cohen, R., David, E., Happer, W., Kelly, M., Kininmonth, W., Lindzen, R., McGrath, J., Nichols, R., Rutan, B., Schmitt, H.H., Shaviv, N., Tennekes, H. & Zichichi, A. 2012, "No need to panic about global warming," *The Wall Street Journal*, New York., http://online.wsj.com/article/SB10001424052970204301404577171531838421366.html

Appleyard, D. 1980, "Livable streets: protected neighborhoods?", *The Annals of the American Acadaemy of Political and Social Science*, vol. 451, no. 1, pp. 106–117.

Bardi, U. 2011, *The limits to growth revisited*, New York. Springer Verlag.

Barnett, M.L. & Pollock, T.G. (eds) 2012, *The Oxford handbook of corporate reputation*, Oxford University Press, Oxford.

Barnett, V. 1998, *Kondratiev and the dynamics of economic development: long cycles and industrial growth in historical context*, Macmillan in association with the Centre for Russian and East European Studies, University of Birmingham, Basingstoke.

Beck, T., Demirgüç-Kunt, A. & Levine, R. 2009, "Financial institutions and markets across countries and over time-data and analysis," *World Bank Policy Research Working Paper Series*, Washington, World Bank.

Beinhocker, E.D. 2007, *The origin of wealth: evolution, complexity, and the radical remaking of economics*, Random House Business, London.

Bentley 2008, *Bentley and CO2*, Bentley & Co, UK.

References

Berger, A.A. 1996, *Manufacturing desire: media, popular culture, and everyday life*, Transaction Publishers, New Brunswick, NJ; London.

Blackman, C. & Srivastava, L. 2011, *Telecommunications regulation handbook*, 10th anniversary edition. Washington, DC: The World Bank. vol. 30.

Block, F. & Keller, M.R. 2009, "Where do innovations come from? Transformations in the US economy, 1970–2006," *Socio-Economic Review*, vol. 7, no. 3, pp. 459–83.

Bloom, D.E., Canning, D. & Sevilla, J. 2003, *The demographic dividend: a new perspective on the economic consequences of population change*, Rand, Santa Monica.

Blowfield, M.E. 2012, *Business and sustainability*, Oxford University Press, Oxford.

Blowfield, M.E. & Dolan, C. 2010, "Fairtrade facts and fancies: what kenyan fairtrade tea tells us about business' role as development agent," *Journal of Business Ethics*, Volume 93, Supplement 1, June 2010, pp. 143–62(20).

Boltanski, L. & Chiapello, E. 2005, *The new spirit of capitalism*, Verso, London.

Boltanski, L. & Thévenot, L. 2006, *On justification: economies of worth*, Princeton University Press, Princeton; Oxford.

Boo, K. 2012, *Behind the beautiful forevers*, Random House, New York.

Bootle, R.P. 2009, *The trouble with markets: saving capitalism from itself*, Nicholas Brealey, London.

Bostrom, N. & Mirkovic, M.M (eds) 2008, *Global catastrophic risks*, Oxford University Press, Oxford.

Briggs, A. 1959, *The age of improvement*, Longmans Green.

Business World "As china costs rise, tech lures US factories back home," *Business World*, 24 July 2012.

Campanale, M. & Leggett, J. 2011, *Unburnable carbon: are the world's financial markets carrying a carbon bubble?* Carbon Tracker, London.

Carbon Trust. 2008, *Climate change—a business revolution*. Carbon Trust, London.

Carter, R.M., De Freitas, C., Goklany, I.M., Holland, D., Lindzen, R.S., Byatt, I., Castles, I., Henderson, D., Lawson, N. & McKitrick, R. 2006, "The Stern Review: a dual critique," *World Economics*, vol. 7, no. 4, pp. 165–232.

Casson, S. 1937, *Progress and catastrophe. An anatomy of human adventure*. Hamish Hamilton, London.

Chakravarti, S. 2008, *Red Sun: travels in Naxalite country*, Penguin, Viking, New Delhi.

Chang, H. 2002, *Kicking away the ladder: development strategy in historical perspective*, Anthem, London.

Christensen, C.M. 1997, *The innovator's dilemma: when new technologies cause great firms to fail*, Harvard Business School Press, Boston, MA.

Clark, G.L. & Monk, A.H.B. 2010, *Sovereign wealth funds: form and function in the 21st century*, Milan. Fondazione Eni Enrico Mattei.

Cleaver, H.M. 1972, "The contradictions of the Green Revolution," *The American Economic Review*, vol. 62, no. 1/2, pp. 177–86.

Club of Rome. 1974, *The limits to growth: a report for the Club of Rome's Project on the Predicament of Mankind*, Pan, London.

Cohen, H. 2000, *Invisible cities: industry trend or event* [Homepage of Standard Media International], [Online]. Available: http://knoke.org/PR/IndustryStandard.htm [2012, 2 October 2000].

The Comptroller and Auditor General's Report on Accounts to the House of Commons: The financial stability interventions. HC 984, July 2011. National Audit Office, London.

Conn, I.C. 2012, "Energy, transport and the environment: providing energy security" in *Energy, transport and the environment: addressing the sustainable mobility paradigm*, eds. O. Inderwildi & D.A. King, Springer, London, pp. 13–27.

Conway, G.R. 1997, *The doubly green revolution: food for all in the twenty-first century*, Penguin, London.

Cortright, J. 2009, "Walking the walk: how walkability raises home values in US cities," Chicago. CEOs for Cities.

Cotula, L., Vermeulen, S., Leonard, R. & Keeley, J. 2009, *Land grab or development opportunity?: agricultural investment and international land deals in Africa*, London, IIED.

Cowen, T. 2011, *The great stagnation: how america ate all the low-hanging fruit of modern history, Got Sick, and Will (Eventually) Feel Better: A Penguin eSpecial from Dutton*, New York. Dutton Adult.

Daly, H.E. 1996, *Beyond growth: the economics of sustainable development*, Beacon Press, Boston.

Dangerfield, G. 1936, *The strange death of liberal England*, Constable & Co, London.

Diamandis, P.H. & Kotler, S. 2012, *Abundance: the future is better than you think*, Free Press, New York.

Diamond, J.M. & Diamond, J.M. 2005, *Collapse: how societies choose to fail or succeed*, New York: Penguin.

Dolan, C.S. 2008, "In the mists of development: fairtrade in Kenyan tea fields," *Globalizations*, vol. 5, no. 2, pp. 305–18.

Drescher, S. 2009, *Abolition: a history of slavery and antislavery*, Cambridge University Press, Cambridge.

Drucker, P.F. 1946, *Concept of the corporation*, The John Day Company, New York.

Durkheim, E. 1893, *De la division du Travail Social: études sur l'organisation des sociétée supérieures*, Paris.

The Economist 2012, 27 October 2012-last update, Urban life: Open-air computers [Homepage of *The Economist*], [Online]. Available: http://www.economist.com/news/special-report/21564998-cities-are-turning-vast-data-factories-open-air-computers

Ehrenreich, B. 2001, *Nickel and dimed: on (not) getting by in America*, Metropolitan Books, New York.

Ehrlich, P.R. 1969, *Eco-catastrophe*, City Lights Books San Francisco, CA.

Eliot, T.S. 1934, *The rock*, London, Faber.

Elliott, F. & Pagnamenta, R. 2012, "Boris bangs the drum and plugs the brand," *The Times*, 24 November 2012.

Etzioni, A. 1989, "Toward an I & We paradigm," *Contemporary Sociology: An International Journal of Reviews*, 18:2, pp. 171–6.

Evans, A. 2009, *The feeding of the nine billion: Global food security for the 21st century*, Chatham House, London.

Ferguson, N. 2005, *Colossus: the rise and fall of the American empire*, Penguin Press, New York; London.

Ferguson, N. 2011, *Civilization: the West and the rest*, 1st American edn, Penguin Press, New York.

Ferguson, N. 2012, *Facebook won't save us; i wish i were a technoptimist*. Newsweek. August 6 2012.

Field, C.B., Barros, V, Stocker, T.F., Qin, D., Dokken, D.J.,Ebi, K.L., Mastrandrea, M.D., Mach, K.J., Plattner, G.-K., Allen, S.K., Tignor, M., Midgley, P.M. eds, 2012. *Climate change adaptation*, Cambridge University Press, Cambridge, pp. 1–19.

Foucault, M. 1979, *Discipline and punish: the birth of the prison*, Penguin, Harmondsworth.

Frank, R.H. 2000; 1999, *Luxury fever: money and happiness in an era of excess*, The American College, Bryn Mawr, Pennsylvania.

Freeman, C. & Perez, C. 1988, *Structural crises of adjustment, business cycles and investment behaviour*. In G. Dosi et al. (eds) Technical Change and Economic Theory. London. Pinter.

Friedman, M. 1962, *Capitalism and freedom*, University of Chicago Press, Chicago.

Friel, H. 2011, *The Lomborg deception: setting the record straight about global warming*, Yale University Press, New Haven, CT; London.

Galbraith, J.K. 2008, *The predator state: how conservatives abandoned the free market and why liberals should too*, Free Press, New York; London.

Gardner, D. 2010, *Future babble: why expert predictions fail and why we believe them anyway*, Virgin, London.

Garnett, T. & Godfray, C. 2012, "Sustainable intensification in agriculture. Navigating a course through competing food system priorities," Food climate research network and the oxford martin programme on the future of food, Oxford, University of Oxford.

Gartner 2010, *ICT marketing strategy*, Gartner Inc., unknown.

Geels, F.W. 2002, "Technological transitions as evolutionary reconfiguration processes: a multi-level perspective and a case-study," *Research Policy*, vol. 31, no. 8–9, pp. 1257–74.

Geertz, C. 1963, *Agricultural involution. The process of ecological change in Indonesia*, Berkeley & Los Angeles, University of California Press.

Gehl, J. 1987, *Life between buildings: using public space*, Van Nostrand Reinhold, New York; Wokingham.

Gendron, B. 1977, *Technology and the human condition*, St. Martin's Press, New York.

Ghemawat, P. 2011, *World 3.0: global prosperity and how to achieve it*, Harvard Business Review Press; McGraw-Hill distributor, Boston, MA; London.

Giles, C. & Bates, A. 2005, "Bright spots can't hide a precarious balancing act," FT.com edn, *Financial Times*, London.

Gimpel, J. 1976, *The medieval machine: the industrial revolution of the Middle Ages*, 1st edn, Holt, Rinehart and Winston, New York.

Glaeser, E.L. 2011, *Triumph of the city: how our greatest invention makes us richer, smarter, greener, healthier, and happier*, Penguin Press, New York.

Godfray, H.C.J., Beddington, J.R., Crute, I.R., Haddad, L., Lawrence, D., Muir, J.F., Pretty, J., Robinson, S., Thomas, S.M. & Toulmin, C. 2010, "Food security: the challenge of feeding 9 billion people," *Science*, vol. 327, no. 5967, pp. 812.

Gordon, R.J. 2012, "Is US economic growth over? faltering innovation confronts the six headwinds". Washington DC. National Bureau of Economic Research.

Government Office for Science 2011, *Foresight. The future of food and farming*, Government Office for Science, London.

Gramsci, A. 1971, *Selections from the prison notebooks of Antonio Gramsci*, International Publishing, New York.

Greenhouse, S. 2012, A part—time life, as hours shrink and shift. *The New York Times*. October 28. A; Business/Financial Desk; online version.

Hagel III, J., Brown, J.S., Kulasooriya, D. & Elbert, D. 2011, "Measuring the forces of long-term change: the 2011 shift index," Santa Clara, CA: Deloitte Center for the Edge.

Hamdi, N. 2010, *The placemaker's guide to building community*, Earthscan, London.

Hammond, A.L., Kramer, W.J., Katz, R.S., Tran, J.T. & Walker, C. 2007, *The next four billion: market size and business strategy at the base of the pyramid*, International Finance Corporation/World Resources Institute, Washington DC.

Harkin, J. 2009, *Cyburbia: the dangerous idea that's changing how we live and who we are*, Little, Brown, London.

Hart, S.L. 2010, *Capitalism at the crossroads: next generation business strategies for a post-crisis world*, 3rd edn, Wharton School; Pearson Education Ltd, Philadelphia, PA; Harlow.

Hawley, J.P. & Williams, A.T. 2000, *The rise of fiduciary capitalism: how institutional investors can make corporate America more democratic*. Philadelphia. University of Pennsylvania Press.

Helm, D. 2008, "Climate-change policy: why has so little been achieved?" *Oxford Review of Economic Policy*, vol. 24, no. 2, pp. 211.

Holstein, W.J., Reed, S., Kapstein, J., Vogel, T. & Weber, J. 1990, "The stateless corporation," *Business Week*, vol. 14, pp. 98–100.

Howorth, F. & Howorth, M. 2012, In *Superyacht Business*, pp. 45–8.

HSBC 2011, *Energy in 2050: will fuel constraints thwart our growth projections?*, HSBC, London.

HSBC Global Research 2012, *Coal and carbon—stranded assets: assessing the risk*, HSBC, London.

Ikenberry, G.J. 2008, "Rise of China and the future of the west—can the liberal system survive," *Foreign Affairs*, vol. 87, pp. 23.

Intergovernmental Panel on Climate Change. Working Group III. 2007, *Climate change 2007. Mitigation of climate change: contribution of Working Group III to the Fourth assessment report of the Intergovernmental Panel on Climate Change*, Cambridge University Press, Cambridge.

IPCC 2012, "Summary for policy makers" in *Managing the risks of extreme events and disasters to advance climate change adaptation*, ed. Field, C.B., Barros, V, Stocker, T.F., Qin, D., Dokken, D.J., Ebi, K.L., Mastrandrea, M.D., Mach, K.J., Plattner, G.-K., Allen, S.K., Tignor, M., Midgley, P.M., Cambridge University Press, Cambridge, pp. 1–19.

Jack, W. & Suri, T. 2011, "Mobile money: the economics of M-PESA," NBER Working Paper No. 16721, National Bureau of Economic Research.

Jackson, T. 2009, *Prosperity without growth: economics for a finite planet*, Earthscan, London.

Jacobs, J. 1962, *Death and life of great American cities*, Jonathan Cape, London.

Jacques, M. 2009, *When China rules the world: the rise of the middle kingdom and the end of the Western world*, Allen Lane, London.

Johnson, S. 2009, "The quiet coup", *The Atlantic*, vol. 52, 1 May.

Kaletsky, A. 2010, *Capitalism 4.0: the birth of a new economy*, Bloomsbury, London.

Kapur, A., Macleod, N. & Levkovich, T. 2006, *The global investigator—the plutonomy symposium: rising tides lift all yachts*, Citigroup, New York.

Kapur, A., Macleod, N. & Singh, N. 2005, *Plutonomy: buying luxury, explaining global imbalances*, Citigroup, New York.

Kapur, A., Macleod, N. & Singh, N. 2006, *Revisiting plutonomy: the rich getting richer*, Citigroup, New York.

Keen, A. 2012, *Digital vertigo: how today's online social revolution is dividing, diminishing, and disorienting us*, 1st edn, St. Martin's Press, New York.

King, S.D. 2010, *Losing control: the emerging threats to western prosperity*, Yale University Press, New Haven, CT; London.

Kostal, R.W. 1994, *Law and English railway capitalism, 1825–1875*, Clarendon Press, Oxford.

Krippner, G.R. 2005, "The financialization of the American economy," *Socio-Economic Review*, vol. 3, no. 2, pp. 173–208.

Kumhof, M., Lebarz, C., Ranciere, R., Richter, A. & Throckmorton, N.A. 2012, *Income inequality and current account imbalances*, IMF Working Paper, Washington, International Monetary Fund.

Lagi, M., Bertrand, K. & Bar-Yam, Y. 2011, *The food crises and political instability in North Africa and the Middle East*, Cambridge MA, New England Complex Systems Institute.

Lessig, L. 2008, *Remix: making art and commerce thrive in the hybrid economy*, Penguin Press, New York; London.

Lévi-Strauss, C. 2001, *Myth and meaning*, Routledge, London.

Lewis, M. 2011, *The big short: Inside the doomsday machine*, Penguin, London.

Lindsay, G. 2010, "Cisco's big bet on New Songdo: creating cities from scratch," 1 February 2010 edn, *Fast Company*, unknown.

Lipsey, R.G., Carlaw, K.I. & Bekar, C.T. 2006, *Economic transformations: general purpose technologies and long term economic growth*, Oxford University Press, New York.

Lomborg, B. 2007, *Cool it!: the skeptical environmentalist's guide to global warming*, Cyan: Marshall Cavendish, London.

Lomborg, B. 2010, *Smart solutions to climate change: comparing costs and benefits*, Cambridge: Cambridge University Press.

Lovelock, J. 2000, *Gaia: the practical science of planetary medicine*, Rev. edn, Gaia, London.

Lovelock, J. 2006, *The revenge of Gaia: why the earth is fighting back—and how we can still save humanity*, Allen Lane, London.

Lovelock, J. 2010, *The vanishing face of Gaia: a final warning*, Penguin, London.

Lukes, S. 1974, *Power: a radical view*, Macmillan, London.

MacIntyre, A.C. & Carus, P. 1999, *Dependent rational animals: Why human beings need the virtues*, Cambridge University Press, Cambridge.

MacKay, D.J.C. 2009, *Sustainable energy—without the hot air*, UIT, Cambridge.

MacNeil, I. & Li, X. 2006, "'Comply or Explain': market discipline and non-compliance with the Combined Code," *Corporate Governance: An International Review,* vol. 14, no. 5, pp. 486–96.

Martenson, C. 2011, *The crash course: the unsustainable future of our economy, energy, and environment,* Wiley; John Wiley distributor, Hoboken, NJ; Chichester.

Marx, K. 1973, *Grundrisse. Foundations of the critique of political economy,* Vintage Books, New York.

Mazzucato, M. 2013, *The entrepreneurial state,* Anthem Press, London.

McCulley, P. 2008, "The paradox of deleveraging will be broken," *Global Central Bank Focus,* PIMCO—http://www.pimco.com/EN/Insights/Pages/Global%20Central%20Bank%20Focus%2011-08%20McCulley%20Paradox%20of%20Deleveraging%20Will%20Be%20Broken.aspx

McKinsey & Co 2005, *The impact of aging* [Homepage of McKinsey & Co], [Online]. Available: http://www.mckinsey.com/mgi/reports/pdfs/demographics/The_Impact_of_Aging_Executive_Summary.pdf [2011, 5/6/2011].

McKinsey Global Institute 2011, *Resource Revolution: meeting the world's energy, materials, food, and water needs,* McKinsey & Company, unknown.

Mearns, E. 2008, "Why oil costs over $120 per barrel," *The Oil Drum: Europe,* http://europe.theoildrum.com/node/4007.

Melchior, A. 2012, *World Trade 1970–2010: Globalisation, regionalisation and reallocation,* Norwegian Institute of International Affairs, Oslo.

Minsky, H.P. 1982, *Can "it" happen again?: essays on instability and finance,* M.E. Sharpe, Armonk, NY NAO 2011.

Moerschbaecher, M.K. 2011, *Energy, environment, and sustainability: a hierarchical analysis of South Louisiana,* Louisiana State University.

Morris, I. 2010, *Why the West rules—for now: the patterns of history and what they reveal about the future,* Profile, London.

NAO 2011, *The comptroller and auditor general's report on accounts to the house of commons: the financial stability interventions,* National Audit Office, London.

Nordhaus, W. D. 2012, "In the climate change casino: reply by William D. Nordhaus," *The New York Review of Books,* New York. 26 April 2012.

Nordhaus, W.D. 2007, *The challenge of global warming: economic models and environmental policy,* Yale University. New Haven, Conn.

Oleksak, M.A. 2010, *Intangible capital: putting knowledge to work in the 21st-century organization,* Praeger; Roundhouse distributor, Westport, Conn.; Hove.

Palma, J.G. 2009, "The revenge of the market on the rentiers: why neo-liberal reports of the end of history turned out to be premature," *Cambridge Journal of Economics,* vol. 33, no. 4, pp. 829–69.

Pearce, F. 2010, *The coming population crash: and our planet's surprising future,* Beacon Press. Boston, USA.

Pearce, F. 2011, "Dubious assumptions prime population bomb," *Nature,* vol. 473, no. 7346, pp. 125.

Perez, C. 2002, *Technological revolutions and financial capital: The dynamics of bubbles and golden ages,* Edward Elgar Publishing, Cheltenham.

Piepenbrock, T.F. 2010, "Toward a theory of the evolution of business ecosystems," PhD thesis, Massachusetts Institute of Technology.

Pieterse, J.N. 2010, "Innovate, innovate! here comes American rebirth". In *Education in the Creative Economy: Knowledge and Learning in the Age of Innovation* Araya, D. and Peters, M.A. Peter Lang. New York. pp. 401–419.

Pietsch, W., Calvillo, N., Halpern, O. & LeCavalier, J. 2012, *Skewing the city*, December 2012 edn, The Electric City. London. LSE.

Plutarch, *Plutarch's life of lycurgus*.

Polanyi, K. 1944, *The great transformation*, New York, Toronto, Farrar & Rinehart, inc. 1944 xiii, 1, 305 p.

Prahalad, C.K. & Hart, S.L. 2002, "The fortune at the bottom of the pyramid," *Strategy + Business*, no. 26, pp. 2–14.

Pratt, M., Sarmiento, O.L., Montes, F., Ogilvie, D., Marcus, B.H., Perez, L.G. & Brownson, R.C. 2012, "The implications of megatrends in information and communication technology and transportation for changes in global physical activity," *The* Lancet vol 380; 9838. pp. 282–293.

Putnam, R.D. 2000, *Bowling alone: the collapse and revival of American community*, Simon & Schuster, New York.

PwC 2011, *Low carbon economy index*, PricewaterhouseCoopers LLC, London.

PwC 2012, *Too late for two degrees?: Low carbon economy index 2012*, PwC, London.

Quinn, T.K. 1962, *Unconscious public enemies*, Citadel Press, New York.

Randers, J. 2012, *2052: a global forecast for the next forty years*, Chelsea Green, White River Junction.

Ratti, C. & Townsend, A. 2011, "The social nexus," *Scientific American*, vol. 305, no. 3, pp. 42–8.

Reed, M.C. 1975, *Investment in railways in Britain, 1820–1844: a study in the development of the capital market*, Oxford University Press, London.

Reich, R.B. 2007, *Supercapitalism: the transformation of business, democracy, and everyday life*, Alfred A. Knopf, New York.

Reinhart, C.M., and Rogoff, K.S. 2009, *This time is different: eight centuries of financial folly*, Princeton University Press, Princeton.

Reinhart, C.M. & Rogoff, K.S. 2010, *From financial crash to debt crisis*, National Bureau of Economic Research. Working Paper 15795. March 2010. Cambridge, MA.

Ritholz, B. 2009, *Bailout nation: how easy money corrupted Wall Street and shook the world economy*, McGraw-Hill Professional, Maidenhead.

Rockström, J., Steffen, W., Noone, K., Persson, Å., Chapin III, F.S., Lambin, E., Lenton, T.M., Scheffer, M., Folke, C. & Schellnhuber, H. 2009, "Planetary boundaries: exploring the safe operating space for humanity," *Ecology and Society*, vol. 14, no. 2, pp. 32.

Rogaly, B. 1996, "Micro-finance evangelism,'destitute women', and the hard selling of a new anti-poverty formula," *Development in Practice*, vol. 6, no. 2, pp. 10012.

Romer, P. 1991, "Endogenous technological change," *Journal of Political Economy*. Vol 98. No 5. Pt 2, October 1990. pp. 71–102.

Rotberg, R.I. (ed) 2008, *China into Africa: trade, aid, and influence*, Brookings Institution Press, Washington, DC.

Roubini, N. & Mihm, S. 2010, *Crisis economics: a crash course in the future of finance*, Penguin Press, New York.

Roy, A. 2010, *Poverty capital: Microfinance and the making of development*, Taylor & Francis. New York and Abingdon.

Royal Society 2009, *Geoengineering the climate: science, governance and uncertainty*, The Royal Society, London.

Ruttan, V.W. 2004, "The role of the public sector in technology development: generalisations from general purpose technologies," *International Journal of Biotechnology*, vol. 6, no. 4, pp. 301–23.

Sassen, S. 2012, "Digital formations of the powerful and the powerless (keynote)," Software Engineering (ICSE), 2012 *34th International Conference on IEEE*, pp. 961.

Schumacher, E.F., Carasso, J., & Gillingham, P. 1979, *Good work*, Harper & Row, New York.

Schumpeter, J.A. 1942, *Capitalism, socialism and democracy*, London. Allen & Unwin.

Scott, W. 1903, *Money and banking. An introduction to the study of modern currencies*, London; New York, pp. x. 381. George Bell & Sons; Henry Holt & Co.

Sealy, L. & Worthington, S. 2007, *Cases and materials in company law*, Oxford University Press, New York.

Shell 2011, *Signals and signposts: shell energy scenarios to 2050—an era of volatile transitions*, Shell International BV, Rotterdam.

Shin, H. 2012, 'Climate fund boosts hopes for Songdo City,' *Korea Times* October 22, 2012.

Shirky, C. 2010, *Cognitive surplus: creativity and generosity in a connected age*, Penguin Press, New York.

Simon, J.L. 1981, *The ultimate resource*, Martin Robertson, Oxford.

Slaughter, A.M. 2005, *A new world order*, Princeton University Press. Princeton. NJ.

Solow, R.M. 1956, "A contribution to the theory of economic growth," *The Quarterly Journal of Economics*, vol. 70, no. 1, pp. 65–94.

SSEE 2009, *Future of mobility roadmap: ways to reduce emissions while keeping mobile*, Smith School of Enterprise and the Environment, Oxford.

Stern, N.H. 2008, *The economics of climate change: the Stern review*, Cambridge University Press, Cambridge.

Stiglitz, J.E. 2002, *Globalization and its discontents*, W. W. Norton, New York.

Stiglitz, J.E. 2012, *The price of inequality: [how today's divided society endangers our future]*, W.W. Norton & Co., New York.

Sukhdev, P. 2012, "Sustainability: the corporate climate overhaul," *Nature*, vol. 486, no. 7401, pp. 27–8.

Tainter, J.A. 1987, *The collapse of complex societies*, Cambridge University Press, Cambridge.

Tegmark, M. & Bostrom, N. 2005, "Astrophysics: is a doomsday catastrophe likely?," *Nature*, vol. 438, no. 7069, pp. 754.

Thompson, E.P. 1963, *Making of the english working class*, V.Gollancz. London.

Thurow, L.C. 1999, *Building wealth: the new rules for individuals, companies, and nations in a knowledge-based economy*, HarperCollins, New York, NY.

References

Tol, R.S.J. 2009, "The economic effects of climate change," *The Journal of Economic Perspectives*, vol. 23, no. 2, pp. 29–51.

Toynbee, A.J. 1946, *A study of history: abridgement of Vol. 1–6 & vols. 7–10*, Oxford University Press, Oxford.

Truman, E.M. & Peterson Institute for International Economics. 2010, *Sovereign wealth funds: threat or salvation?* Peterson Institute for International Economics, Washington, DC.

Turkle, S. 2011, *Alone together: why we expect more from technology and less from each other*, Basic Books, New York.

Tushman, M.L. & Nadler, D.A. 1978, "Information processing as an integrating concept in organizational design," *Academy of Management Review*. Vol 3 No. 3. pp. 613–24.

Veblen, T. 1899, *The theory of the leisure class: an economic study in the evolution of institutions*, Macmillan Co, New York.

Victor, P.A. 2008, *Managing without growth: slower by design, not disaster*, Edward Elgar, Cheltenham.

Walker, G. & King, D.A. 2008, *The hot topic: how to tackle global warming and still keep the lights on*, Bloomsbury Pub., London; New York.

Wampler, B. 2007, *Participatory budgeting in Brazil: contestation, cooperation, and account-ability*, Penn State University Press. University Park. PA.

WEF & Accenture 2012, *More with less: scaling sustainable consumption and efficiency*, World Economic Forum, Geneva.

White, B. 1991, *In the shadow of agriculture: economic diversification and agrarian change in Java, 1900–1990*, Institute of Social Studies, The Hague, The Netherlands.

White, J. 2012, "The call of the sea," *New Scientist*, London.

Wilkinson, R.G. & Pickett, K. 2010, *The spirit level: why equality is better for everyone*, Penguin, London.

Williamson, D. & Lynch-Wood, G. 2008, "Social and environmental reporting in UK company law and the issue of legitimacy," *Corporate Governance*, vol. 8, no. 2, pp. 128–40.

Womack, J.P. 1990, *The machine that changed the world*, Maxwell Macmillan International, New York; Rawson Associates; Oxford.

World Bank 2012, *Maximizing mobile*, World Bank Group, Washington DC.

Žižek, S. 2011, *Living in the end times*, Verso Books. London.

Index

3D printing *see* additive manufacturing

absolute decoupling *see* decoupling
accelerating transformation, 192, 212, 217–223
additive manufacturing, 152–155, 175, 179, 196, 224
 3D printing, 152–155, 159, 193, 226
agricultural productivity, 25–27
agricultural yields, 26, 44, 45–46
agriculture *see* food
Airbus seat buckle, 152–153
albedo effect, 64
apocalypse, 7, 42
Apple, 98, 118, 119, 149, 157–158
Arab Spring, 17, 45, 57, 66
Arkwright, Richard, 91, 104, 112, 119, 147
aviation, 33–35

banking crisis, *see* financial crisis
Barcelona, 193, 195, 203, 208, 221
basic needs, 73, 125, 147, 166, 168, 204, 207
beruf, 87, 202
biodiversity, 45, 55, 75
biomimicry, 116
blackout, 107
Bloomberg, Michael, 17
Boltanski, Luc, 89, 104–107, 113, 206, 222
bottom billion capitalism, 18, 37, 168, 173, 175, 203, 207
bottom of the pyramid *see* bottom billion capitalism
bottom-up governance *see* governance, open
Bowling Alone, 124
business as usual, 30, 70, 72–73, 135, 175
business risk, 54, 58
business, norms of, 107–109

capital expenditure, 134, 137, 139, 148, 158, 203, 215, 219, 223
capital, predatory, 55, 115, 121, 218
capital, raffendes, 121
capital, schaffendes, 121
carbon credits *see* carbon price

carbon dioxide removal technology, 80, 91
carbon intensity, 16–17, 29–30, 33, 84, 126, 130
carbon price, 35, 66, 73
carbon taxes, 35, 66, 73, 221
Carnegie, Andrew, 112, 115, 146
China, 13, 40–42, 47, 150–152, 212, 214, 221
 and food crisis, 41
 and water, 42
 and oil/energy, 47, 100
 and political power, 50–51
 and resource acquisition, 51
 alternative governance visions, 56
 economic stimulus, 74
 smart cities in, 131
 and sovereign wealth, 132
 and the Petropolis, 149
 labour costs, 150
Citigroup, 17
cleantech *see* green technology
climate change, 27–35, 66, 72–75, 80–81
 adaptation, 26–27, 32, 82, 87
 economic dimensions, 72–75, 77–79, 81–87
 environmental consequences, 100–102
 existential threat of *see* existential risk
 policy, 47, 109, 211
 social disruption, 126, 136, 139
 summit
 mitigation, 27, 30, 32, 73–75, 83, 87
co-innovation, 180
collaboration, 157, 159, 193, 195, 216, 221
 with incumbents, 180
collapse, financial, 113–115, 118, 122–123
collapse, societal, 7, 38, 58, 70, 108–109, 122, 189
commodities, 38–41, 52, 88, 126, 136
congruence, 60, 68–69, 72, 76, 80, 85, 91, 93, 94, 102–107, 108–117, 121–124, 143–144, 200, 203, 211–212, 220
 external, 68–69, 80, 91, 93, 102–106
 internal, 68, 102–106
 Schumpeterian, 110–111

Index

consumer *see* consumption
consumerism *see* consumption
consumption, 11–13, 21, 40, 63, 66, 78, 87, 98,
    107, 122, 124–125, 139, 143, 146, 150,
    163–166, 197
  theory of the leisure class, 116
  consumer capitalism in Cyburbia, 197
  and technology, 163–166
  from consumer to producer, 197–208
cost reduction, technology related, 11, 19, 40,
    75, 80, 112, 125, 131, 146, 148, 152, 161,
    168, 179, 182
creative capital, 121, 218
creative destruction, 97, 100, 110, 112, 115,
    126, 146, 167, 210
examples of , 171–175
crisis of humanity, 17
crisis, definition of, 14
crisis, existential *see* existential risk
crowd-sourcing, 157, 159, 173, 174, 196, 200,
    207, 219
cyburbia, 129–135, 147, 202, 214, 220
  benefits of, 133
  examples of, 130, 131, 212
  logic of, 132
  model of, 130
  obsolescence of, 139
  weaknesses of, 135–138
Cyclone Nargis, 102

D.Light, 161–164, 169
debt crisis, 13, 47–49, 88, 123
decarbonising, 30, 64, 69, 79, 84–85
decay *see* entropy
decoupling, 33, 45, 78, 204
demographic change, 17, 36–45, 83, 108–109,
    168, 203
  business implications of, 44–45
  demographic dividend, 42–43
descriptive economics, 82, 88
Destiny, FL, 131
Dickens, Charles, 105
discount rate, 74, 77, 82
disembeddedness *see* embeddedness
distributed city *see* distributed economy
distributed economy, 147, 157, 158–159,
    161, 166, 181, 189, 191, 197, 202–205, 207
  distributed energy, 197
  distributed outcomes of Oracles, 93
Drogba, Didier, 161
drought, 42, 82, 165
Drucker, Peter, 15, 168

eco-city, 136, 214
eco-vibrator, 98
economic crisis, 19, 46–52, 65, 73, 99, 211
  see also financial crisis

economic growth, 13, 23, 30, 32, 35, 44, 72–73,
    77, 78, 81–83, 89, 90, 93, 110, 143, 150,
    175, 197, 203, 205
  demographic change and, 44
  emerging markets and, 90, 150
  ideology of, 89
  parallel shift in, 175
  uneconomic growth, 78
ecosystem change, 17, 38, 41, 70, 75, 83, 86,
    101, 136
ecosystem degradation *see* ecosystem change
embeddedness, 110, 115
employment, 18, 20, 51, 64, 92, 134, 158,
    202–204
energy
  alternative, 29, 33, 84, 122, 189, 190, 204,
    222–224
  efficiency, 27, 31, 33, 65, 189, 205
  gap, 33
  mix, 31–33
  energy return on energy invested (EROEI),
    20, 120
  nuclear, 30, 31, 33, 70, 85
entrepreneurial state, 209–210, 215–223
entropy, 109, 117
extensive economy *see* distributed economy
external fit *see* congruence, external

Fab Lab, 158, 193, 194, 203, 204, 206,
    218, 221
financial crisis, 15, 21, 47, 49, 99, 122–123
financial economy, 121–123
food, 15, 25–26, 39, 40–41, 45, 52, 66, 91, 147,
    165, 170, 172
Ford, Henry, 10–13, 18, 44, 63, 67, 146,
    148, 157
fossil fuels, 13, 22, 31, 32, 35, 47, 77, 78, 100,
    112, 119, 123, 126, 219
frenzy, 48, 113, 119, 122, 123, 124, 176, 218
Galbraith, JK, 116, 125, 157
gas *see* fossil fuels
gated community, 76, 136
GDP, 13, 16, 21, 31–32, 43, 49, 72, 73–74, 77,
    80, 83, 85, 113, 120, 121, 198
general purpose technology (GPT), 19,
    63, 97, 102–103, 113, 117, 135,
    137, 139, 140, 144, 146, 147, 176,
    177, 178, 185, 192, 200, 210–211,
    218–220
  financing of, 220
  ICT GPT, 146–148
geo-engineering, 29, 70, 79–80, 89, 91, 93, 144,
    177, 219
  technological wild cards, 85
geo-political shift, 22–23, 46–52, 101
  see also economic crisis
GeoSpring water heater, 150–151

governance, 21, 22–23, 47, 52–62, 65, 66, 80, 85, 134, 199–202
  civil, 199–202
  geoengineering and, 91–92
  industry self-governance, 122
  open, 186, 195, 202, 223–224
government role, 209–212, 215–223
great stagnation, 14, 134, 146
green business as usual, 30, 32, 70, 73–75, 83–85, 203
green economic stimulus, 74, 84, 123
green new deal *see* green economic stimulus
Green Revolution, 42, 46, 91
green technology, 85, 135, 152, 203

Hello Kitty, 87, 124, 125
high carbon fuels *see* fossil fuels
high-frequency trading, 99, 121
Hurricane Katrina, 8–9, 12–14, 101–102, 147
Huxley, Aldous, 13

ICT, 48, 64, 92, 98–100, 100–102, 118–124, 134–136, 146–149, 168, 172, 177, 179, 182–183, 186, 193, 200, 203, 212, 219–220
  and energy, 100
  and productivity, 146–149
  era, 118–124
  waves of, 182–183
IFPRI, 25–26
illth, 121
income inequality, 13, 67, 122, 150
incongruence *see* congruence
incumbent industries, 119, 138, 155, 167, 170–171, 176–178, 178–182, 189, 215–217, 226
  ICT and, 119
  innovators and, 170–171
  strategies for, 178–182
Indexmundi Commodity Price Index, 41
India, 47, 49, 53, 56, 84, 100, 161, 174, 187, 200
industrial economy, 121, 123, 202
installation, 112–113, 118–119, 124, 126, 218
Intergovernmental Panel on Climate Change (IPCC), 83
interdependency, 26, 37, 65
internal fit *see* congruence, internal
internal rate of return, 84
irruption, 112, 118, 119, 122, 146, 176, 182, 216, 217–218

Jackson, Tim, 16, 70, 74, 78, 87
justifications of capitalism, 104–106, 114, 125, 144, 147, 202, 206, 226

Kaletsky, Anatol, 54–55
Kardashian, Kim, 119, 121, 122

Kasparov, Gary, 98
Kenya, 40, 162, 163, 165, 174, 199, 200, 213
Kickstart, 159, 166–167, 173, 180, 192, 208
Kilimo Salama, 165, 170, 180, 181, 215, 216
Kondratiev, Nikolai, 14, 11
Konza City, 213–215

labour costs, 148, 150, 159, 182, 226
land, 41, 42, 46, 51, 52, 76, 82, 91, 108, 137, 165, 212, 215
Lerner, Jaime, 135, 198, 199, 201
liquid democracy, 23, 53, 57
local production, 182, 191
  waves of production, 191
localized manufacturing *see* local production
Lovelock, James, 80
Low Carbon Economy Index, 29, 84
low-carbon economy, 27

Macaulay, Thomas B., 8
Malthus, Thomas Robert, 40, 44, 46, 77
Mama Felix, 162–165
manufacturing costs, 186, 215
manufacturing, decline of, 48
market disruption, 170–171, 179
market exit, 69
market moderation, 69–72, 86
market solutions, 79–80
Mars, fixer upper planet, 145
mass era *see* mass production
mass production, 10–13, 25, 31, 35, 37, 53, 63–67, 77, 94, 98, 106, 117, 146, 158–159, 175, 182, 206–207, 219, 222, 224, 226
  challenges to, 149, 214
  hidden costs of, 151
  incongruence of, 106
  logic of, 148–149
maturity, 19, 115, 126, 167, 177, 211, 216, 222
McCartney, Stella, 75
McNamara, Robert, 12
megacity, 38, 43, 87, 132, 136, 214
megatrends, 25–62, 178, 182
Memmento, 98
micro- insurance, 165, 169–171
micro-grids, 187, 189, 190, 215, 224
M-KOPA, 164–165, 170, 215–216
mobile telephony, 11, 57, 76, 112, 121, 160–167, 168, 171, 174, 180, 200, 201
Model T Ford, 10–12, 112, 146, 148, 155, 157, 161
monetary economy, 123
MOOC, 174
moral hazard, 91, 145
morality, 37, 74–75, 78, 87, 89
  of discount rates, 74–75
  of green plutonomy, 75
M-PESA, 163–166, 170, 176, 181, 212, 215, 216

nanotechnology 100, 154, 159, 161,
     75, 212
NASDAQ, 119
net present value, 82
new energy economy, 189
non-resilient *see* resilience
Nordhaus, William D., 72, 74, 82

Occupy Movement, 18
oil sands, 20, 100
oil *see* fossil fuels
Olduvai Gorge, 140, 161
open source technology 158, 161
opportunity analysis, 180
optimism, 14, 27, 37, 72, 79–80, 91, 97, 118,
     126, 132, 144–149, 226–227
   demographic optimism, 37
   demographic pessimism, 37
   reluctant, 118
   techno-, 72, 79–80, 91, 144–149
orders of worth *see* justification
outsourcing, 13, 20, 132, 151, 152, 215
overshoot, 77–78

participatory budgeting, 201, 224
Paul, Ron, 22
peak oil, 20, 77
Pecan Street, 187–190
Perez, Carlota, 110, 112, 113, 114, 146, 171,
     176, 177, 178, 192, 212, 215
petropolis, 9, 67–69, 107, 118, 125–127,
     129, 132, 143, 147, 161, 212,
     214, 215
pinch points, 65–66
plutonomy, 18, 70, 75–76, 166
   green plutonomy, 75–76
   medical, 145
polis, 147, 224
power grid, 187–188
predatory capitalism, 55, 115, 121
prescriptive economics, 74
   see also business as usual
producer capitalism, 215, 223–226
productive economy, 205, 207
product-in-trash-out (PITO), 137, 218, 225
productivity, 10–11, 19, 42, 63, 63, 67, 78, 89,
     92, 97, 105–106, 125, 131, 138, 140, 146,
     148, 161, 163–166, 170, 171, 174, 175,
     177, 192, 202, 204, 214, 222, 224
   ICT and, 98–99, 182, 204, 214
   increase in, 163–166
   rural, 171
profit, 21, 53, 66, 69, 87, 90, 92, 104, 157,
     167–168, 207
prosperity without growth, 70, 77–79,
     85–89, 93

quant, 99

rapid prototyping, 161, 179, 193, 203
real economy, 120–123, 125, 146–147, 192
regulation, privatization of, 53–55
regulators, 23, 53–54, 57–58, 186, 211
relative decoupling *see* decoupling
renewable energy, 29, 33, 84, 189, 190, 204,
     222–224
representative social institution, 15, 68, 102
re-shoring, 151–152, 183
resilience, 8, 9, 53, 135–136, 138–139, 187,
     189, 197, 221
   non-resilient city, 138–139
return on assets, 19, 67, 92, 123, 144,
     146, 214
Richard, Cliff, 218
Richards, Keith, 218
rising waters, 82, 93
Ruskin, John, 121

Schumpeter, Josef, 97, 110, 111, 117, 121, 146,
     167, 210
   see also creative destruction *and* S-curve
S-curve, 110–111
Shift Index, 19, 20, 67, 92, 214
Singularity, The, 144–145
slavery, 105, 110, 114
SLEPT, 68–68, 102, 108
Slingshot, 165, 180
smart city, 130–132, 134–139, 185, 186, 214,
     215, 216, 220
social cost of carbon, 74, 77, 83
social exclusion, 135–137
   civic disengagement, 137
   environmental disconnection, 137
solar 29, 57, 85, 161, 164, 166, 170, 188, 197,
     205, 221, 226
   panels, 29, 166, 188
   power, 85, 161, 170, 221
solar radiation management technology,
     79–80, 91
Solyndra, 85
Songdo, 129–131, 134, 135
sovereign debt, 13, 15, 47, 49, 51
stagflation, 116, 118
stateless corporation, 51
stationary state, 70, 78
steady state growth, 70, 78, 85, 88
Stephenson, George, 48, 112, 119,
     146, 211
Stern, Nicholas, 32, 73, 74, 77, 83, 203
Stiglitz, Joseph, 55, 66, 146
stranded assets, 32, 36, 100
subtractive manufacturing, 154–155, 223
suburbia, 132

supply chain, 151, 211
synergy, 114–115, 122, 126, 171, 177, 180, 192
  and the entrepreneurial state, 215–216

techno-economic paradigm (TEP), 48, 69,
  98–99, 103, 110, 111–112, 116–118,
  119, 121, 124, 139, 145, 176, 226
techno-optimism, 72, 91, 144–149
TEEB, 75
Tesla, 64, 145
there is no alternative, 67, 126, 226
Thévenot, Lauren *see* Boltanski, Luc
tight oil, 77
Toyama, Kentaro, 101, 197
Trafigura, 57
transformation pathway *see* transition
  pathway
transformation *see* transition
transition, 88–89, 145, 171, 178, 192
  accelerating, 192
  incongruence and, 109
  management, 178

pathway, 88–89
  see also S-Curve
TrillionthTonne, 29
turning point, 113–114, 121–123, 177
twin test of alternative approaches, 67–69, 76,
  77, 80, 132, 145, 226
  achievability, 68–69, 76, 132, 145, 226
  adequacy, 67–69, 77, 132, 145, 226

Ushahidi, 200

Veblen, Thorstein, 68, 102, 116, 211, 222
Vestas, 51
Vives, Antonio, 193, 202, 224

Weber, Max, 87, 202
wellth, 121
West, decline of the, 15, 49, 53, 191
wicked problems, 25
Wikispeed, 155–158, 159, 171, 192, 194, 206
Wolf, Martin, 22
World Economic Forum, 40, 65, 211